# THE ART OF BEING A

# The Omega Uniform Edition of Teachings by Pir-o-Murshid Hazrat Inayat Khan

*The Art of Being and Becoming*
*The Awakening of the Human Spirit*
*The Complete Sayings*
*Mastery*
*The Music of Life*
*Spiritual Dimensions of Psychology*
*Tales*

# THE ART OF BEING AND BECOMING

Hazrat Inayat Khan

**OMEGA PUBLICATIONS, INC**
New Lebanon

**Cover:** *The Magic Fish* by Peter Birkhauser. Reprinted with permission from *Light From The Darkness: The Paintings of Peter Birkhauser,* published by Birkhauser Verlag. Commenting upon this painting, Marie Louise von Franz writes: The future world savior in his double form still hidden in the fish in the depths of the sea. The fish's eye is like a flower--earth's answer to the light of the sun. The huge blue eye at the top left suggests that something in the cosmic background "sees" everything. Within the fish, mortal and immortal man hold each other in a close embrace.

Third printing 1994
Omega Uniform Edition, 1989
©1982 Omega Publications
Originally published as *Personality: The Art of Being and Becoming*

Published by:
 OMEGA PUBLICATIONS
 RD 1 BOX 1030E DARROW RD
 NEW LEBANON, NY 12125-9801

0-930872-41-X
Printed in the U.S.A.

## PART I: PURIFICATION

## PART II: SELF-CONTROL: THE MORAL OF RENUNCIATION

## PART III: THE ART OF PERSONALITY

## PART IV: THE DIVINE MANNER

# FOREWORD
## by
## Pir Vilayat Inayat Khan

At a time when spirituality spelled otherworldliness, Hazrat
Inayat Khan was demonstrating by example how one can
bring sparkle to one's own personality by incorporating the
very splendor that one had been searching beyond. "If you
do not see God in man, you will not see Him anywhere," he
said, in line with the Sufi dervishes. The Sufi Niffari asks,
"Why do you look for God up there? He is here!" and Rumi,
after meeting Shems-i Tabriz, exclaimed, "The one I have
worshiped all my life as God appeared to me today in the
form of man!"

Rather than alienating himself in splendid aloofness, Hazrat Inayat Khan valued immensely the human being, in
whom life throbs and thrives and strives surreptitiously to
perfect the expression of all the many-splendored bounty
invested in it. The master was known to treat both his pupils
and strangers with reverent respect. A street sweeper was
enraptured when the "grand seigneur," as they called Hazrat
Inayat Khan, walking majestically in the street, took his hat

off to him, bowing royally. His pupils were nonplused when they came for audiences with him, expecting to sit humbly at the master's feet, chela fashion. Instead he rose, greeting them with both hands outstretched, inviting them to sit with him on the sofa, treating them as venerable friends, and showing a dedicated interest in their problems and well-being. He spotted the potentialities in those who approached him, looking into their souls rather than assessing them on the basis of the apparent features of their personalities. Such was the impression of a visitor who said, "I had read so much about the soul, but it never seemed real to me until, looking at Hazrat Inayat Khan as his gaze turned towards me, I could see that he was glancing into my soul."

For the master, the personality is the fruit on the tree of life, the fulfillment of the purpose of our existence on the planet. God's creativity is extended in man, and our personality is the ultimate masterpiece. In typical oriental metaphor, we are both the gardener and the garden he/she cultivates. As the celebrated Sufi metaphysician Ibn al-'Arabi said, "Man is the created creator and the creating creature."

The accent in Sufism is truly on creativity. Admittedly, we must first accept ourselves and others with both our qualities and defects, without being judgmental. Yet the human being is remotely aware of dimensions of his/her being that have not yet come through in the personality and he/she entertains a longing to materialize these potentialities. In all of us, as is exemplified in the case of the artist, imagination serves as the transducer whereby we may draw archetypes from the "storehouse of all knowledge" of which Hazrat Inayat Khan muses, marking our personality with this splendid stamp that we idealize and which we seek in others. We all carry the divine inheritance as our heritage, emphasizes the master, having continually in mind Christ's exhortation, "Be ye perfect as your Father."

No doubt it takes a powerful, sometimes traumatic impact to trigger off a change in a person. One has to free oneself from one's tendency to confine one's thinking to the middle ranges of understanding and, having accepted the idiosyncracies of one's self-image, free onself from the limitation of that image. This means extending the compass of one's mental grasp and personal emotions beyond one's concept of a quality one would like to see in oneself, so as to include at the limits of one's reach what this quality would be like in a perfect archetypal state before becoming circumscribed by human limitation. Paradoxically, while one thinks one is reaching out or up into the divine condition, one is in reality simply responding to the divine condition that is contriving to come through one.

To appreciate Sufism, one has to learn to reverse one's usual way of viewing things. The human being is never the one who knows or wills or becomes, nor even the object seen or transformed; he/she can only lend him/herself to the divine action. This is the meaning of the *significatio passiva* of the early Christian fathers. This is why Hazrat Inayat Khan says, "It is not by self-realization that one realizes God, it is by God-realization that one realizes self."

One cannot satisfactorily improve one's personality without calling into action all the dimensions of the web of reality. Since a point has no surface, one is both the intersection of the web and also the whole web. Forestalling the present paradigm shift towards holism, the master sixty years ago was teaching his pupils to take into consideration the whole person. It is all one reality, only relatively divisible. One might consider this as the rendering of the Sufi proclamation *La illaha illa 'llah hu,* "Nothing exists save God."

# INTRODUCTION

There is a difference between individuality and personality, as there is a difference between nature and art. As much as nature is near to man's soul, art is closer to his heart. If it were not so, man would have preferred to live in the forest, he would have roamed about in nature and would have been quite satisfied in the wilderness, he would have found the greatest charm in the beauty which is to be seen in the forest. But instead of all that, man has created a world for himself, and in that world he has made a nature of his own imagination, a nature which he calls art.

If that is art, then on art much depends. People may say, "Is it not an imitation of nature?" Yes, it is an imitation of nature. They might say, "Then it is not as great as nature." But I say, "Both nature and art are made by the same Artist." Nature is made directly by the Artist, and art is made indirectly, through the pen of the artist. Nevertheless, art is the finishing of that beauty which begins to manifest in nature. A person who has not come to this conception of art does not yet know the divinity of art.

Coming to the question of what art has to do with personality, personality is art itself and the greatest art. Once a person came to me and said, "My parents brought me up just like a plant in the wilderness, growing naturally." I said, "It is a great pity," and she was surprised. What is education, what is culture, what is self-development? It is all art; it is all the way for individuality to culminate in personality.

In ancient times, religious education and human culture in every form had personal culture as their central theme. Today we are expected to learn mathematics, geography, history, and never the art of personality, which is of greatest use in life—apart from its spiritual significance. In our everyday life we see a salesman who is pleasant, who is courteous, whose manner is good, become a successful salesman. If a seller lacks manners, if he is repellent, though he may have beautiful things in his shop he will have no success. If a clerk in an office, a secretary, an assistant, a supervisor, has a charming personality, if he has a kindly manner, if he has a sympathetic attitude, he will win the affection of all, and everything will be light and go smoothly. If a person lacks the art of personality, despite all the qualifications he may have, though he may be the most capable person, yet things will not run smoothly. And so it is at home. A person may be a barrister, a solicitor, a doctor, a most qualified person, but if the art of personality is not developed, he will be disagreeable and unpleasant in his own home and in all walks of life.

The art of personality is the main thing to develop, and if it is not developed, a person has missed a great deal. If the love of this art has not been given, then what happens? The human being becomes no better than the lower creation. Is a human being greater because he possesses wealth, or because he has read many books, or because he has much learning? No. Man is greater when he has changed from an individual into a person. Very few of us distinguish between individuality and personality. Individuality is that which we have brought with us at birth. We are born as a separate entity; that in itself makes us an individuality. But personality is something that is acquired: it has not come with us, it is something we gain. If a tree from the forest grew in a garden in the same way, the gardener would say, "You are not welcome here; you do not fit in with the surroundings. This is a garden, not a forest."

Moreover, the art of personality is not only something that a person should learn in order to become pleasant to others: the art of personality fulfills the purpose of life.

Now comes the question, what is the art of personality? Is the art of personality mannerism, is it putting on different ways of expression, extra politeness, a society rhythm? Not at all. That is a falsehood that people adopt, being unnatural and acting unnaturally, but instead of giving a better impression, they give a worse one. It is something which expresses itself spontaneously. You do not need to act in a certain way, you do not need to put something on: it is the expression of your self that is the art of personality.

Moreover, it is the sign of the great that they express the art of personality. Whether knowingly or unknowingly, a person may have developed himself to that manner, and it is wonderful to watch. In India I was very fond of seeing the celebrities of our country, and one day I heard that a great wrestler was visiting our town. I had never approved of something that makes one win and the other fail, but because this man was a celebrity I wanted to see him. One would have expected very little from the personality of a wrestler, but in his personality, instead of muscular and nervous strength, there was such a kindly manner, such a sympathetic look, such an outgoing attitude, and such serenity that I thought, "Even a wrestler, who does the most material and physical work, can show that it is his personality and not something material that has made him great."

One might ask, "If a person has a personality, why must he develop it?" But even a diamond must be cut. It has the light in it, yet cutting is required: it cannot show that glow and that brilliancy before it has been cut. The same thing applies to personality.

Then one may ask, "How is personality regarded, in how

many different aspects?" The first aspect of personality is the action, the movement. Very often, before a person has spoken a word he makes a movement that jars upon the delicate sensibility of a person who sees it, who may form an opinion of that person before he knows about him, only by his movement. In one movement a person shows his state of mind, unless he has the power to control it. One can show stubbornness, weakness, foolishness: all things can be traced when a person walks, or sits, or stands up. For those who can recognize a person in the twinkling of an eye it is not necessary to study physiognomy. One movement shows them whether a person is evolved or unevolved. And when his movements are not directed, when this science is not taught or understood, a person may make movements that will make an impression upon his spirit and turn his whole being into wrong. Very little attention has been given to this by education.

Now coming to the other aspect of personality, which belongs to speech. The more we understand about this, the more we know that for every word there is a time and for every word there is a place. Everything you say that is in its own place and is a fitting thing will be good. It becomes wrong when it is spoken in a place which is not its place. People generally do not think about this. Very often people are outspoken; they do not mind when they speak, what they speak, where they speak. A person who has no control over his speech becomes like a kind of machine which goes on and on and on, without any will at the back of it. Remember that not only do such people not gain the affection and approbation of others, but they repel others. They cannot keep any secret because they have the habit of saying everything, they have no control over it.

Once a woman went to a healer and said, "Can you help me? I am in distress." The healer asked, "What is the matter?" She said, "When my husband comes home, he is in such a state that there is always a disagreement." "Oh," said the healer, "that is the easiest thing to do. I will just give you these magnetized lozenges. When your husband comes home, you take one in the mouth and keep it there." When her husband came home, tired and fatigued, he was inclined to war as usual, but she was quiet and did not answer. He was grumpy for a little while but then became quiet. And so the home became more harmonious. Then, before the lozenges were finished, she went to the healer and said, "Give me one more pack of these," and he answered, "Lady, learn from this that it is not the lozenges, it is the closed lips. When your husband is tired, he does not know his mind. And when you do not encourage him to quarrel, he will not quarrel."

The art of personality is not so difficult to learn: it is to learn to be thoughtful. Those who say much very often say so little. Others, who say little, say much. It depends upon how it is said. The Bible says, "First was the Word and the Word was God." That shows what power the word has. If we control our speech, if we know how to use a word, we know the chemical science of life and use it to the best purpose of life. Sometimes a person can change a situation by one word when others cannot change it by a hundred hammers. There is a way to hammer and break a rock, and there is the way of the water. If the rock is in the way, the water will not hammer at it, the water will surround it, will run smoothly over it and make its way on the top of the rock, and in this way the waves will proceed.

If one only knew the art of personality. If a person is upset among ten people who want to console him, there are nine who will upset him more, and there is rarely one who will console him. That consolation also belongs to the art of personality.

Thus we come to another aspect of the art of personality, and that is sympathetic and right thinking. By right thinking all that one says and does naturally becomes right, because the root of every speech and action is in the mind. Naturally, by right thinking one speaks rightly and acts rightly; one cannot do otherwise. But what generally happens is that one

never thinks about right thinking in connection with oneself, one always thinks about it in connection with others.
If there is any wrong, it is in the other. And the most wonderful thing is that the one who is most in the wrong is the
one who sees most the wrong in others. You will see that
that person who is full of wrongs knows a thousand wrongs
about a thousand people. Besides, our experiences make us
so pessimistic that if someone says, "I have seen such a nice
and kind and good person," we begin to doubt it; unconsciously our first thought is, "Can it be true? It cannot be
true; there is no such a thing as good in the world." But as
soon as a person says, "I have seen such a wicked person,"
everybody is interested, because they believe it. That shows
that we hardly expect any experience that can ever be right.

The fourth aspect of the art of personality is feeling. The
great drawback of modern civilization is that man today
thinks what is balanced and practical is to think with the
brain, to reason things out. But he thinks that to feel with
the heart is not practical, is not common sense. Therefore
today a "normal" and "balanced" person is the one who
lives in his brain, and the one whose heart is developed is
called a fanatic, or unpractical. Imagine, after reading in the
Bible that God is Love, we come to believe that the one who
has less God in him is the more practical and the one who
has more God in him is good for nothing. When there is a
discussion among intellectual persons, it is understood to
keep away from sentimentality: "Just discuss the point, that
keeps your reasoning clear."

But this takes away the beauty of life. The art of personality is in that profound, deep feeling which directs every
thought, speech, and action of man. When Jesus Christ said
to the fishermen, "Come hither and I will make you the
fishers of men," he spoke to those who were absorbed in
catching fish at the sea shore: in other words, "Come here,
I will teach you the art of personality." It is therefore not a
new subject that I bring before you, it is a subject that Christ
taught. It is the art of personality that the prophets proved

in their own lives to be of the greatest importance. What is the impression Buddha has left upon millions of people in the East who keep his image in temples and see the expression of God in him? Is it the theories and dogmas and teachings he gave? No, it is his personality which has made such a deep impression upon people that for centuries they have held it sacred. It has proved to be more precious than anything in the world.

This is not a subject of which one can say, "It is no better than any other subject." On the contrary, it is a subject of the greatest importance. There are millions of Muslims whose eyes are full of tears on hearing the name of the Prophet. Why is it? Is it the teaching the Prophet gave? What touches them is the personality of the Prophet; his personality has made a deep impression that never can be erased, that remains there still. The art of personality therefore is a magic. The fishermen among whom Jesus Christ had to walk were incapable of knowing the greatness of the master and not ready to understand the message he had brought, and yet they used to stand spellbound in the presence of the master, they were deeply impressed by the personality of the teacher. What was it? It was not a new teaching they received, it was the example before their eyes.

The Sufis of all ages have considered the art of personality of the greatest importance. The yogic theory of asceticism has nothing to do with the art of personality; it is another thing. But the wise of all ages who have taught that God Himself has manifested in the form of man, who from an individual develops into a person, see in this the fulfillment of life's purpose.

And now one might ask, "How does one learn the art of personality?" In the same way as one learns the art of painting or drawing. In the first place one learns how to draw a straight line, a horizontal line, a circle, a curve. In the art of personality one learns how to say a thing, how not to a say a thing, how to avoid saying a thing, and how to say a thing without saying it.

Then one learns the art of light and shade, which is the next thing: how to hide a certain aspect in conversation and to bring the other part brought to prominence. And then there is coloring. There is a great variety of colors: every feeling, every thought, every idea has its particular color, and when a person knows how many of these colors there are, when he composes with them all he says and does in life, then it becomes an art of personality. It is nothing if a person has collected diamonds, or if he has pearls or rubies. What is it worth if he has not developed in his personality that precious quality which makes a person precious? All those things are nothing.

There are four grades through which one develops in the art of personality. In the first grade a person has become thoughtful. Then he begins to observe his thoughts, to see his actions. In the second grade he not only observes his thoughts and actions but is able to control them. In the third grade a spontaneous outflow of sympathy comes naturally from the person; his attitude is outgoing, his personality attracts and becomes a blessing. And the fourth is a grade where no effort has to be made by the artist to make the art of personality. In this grade the artist becomes art itself, and whatever he does, it all becomes a beautiful picture.

The art of personality is not a qualification. It is the purpose for which man was created, and it leads man to that purpose in the fulfillment of which is his entire satisfaction. By this art man not only satisfies himself, but he pleases God. This phantom play on the earth is produced for the pleasure of that King of the universe whom the Hindus have called Indra, before whom gandharvas sang and upsaras danced. The interpretation of this story is that every soul is destined to dance at the court of Indra. The art of personality is, in reality, learning to dance perfectly. But the one who says, "How can I dance? I do not know how to dance," defeats his purpose. For no soul is created to stand aside and look on. Every soul is created to dance in the court of Indra.

The soul who refuses certainly shows its ignorance of the great purpose for which the whole play is produced on the stage of the earth.

Any efforts made in developing the personality or in character-building must be for the sake not of proving oneself superior to others but of becoming more agreeable to those around one and to those with whom one comes in contact. Conciliation is not only the moral of the Sufi, it is the sign of the Sufi. This virtue is not learned and practiced easily, for it needs not only goodwill but wisdom. The talent of the diplomat consists in bringing about such results as are desirable with mutual agreement. Disagreement is easy (among the lower creation one sees it so often); it is agreement that is difficult, for it needs a wider outlook, which is the true sign of spirituality. Narrowness of outlook makes man's vision small: the person with a narrow outlook cannot easily agree with another. There is always a meeting ground for two people, however much they differ in thought, but the meeting ground may be far off, and when that is so a person is not always willing to take the trouble to go so far in order to come to an agreement. Very often this is due to his lack of patience. What generally happens is that each wants the other to meet him at the place where he is standing; there is no desire on the part of either to move from the spot.

This does not mean that in order to become a real Sufi one should give up one's own ideas so as to agree with someone else. There is no advantage in always being lenient towards every thought that comes from another, nor in erasing one's own ideas from one's heart; that is not conciliation. The one who is able to listen to another is the one who will make another listen to him. The one who finds it easy to agree with another will have the power of making another agree easily with him. Therefore in doing so one really gains, in spite of the apparent loss which may sometimes occur. When a man is able to see both from his own point of view and from that of another, he has complete vision and a clear insight; he so to speak sees with both eyes.

No doubt friction produces light, but light is the agreement of the atoms. Two people having their own ideas and arguing about them can be a stimulus to thought, and then it does not matter so much. But when a person argues for the sake of argument, the argument becomes his game; he has no satisfaction in conciliation. Words provide the means of disagreement and reasons become the fuel for this fire; but wisdom is found where the intelligence is pliable, where it understands all things, even the wrong of the right and the right of the wrong. The soul who arrives at perfect knowledge has risen above right and wrong. He knows them, and yet he knows not; he can say much, and yet what can he say? Then it becomes easy for him to conciliate each and all.

There is a story of two Sufis who met after having travelled their different ways. They were glad to meet each other after many years of separation as they were both pupils of the same murshid. One said to the other, "After all this time of study and practice of Sufism I have learned one thing: how to conciliate another; and I can do it very well now. Will you please tell me your life's experience, what you have learned?" The other one said, "After all this time of study and practice of Sufism I have learned how to master life. All that there is in this world is for me, and I am the master. All that happens, happens by my will." Then came the murshid, whose mureeds both of them were, and they spoke to him of their experiences during their journey. The murshid said, "Both of you are right." In the case of the first it was self-denial in the right sense of the word that enabled him to conciliate others; in the case of the second there was no longer any of his will left; if there was any will, it was the will of God.

In human beings one finds millions of qualities. Every quality has its origin in heredity, and is in reality a mixture, a kind of solution, of different qualities. So every person will have qualities unlike those of others, and every person is unique in his way. In this lies the secret of the oneness of God. Not only is God one, but man is one too.

One should never be discouraged or disappointed in life. Man has the key to his own life in his hand, if he only knew it. It is absurd to say, "I do not have that quality"; there is no quality in the world that man does not have, either good or bad. The soundest psychology is to say to oneself that one has the quality one thinks most desirable, most attractive, and has not that quality which one does not think desirable.

There is infinite variety in personality. The law of variety comes from the nature of manifestation: every current, taking a different direction, becomes different and manifests differently. Variety is also caused by time and space, and every personality differs because of time and space. A person born in one year will be different from a person born in another year. A person born in one month or on a certain day will be different from a person born in another month or on another day. Every moment makes a difference because of the difference in people's breath. The difference of personality comes also through the difference in the direction of one's thought: one's personality depends on the direction in which one's thought goes, and also on one's action, motive, expression. All these things cause differences in personality.

There is a story of a dervish who was standing in the middle of the street when the procession of the king was approaching. First came the pages who ran before the procession, and they pushed him and said, "Don't you see, the king is coming! Go away!" And the dervish smiled and said, "That is why," and he remained in the same place. Then there came the horsemen, the bodyguards. They said, "Get out of the way, the procession is coming!" The dervish smiled and said, "That is why." Next the courtiers came and saw the dervish standing there, and instead of telling the dervish to go away, they moved their horses a little away from where he stood. And again the dervish said, "That is why." Finally came the king, and when the king saw the dervish standing there, he greeted him first; and the dervish in reply said, "That is why." An intelligent young man asked him, "What is it you mean by this remark?" The dervish answered, "You can see that is why he is what he is."

People have wiped this ideal away from their minds. Where is democracy? The kingliness of greeting the dervish, that is democracy. But the man who is not evolved, who is pulling the most evolved down to his level, has a wrong conception of democracy; it is going downwards instead of upwards. If lack of manners and consideration can be democracy, it loses its real ideal and true spirit. Democracy is the result of aristocracy. When the spirit of aristocracy has evolved sufficiently, it becomes democracy. Then a person thinks, "I am the equal of any person in the world; there is no person lower than I." But if a person says, "There is no person higher than I," that is not democracy.

In Burma one finds Buddhists of a very wonderful kind. They are the only race that for centuries has believed that there is no religion that is not as good as their own. Imagine, today, when the followers of most religions look down upon the followers of another! These people say, "Whatever be the religion, Christian or Muslim or Jewish, it is not worse than ours. Perhaps it is better." They all had this same thought, and even today they still hold this belief. That is something wonderful. But when a person says, "Nobody is better than I am," it is not democracy; it is sinking lower, because it means closing one's eyes to what is greater, higher, and better. If one cannot appreciate or see it, one cannot rise to it. One can only rise towards that which one values and that towards which one aspires.

If I were to speak before the world today about occult power, psychic power, spirit communication, breathing practices, people would be glad to listen, but if I say simple things like this, it means nothing to them. Yet suppose one did not develop personality, what about spirituality? A person must be a person first, and spiritual afterwards. If he is not a person, then what is the use of being spiritual? It is going back instead of going forward. Man is born to fulfill the purpose of his life; he is made to prove he is a human being: a person who can be relied upon, a person whose word carries authority, who uses thought and consideration, whom one can trust with one's secret; a person who will not humiliate himself under any conditions, who will lose his life rather than humble himself, who will not deceive or cheat anybody, who will never go back on his word; a person who will carry through what he has once undertaken. All these qualities make a person a human being.

Today our condition is such that we cannot believe in one another's word. We have to have a stamp on a contract. Why are we in such a condition? Because we are not evolving towards the ideal the ancient people had. That is why we cannot trust each other individually; that is why nations cannot trust one another. Human beings live only from day to day, striving and working for a loaf of bread. That is all. But is that all there is in life, to earn a loaf of bread? In that case we do no better than the animals in the forest, and even they appear better than we. Rich and poor, all are wretched in every walk of life, whether it be business, a profession, or politics, because there is nothing but competition between individuals, nations, parties, and communities. We have made our lives wretched. What are we here for? If we were born only to meditate and to be spiritual, then we had better go into the forest and into the caves of the mountains: it would not be necessary to be in the world. If we had only to live as the animals do, we could do as the worldly person is mostly doing today, and accomplish nothing. Therefore the first necessity for those who are seeking after truth is to develop the spirit of personality. Personality is more valuable than wealth. How strange it is that there is such a large population in this world and that there are so few personalities! Think of that Greek philosopher who went about with a lighted lantern in daytime. People asked, "What are you looking for?" He said, "For a human being."

Very often when I speak of the development of personality, people ask me, "What about annihilation?" But it depends on what form of annihilation they mean. One can only be a spendthrift if one has wealth; one cannot annihilate what one does not possess. When an individual has no personality he can annihilate nothing; there must be something first. If a person started in life with self-effacement, he would never become a self. What would he efface? Effacing comes afterwards. First he must be a self, a real self that is worth being.

One makes one's nature by one's likes and dislikes, by what one favors or disfavors. When a person says, "I don't like this food," he has built something into his nature; and then that food, when eaten, will often disagree with him. It is not that it was meant to disagree with him, but he made it disagree by disliking it. By control, bravery, endurance, steadiness, by all such qualities one makes one's nature either agreeable or disagreeable. Either one makes one's nature as hard as a rock that will not allow anything to pass, or one makes one's nature as pliable as water.

One may ask if it is not conceit to try to be better than others. There are many thorns and few flowers. We should not try to become a flower in order to feel ourselves superior to a thorn, but only for the benefit of others. All that trouble and pain and difficulty should be suffered for others; if among so many thorns we turn into a flower, it should be for others. That must be the idea. Besides, it is not an easy task to become a flower; it is far easier to become a thorn. For one is naturally born a thorn, and one has to become a flower. It is easy to say, "You have hurt me, insulted me, disturbed me, troubled me." But one does better to ask oneself if one has not harmed or disturbed someone else. One never thinks enough about this. Therefore to develop personality one learns self-effacement. It is an annihilation, a continual, unconscious annihilation which turns the self from a thorn into a flower.

One may also wonder whether with the development of personality one would not develop self-consciousness. But personality contains all: spirit, mind and thought, and body.

A self-conscious person is not necessarily one who has developed his personality, although development does sometimes give a tendency to vanity. But vanity is the power which can lead man either to good or bad. It is the living spark of the ego: the soberness of the ego is divine vanity, and the intoxication of the ego is the conceit of man. Conceit is difficult to conquer; it is almost impossible to get rid of. The reason is that wherever there is light there is darkness; wherever there is a form there is a shadow.

The word vanity is generally used in a very ordinary sense; there is no really good expression for the higher form of vanity. It is difficult to express this in any other way. The Hindus call it *vairagya,* and the Sufis use the word *kibria* for divine vanity. It is God's satisfaction in the manifestation which He wanted to create; but this is not the same as the satisfaction of the ignorant soul in its limitation. When it is in its proper place it is divine virtue; when it is out of its proper place it is a sin.

The understanding of vanity is the most fascinating vision of the phenomenon of life, and what the Sufi calls wine is the pleasure he derives from it. When this phenomenon is disclosed to him and he sees what activates all the different lives, it is almost like wine. What Omar Khayyam has called wine is the amusement one gets by looking at the phenomena of life, which lifts one above the worries of life. One will always find that the most evolved sages can be amused; that is why they are pleasant to meet and to speak to. Worrying comes from self-pity and fear, and fear is made of the clouds of ignorance; the light will dissolve it. Humor is the sign of light: when the light from above touches the mind it tickles the mind, and it is the tickling of mind which produces humor.

The one who develops his personality enriches and ennobles himself in manner, principle, and ideal. This subject has been much overlooked. It is not that man is not capable of it: man is more capable of it than ever before because he has to suffer so much. This life as we live it is a most painful life;

it crunches and grinds a person, and in that way can make him a better person. If he gave his thought to it, he would profit by it and become a better person. In ancient times people willingly went through different sufferings, trials, and tests. Today we do not need to do so; we have other trials. We do not need to look for them if we only learn how to profit by them; otherwise this experience is lost. Nowadays man can make use of all the skin and bones and nails of every animal in some way or another, and yet we do not use our own life's experience which is more precious than anything else. When people hear of an oil well or of a gold mine they are all interested in it, but they are not interested in this gold and silver mine, this mine of jewels and gems, the cultivation of which will produce all that can be produced. What is most valuable they do not even think about.

There is, however, no need to scorn a rich person. With all the money he has in the bank, his condition is sometimes much worse than that of the poor person. It is a mistake to say a person is rich because he has money or high rank; besides, the question whether a person is poor or rich has nothing to do with personality. One can develop personality regardless of being rich or poor; neither poverty nor riches necessarily draws one back from spiritual progress, for all that exists in the world is there for our use. If one has wealth, so much the better; if one does not have it, it is better still.

The great gurus and teachers of all times have taught that to give one's thought and mind to the development of personality is of the greatest importance for those who wish to seek for truth.

# PART I
# PURIFICATION

*Chapter 1.*

# PURITY OF LIFE

Purity of life is the central theme of all religions which have been taught to humanity in all ages. Purity of life has been their central idea, and they differ only in how they look at it. It seems that not only has purity of life sprung from religion, but it is the outcome of the nature of life; one sees it working out its destiny, so to speak, in all living creatures in some form or other. One sees this tendency in the animals, who look for a clean place to sit, and among the birds, who go to a lake or river to bathe and clean their feathers.

In humanity one sees the same tendency even more pronounced. A person who has not risen above the material life shows this faculty in physical cleanliness, but behind it there is something else hidden. And that which is hidden behind it is the secret of the whole creation, the purpose for which the whole world was made.

Purity is a process through which the life rhythm of the spirit manifests. It has worked for ages through the mineral, the vegetable, the animal, and the human kingdoms, passing through and arriving with all the experience it has gathered on its way at that realization where the spirit finds itself pure in essence, in its pure and original condition. The whole process of creation and of spiritual unfoldment shows that the spirit, which is life and which in life represents the divine, has wrapped itself in numberless folds, and has thus so to speak descended from heaven to earth. And its next process is to unwrap itself, and that unwrapping may be called the process of purification.

The word Sufi, which means unfoldment of the spirit towards its original condition, is derived from the Arabic word *safa* or *saf*, which literally means pure: i.e., pure from distinctions and differences.

What exactly does pure mean? When a person says water is pure, he means it is not admixed with sugar or salt; it is pure, it is original. Thus "a pure life" is the term used to express the effort on the part of man to keep his spiritual being pure or free from all impressions of worldly life. It is the search for one's original self, the desire to reach this original self, and the means of getting to one's original self that really speaking are called a pure life. But this can be applied with the same meaning in any part of one's life. If it is used pertaining to the body, it means the same: that what is foreign to the body must not be there. This is cleanliness, the first stage of purity.

And so it is with mind. When a person says pure-minded, what does it mean? It means what is foreign to the mind does not belong to it, but what is natural to the mind remains. And what is natural to the mind? What one sees and admires in the little child; the tendency to friendliness; readiness to see or admire something beautiful, instead of criticizing; willingness to smile in answer to anybody's love or smile, and to believe without questioning. A child is a natural believer; a natural friend, responding and yielding; a natural admirer of beauty, without criticism, overlooking all that does not attract, knowing love but not hate. This shows the original state of mind, natural to man. After the mind has come into this world, what is added to it is foreign. It may seem good for the moment, it may seem useful for the moment, but still the mind is not pure. A person may be called clever, a person may be considered learned, a person may be called witty, but with all these attributes the mind is not pure. Beyond and above all this is the man of whom it can be said that he is pure-minded.

Is it then desirable for a child never to learn anything which is worldly, and remain always a child? This is like asking, "Is it desirable for the spirit never to come to earth, but to remain in heaven always?" No. The true exaltation of the spirit is in the fact that it has come to earth and from here has risen to the spirit state and realized its perfection. Therefore all that the world gives in the way of knowledge, in the way of experience, in the way of reason, all that one's own experience and the experience of others teaches us, all that we learn from life, from its sorrows and disappointments, its joys and opportunities—all these contradictory experiences help us to become more full of love and kindness. If a person has gone through all these and has held his spirit high, not allowing it to be stained, that person may be called pure-minded.

The person who is considered pure-minded but who has no experience of the world and who does not know good or evil has no credit. He is a simpleton, no better than a rock. A rock does not know what is evil. The greatness of man is that he goes through all that which takes away that purity of mind with which man is born and rises through it, not being pushed under but holding to the mind's original purity, rising above all that pulls him down and keeps him down on the earth. It is a kind of fight throughout life. He who has no cause to fight does not know life. He is perhaps an angelic person, perhaps a pious person, and that we can call him out of respect; but plainly speaking, he is a simpleton.

There are so many phases through which one passes during life that a phase through which one has passed seems of no importance. It is the phase that one is passing through that is of importance. Outward purity matters little when a person goes through the inward purity of life, but the first purity is the purity of the physical world, where one keeps to the laws of cleanliness, the laws of health, from the psychic, the physical, the hygienic point of view; and in doing so, a person takes one step onward towards spirituality.

The next step is what is called in general purity of life. That purity of life is the purity of one's conduct in dealing with others, and very often a person takes to purity of life in one direction and in another direction forgets it. The churches, the religions, national and social laws very often make rigid principles about purity of life, and a person begins to know manmade purity, which the individual soul has to break through to find that of a higher plane.

However, one can learn from anything the principal rule of purity of conduct, and that rule is this: in speech or action, that which brings fear, which produces confusion, which gives a tendency to deception, which takes away that little twinkling spark in one's heart, the spark of trueness, that in which one would feel embarrassed, ashamed of oneself, uncomfortable, full of anxieties—all these things keep man away from what is called purity of life. One cannot point out that a particular action is a wrong action or a right one, and a person may not always be able to tell when a particular action is right or wrong in regard to circumstances, but one can always remember and understand for oneself the psychological principle that in every action that is wrong which is seen to take away that natural purity and strength and peace and comfort of mind which are man's natural life, in which man feels comforted. When a religious authority says, "Oh, this person is guilty of a fault," he is often wrong; he does not know the condition of the other person. No one can judge another person; one can judge one's own action best oneself. Therefore, there is no use in making rigid standards of moral or social purity. Religion has made them, schools have taught them, and many people make laws for purity of life; yet with all these manmade laws the prisons are full of criminals, and in the newspapers one finds every

Noor-un-nisa Inayat Khan

day more and more about the faults and crimes of the world. No external law can stop crime. It is man himself who must understand what is good for him and what is not good for him, who must be able to discriminate between poison and nectar. He must know, weigh, measure, and judge, and that he can only do by understanding the psychology of what is natural to him and what is unnatural. The unnatural action, thought, or speech is that which makes one uncomfortable before, during, or after doing it. That means that all things that give discomfort are not the wish of the soul. The soul is ever seeking for something that will open a way for its expression and give it comfort and freedom in this physical life.

It seems as if the whole life is tending towards freedom, towards the unfoldment of something which is choked up by coming on earth. This freedom can be gained by true purity of life. Of course it is not for everybody to understand what action, what thought brings remorse or causes discomfort. Moreover, the life of the individual is not in his control. Every rising wave of passion or of emotion or of anger or of wrath or of affection carries away one's reason, blinds one for the moment, so that in a moment's impulse one can easily give way to an unworthy thought or action. Then comes remorse. But still a person who wishes to learn, who wishes to improve himself, a person who wishes to go further in his progress will go on at the thought of his faults and mistakes because every fault will be a lesson, and a good lesson. Then he does not need to read in a book or learn from a teacher, because his life becomes his teacher.

However, one should not wish for the lesson for one's personal experience. If one were wise, one could learn the lesson from others; but at the same time one should not regard one's fault as one's nature: it is not one's nature. A fault is what is against one's nature. If it were in one's nature, it could not be a fault. The very fact that it is against one's nature makes it a fault. How can nature be a fault? When one says, "I cannot help being angry and I cannot help saying what I want to say when I feel bitter," one does not know that one could if one wished to. I mean to say that when one says, "I cannot help it," one does not wish to help it. It is lack of strength in a person when he says "can't." There is nothing that one can't. The human soul is the expression of the Almighty, and therefore the human mind has in its will the power of the Almighty, if only one could use that power against all things which stands in one's way as hindrances on the journey to the goal.

By regarding some few things in life as faults, one often covers up little faults that are sometimes worse than the faults that are pointed out by the world. For instance, when a younger person is insulting to an elderly person, people do not call it a very great fault. Yet sometimes such a little fault can rise and have a worse effect upon his soul than the faults which are recognized as faults in the world. By a sharp tongue, by an inquisitive nature, by satiric remarks, by thoughtless words, a person may commit a fault that can be worse than so-called great sins.

You do not know what is in an action. You cannot always judge a thing from the action. The judge has to see what is behind the action; and when a person has arrived at this stage of judgement, then he never dares to form an opinion, to judge. It is the ordinary person, the person who makes a thousand mistakes every day and overlooks them, who is ready to judge others.

We have seen what purity of the body and purity of the mind mean. However there is a further purity, the purity of the heart. This is reached by making the heart free from all impressions that come from outside, that are foreign to one's nature. This can be done by overlooking the shortcomings of others, by forgiving the faults of one's friends. By an increase of love one gives way to desirable impressions, which come upon one's heart and collect there. And in that way one keeps one's heart pure.

If during the day an ill feeling comes to a person towards a friend or relative—a feeling of hatred, a feeling of annoyance, a feeling of criticism, a feeling of bitterness—and he wishes to protect his heart from such an impression, he should not think about it; knowing it to be poison, he should not let it enter. Allowing it to enter is just like taking a poison into one's blood, introducing a disease. Any bad impression from outside kept in one's heart produces disease. The bitterness that one takes from others who perhaps have done something one did not like or toward whom one feels bitter is kept in one's heart. This is just like injecting poison into one's heart, and that poison develops there till it breaks out as a disease in one's physical being. Such illnesses are difficult to heal because they do not arise from a physical source but from an inner source. It is taking the poison of another into one's own self, and that becomes lasting, even incurable.

External purity or cleanliness does not have much effect on one's purity, but inner uncleanness, such as bitterness and spite against another, causes disease both inwardly and outwardly. However, when one has gone through this process and has tried to keep one's body and mind, one's life and character pure, then there comes a stage of still greater, higher purity. That is attained by a good ideal, by a righteous path, by good action, by good thoughts. One has to train oneself to become free from all foreign impressions. In this phase of one's journey one has to keep one's mind away from all but God. Then all that one thinks about, all that one feels, all that one sees and admires, all that one touches and perceives, is God. This is the greater purity, in which no thought or feeling is allowed to come into the heart but that of God alone. For instance, in the picture of an artist such a person sees God; in the merit of the artist he sees God; in the color and brushwork of the artist; in the eye of the artist, which observes nature; in the faculty of the artist, which produces the picture, such a one sees the perfection of God. And therefore to him God becomes all and all becomes God.

When he has arrived at this purity, many things will come in his life to test him: his enemy, who annoys him; those whom he cannot bear; those whom he does not like; those who are intolerant to him. He will come in contact with situations that are difficult. An occasion always comes for him to give up that purity for a moment; and every moment in the life of a sage at which that purity becomes poisoned, is for him a sin. I remember the words of my murshid, who said, "Every moment that God is absent from one's consciousness is a moment of sin, and when God is continually in one's consciousness, every moment is virtue."

When a person has arrived at that pitch, he lives in virtue. For him virtue is not a thing which he expresses or experiences from time to time, but his life itself is virtue. What he says and does and what is done to him is all virtue. And that shows that virtue is not one little experience: virtue is purity of life. Really, I would not consider virtue a worthwhile thing if it came and went away. It is only worthwhile when it lives with us, when we can depend upon it, and when we can live and move and have our being in it. That is worthwhile. If it only visited us for one minute, it would not be a virtue and we would rather not have it. We would prefer poverty to the wealth which came for a moment and went away. Therefore, this is the stage when man begins to understand what virtue means, when he begins to see a glimpse of virtue. What he knew before he thought to be virtue, but now life in its entirety becomes virtue to him; he lives in it, and life to him means virtue. Properly speaking, it is lack of life that is sin.

But then there is a further purity, and that is the purity of freedom from the thought of oneself. By thought of oneself I do not mean the thought of one's real self, but of one's limited self. Thought of one's limitation covers what is true in one's being, one's true self. It is this limitation that makes one feel at times that, "I am good," or, "I am bad." In this final phase one realizes, "I am perfect, nor does badness make me imperfect." Good and bad do not exist when one is above them, for then one is pure from all shapes and colors, from all forms of life. It is like rising above heaven and hell; it is like touching the throne of God, it is like bathing in the truth of God. This is real exaltation, when one has risen above one's limitation and has become conscious of that perfection whom we call God, whom we worship and whom we love, and who is the ultimate purpose of our life.

*Chapter 2.*

# THE PURIFICATION OF THE MIND

The real purification of the mind is in purifying it from the thoughts and impressions which live in it as germs of disease. The best way of cleansing the mind from all this is to empty it of any thought, feeling, or impression. To be pure means to be natural. The spirit in man in its natural condition is not thought but mind, not love but heart. For as the thought is the outcome of the mind, so is love the outcome of the heart. To attain to the purity which is the seeking of the mystic, one must be able to purify one's spirit from every thought and feeling, however deeply impressed or engraved in one's heart. The mystic goes as far as purifying himself from his identity, by removing it for a certain time and putting something else in its place. From beginning to end, the whole process of spiritual development depends upon this.

All that exists lives on its own element, springs from its own element, and returns to its own element. So earth to earth, water to water, fire to fire, and air to air. Purification means to make a certain object itself, with nothing foreign added, nothing attached to it that does not belong to it.

These two rules make one understand the process by which the mind can be nourished and purified. It is nourished by thoughts and impressions that are harmonious and productive of beauty and that result in satisfaction, for harmony is the nature of the soul and beauty is its source and goal. Thus by harmony and beauty the mind is nourished, as it is made of harmony and beauty. And the same elements are needed to purify the mind of all undesirable thoughts and impressions, harmony as water and beauty as soap, purifying the mind of all thoughts which are void of harmony and beauty.

The first thing in purifying the mind is to be able to discern the foreign element there. As all that is foreign to the body does not agree with the body, making it ill, so all that is foreign to the mind disturbs its peace, and that is what proves that it does not belong to the mind. Such things are worry, anxiety, fear, sorrow, or any sort of disturbance that takes away the tranquility of the mind, preventing it from experiencing that joy and peace for which it longs and in which alone is its satisfaction.

There are many who do not know the importance of keeping the mind in a pure and harmonious condition, and the few who do know it find it difficult to bring about better conditions in practical life. In the first place it is difficult to accomplish outward duties, to answer the demands of life, and yet, keep the mind in perfect tranquility. To do this one needs the knowledge of purifying the mind of all external influences. And the way one can manage it can be said in a few words: to throw away inharmony by the power of harmony, and to wash away all that lacks beauty by preserving the great power of beauty within oneself.

Anything that weighs upon the mind, such as a worry, a fear, or a feeling of remorse, keeps the mind below the pitch at which it is meant to be. When the mind is weighed down by anything, however learned a man may be, however capable and efficient, he can work very little. Learning does not help the mind that is not in its right place. So it is seen to be with many learned people: though most capable and efficient, yet they are incapable of accomplishing anything important in life. This is usually found in life, and rare is the case where it is not so.

All the affairs of life are accomplished by the power of mind. External conditions are nothing but mechanisms with which the mind works as an engineer, producing from life all that is desired. Therefore, whatever be one's condition in life, the principal thing is to shake off all that weight upon the mind, thus making it free to fulfill its task through life.

Often people find themselves helpless before a difficult situation, but very few stop to think that it is not only the situation that is difficult, but there is some difficulty in one's own mind. One hardly gives a thought to this question, for every man's eyes are fixed upon the difficulty of the situation alone. It is like seeing a wall standing before one and yet not realizing that one has a hammer in one's hand. If one realized the power that the mind has, whatever was standing before one—not only the wall but even mountains,—could be removed. Many seek for power from without, ignorant of the fact that all power is hidden within. When by freeing his own mind from all that weighs it down man realizes the power he inherits from the source of all beings, he will realize in himself an enormous power. The master mind is the master of life.

Purifying the mind from fear is of great importance, and this can be best done by analyzing what causes one fear. Fear is an outcome of long-collected, unsolved problems. When once a person looks his own problems in the face, he gets an insight into the cause of fear; and as in the sun many germs are destroyed, so the germs of fear are destroyed by the light of intelligence. Fear comes from weakness in facing the consequences of one's condition, attitude, and deeds. Once a person has solved the problem of how he will meet the consequences, the fear is done with. The best way of getting over the fear of swallowing a bitter pill is to swallow the pill and so to experience that it is not more bitter than it is.

Fear comes also by being too cautious with one's health,

morals, and reputation; by being too considerate of the feelings of those whom one loves and too regardful of those under whose influence one is; and by taking what others say too much to heart. Fear very often remains in the heart of man in the guise of virtues, and often a timid person is taken for a righteous one. But the timorous well-doer is worse than a fearless sinner.

The best practice one can do is to speak with one's own fear to dispute with it, to root out the reasons on whose foundations it rests. What generally happens is that one fears even to think of all the things one fears. But the solution—getting above fear—lies in analyzing the cause of the fear and so making it nonexistent. Man by nature possesses a tremendous power hidden in his heart, a power that waits constantly to become manifest. This power is hidden by fear. The day when fear disappears, this latent power manifests to view.

The nature of the memory is to hold an impression, agreeable or disagreeable. Therefore a person holds a thought in the mind, whether it is beneficial to him or not, without knowing the result that will come from it. He is like a child who holds a rattle in his hand, hits his head with the rattle, and cries at the pain, and yet does not throw the rattle away. There are many who keep in their minds thoughts of illness or thoughts of unkindness done to them by another, and who suffer from it, yet not knowing what it is that makes them suffer so or understanding the reason of their suffering. They go on suffering, and yet hold on in memory the very source of suffering. Memory must be one's obedient servant; when it is master, then life becomes difficult. Someone who cannot throw away from his memory what he does not desire to keep in mind is like a person who has a safe but has lost the key to that safe. He can put money in, but he cannot take it out. All faculties in man become invaluable when a person is able to use them at will, but when the faculties use the person, then he is no longer master of himself.

Purity of mind requires the destroying of all bad impressions collected there or received at present. One can destroy these impressions by five methods, and the method is chosen according to the impression one has to destroy. Some impressions need to be washed off the mind; some require to be erased from the surface of the mind; some have to be shaken off, like dust from one's clothes; some need to be burnt, like the wood in the fire, which after its test by fire turns into ashes; and some impressions must be drowned, so that they will never come up again. Bury certain impressions like corpses. Find every way of annihilation that is suited to each impression, so that your mind may be clear. The mind is not only a means of thinking or reasoning but the king of one's being and upon the condition of the mind one's health, happiness, and peace in life depend.

Now the question is what to destroy and what to keep in the mind. Collect and keep all that is beautiful, and destroy all that is void of beauty. Collect and keep all that is agreeable, and destroy all that has a disagreeable effect upon you. Collect and keep all that is harmonious, and destroy all that creates inharmony in yourself. Collect and keep all that is restful, and destroy all that disturbs the peace of your life. As dust gets into the works of a clock and stops the clock, so the effect produced by all impressions that are void of beauty and harmony and that which disturb your peace keeps you from progress. The mind cannot act properly when it is hindered by impressions that have a paralyzing effect upon it. Life is progress, and stopping progress is death. Failure does not matter in life. To a progressive person even a thousand failures do not matter: he has before his view success, and success is his, even after a thousand failures. The greatest pity in life is the standstill when life does not move further. A sensible person prefers death to such a life as that. It is a paralysis of the soul, of the spirit, which is always caused by holding bad impressions in the mind. No soul is deprived of happiness in reality; the soul's very being is happiness. Man brings unhappiness upon himself by holding in his hands the clouds of bad impressions, which fall as a shadow upon his soul.

Concentration is taught by the mystics in order to exercise the will, making it capable of using all faculties. A person with will power can remember what he wishes to remember and can forget what he wishes to forget. All things that deprive one of one's freedom in life are undesirable. The mind must be free from all bad impressions of life, which take away life's rest and peace. By concentration one is able to hold a certain thought one desires and to keep away all other thoughts, and when one is able to keep away all the thoughts one does not wish to have, it becomes easy to throw away the impressions of years, if one wishes to forget them. Bad impressions, however old and intimate, are like accumulated rubbish, which should be removed in order to make the house clean. The human heart is the home of the soul, and upon this home the comfort and peace of the soul depend.

The action of every illness or weakness is more manifest in its impression on the mind. There are many people who after an illness that has lasted some time become so much impressed by it that the impression remains even after their cure. To those who suffer for many years from an illness, their illness becomes natural—it becomes a part of themselves—and the obstacle to their cure is not the illness but the impression engraved on their mind.

So it is with weakness or a defect of any sort. Very often a person confesses, "This is my defect, but I cannot help it." If there is any weakness or defect, it is merely in the impression. When a person says, "There are moments when I lose my temper," or when he says, "I would like to tolerate, but I cannot stand that person," his weakness is nowhere but in the impression he has in his mind. Therefore the best cure for every illness and weakness is denial of the same. Affirmation deepens the impression, and contemplation of it makes it worse. There is no harm in denying one's illness or weakness, for that is not telling a lie as it does not exist in reality; it is merely a shadow. Truthful confession of something that is unreal is worse than lying. One must first deny that to oneself and then to others.

The Sufi's ideal through life is the realization of God and His perfection, and after realizing his ideal he cannot say, "I cannot tolerate or endure or stand anybody," and he cannot say that he cannot think, act, or feel as he thinks right. The idea of the Sufi is always to suggest to himself that which he wishes to be, that which he would like to be; and when he finds that he has failed to think, speak, or act as he wishes to, he must think that the condition of the process is to fall several times before one gets one's balance, instead of thinking, "It is my weakness, I cannot do otherwise." Those who walk toward the perfection of power and wisdom take every step forward with new hope and new courage, and weakness to them is a story of the past: it does not exist anymore; they don't recognize such a thing as existing. They can't accept themselves as being what they don't wish to be. They picture themselves as their ideal, what they would like to be. Sometime or other in their lives, if not sooner, later, they certainly succeed in molding their life to their ideal. Not only are there bad impressions that disturb the tranquility of the mind, but many feelings of resentment and resistance against things which do not agree with one's own idea also disturb one's mind. The person who has some business to carry on or some profession requires a tranquil mind, but the one who journeys on the spiritual path needs tranquility of mind most. Prayers, concentrations, meditations have no effect if the mind is not purified from all disturbances. Therefore for an adept no cost and no sacrifice are too great for keeping harmony within himself. A Sufi tries to keep harmony in his surroundings, the harmony which demands many sacrifices. It makes one endure what one is not willing to endure, it makes one overlook what one is not inclined to overlook, it makes one tolerate what one is not accustomed to tolerating, and it makes one forgive what one would never have forgotten if it had not been for the sake of harmony.

But at whatever cost harmony is attained it is a good bargain, for harmony is the secret of happiness, and in the absence of this a person living in palaces and rolling in gold can be most unhappy.

Harmony is brought about by attuning oneself to all beings, to all things, to all conditions, to all situations. He who cannot tune himself tries to tune others, and in setting about tuning others he breaks the string. It is as if a person with a violin in his hands tried to tune the cello. If he wishes to be in tune with the cellist he must tune his violin to the cellist's pitch. Every soul, as is its nature, constantly seeks harmony, but rarely is there to be found a soul who really knows how to create it. If someone says, "This noise that always goes on close to my ears drives me mad," he cannot stop the noise. He must know how to close himself to that noise; if he cannot close himself to accustom himself to it so it no longer create inharmony.

It is very difficult to evolve oneself and at the same time to keep in tune with the unevolved ones through life. It is like being drawn from above and at the same time being pulled from below. And if there is anything that can save man from being torn to pieces in life there is only one way, and that is to resound, to respond to all that is asked of him. It is this principle that was taught by Christ in the Sermon on the Mount. The Sermon on the Mount may seem to teach willing surrender to all, but that is not the way to look at it. The real lesson that one can learn from it is to try and harmonize with all instead of with one note. As every note is fixed in its place, so is every man fixed in his ideas and ways. But the one who treads the spiritual path is all notes, and he is no note in particular. Therefore he may rightly be called the keynote, the note which makes a consonant chord with every note that is played with it. There is no beauty where there is no harmony. Harmony is the fruit of love; therefore by attaining harmony in life one reaches the perfection of all three, love, harmony, and beauty.

*Chapter 3.*

# THE PURIFICATION OF THE HEART

The real purity is experienced not by means of outer ablutions nor by keeping away evil thoughts, but by keeping the heart pure from feelings that disturb the rhythm of the mind and thus upset the whole spirit. Feelings have a greater power than thoughts. If evil thoughts are monsters, evil feelings are demons. Such feelings as the desire to rob someone of his rights or his belongings have a very disturbing effect upon the spirit. Before such a feeling is put into action the effect is greater, while it is being acted upon it is less, but afterwards the effect is greatest. Life rightly and honestly lived has inner struggles, but by adding to it feelings that disturb life's tranquility one only adds to one's troubles in life, which then become endless. Purity of heart must not be considered a virtue but a necessity, a necessity not only to be considered for the good of others but for one's own life. The main thing that must be remembered is that the soul is pure and it cannot bear the lack of purity without feeling restless. The spirit has a tune and a rhythm. When it is out of tune and out of rhythm, though the riches of the whole world be given to it, it is worth nothing. It is purity and peace which are the soul's constant seeking.

As rust is natural to iron and as milk turns sour, so the feeling of the heart which by nature is as pure as milk, turns when it becomes rusted. Then nothing in the world is tasteful to a person and life with all its beauty becomes worthless. This condition must be avoided. An adept must keep his mind pure from rust.

The rust comes from allowing the heart to bear malice and spite against anyone, by having hatred and prejudice against anyone, by wanting to take revenge, by looking down upon another with contempt, and by the feeling of jealousy, rivalry, or envy. The heart wants constant care to keep it from getting rusted, for the nature of this life of illusion is such that the heart may be affected by little, unimportant things that are not of the least value coming from the outer life, and rust may be produced, as the mere touch of water can produce rust upon iron. Once the feeling has become soured it is difficult if not impossible to turn it sweet again, as it is impossible to make sour milk sweet.

A soul has brought from heaven its love for sweetness. It may after coming on earth develop a taste for salt, sourness, or bitterness, but its innate longing is always for the sweet. What its life needs most is not sugar (which is required in some degree for physical health) but the sweetness that is the original property of the heart and is needed most for true happiness and real well-being.

The process of purifying the heart does not differ very much from the process of cleaning or washing any object. Water poured upon any object washes it, and if there is a spot that cannot be washed away by water, some substance that can take that spot away is applied, to wash it thoroughly. The water that washes the heart is the continual running of the love stream. When that stream is stopped, when its way is blocked by some object that closes the heart, when the love stream is no longer running, then the mind cannot remain pure. As water is the cleansing and purifying substance in the physical world, so is love on the higher plane. Sometimes when it is difficult for love to take away impressions that are disagreeable, that block the way of the love stream, they may be washed away by some element that can destroy them. The whole life is a chemical process, and knowledge of its chemistry helps man to make life happy. An unhappy person, being unhappy himself, cannot make others happy. It is the wealthy person who can help the one who is hard up, not the poor person, however much desire the latter may have to help. It is the same with happiness, which is a great wealth: a happy person can take away the unhappiness of another, for he has enough for himself and more besides for others.

Earthly pleasures are the shadows of happiness, because of their transitoriness. True happiness is in love, which is the stream that springs from one's soul. He who will allow this stream to run continually in all conditions of life, in all situations however difficult, will have a happiness which truly belongs to him, whose source is not without but within. If there is a constant outpouring of love one becomes a divine fountain, for from the depth of the fountain a stream rises, and on its return it pours upon the fountain, bathing it continually. It is a divine bath, the true bath in the Ganges, the sacred river. When once one has the key to this fountain one is always purified every moment of one's life, and nothing can stay in the mind causing unhappiness. Happiness alone is natural, and it is attained by knowing and by living naturally.

Antipathy turns into malice, and malice culminates in bitterness. To possess it in one's heart is like possessing a poison, a poison that clouds the wit and produces obscurity. If one keeps one's heart free from malice one has accomplished a great deal, for it is in the clear heart that the light from above is reflected. Often malice of which one is unconscious enters without one's intention. Often the one who possesses malice is quite innocent, for his heart is reflecting the malice projected from another heart. Therefore care must be taken to keep one's heart free from the impressions and influences coming from others. The question, "How can one avoid this?" is answered thus, that the heart will focus itself on a person or an influence which is akin to its own quality; that is the nature of the heart.

Therefore even if the impression comes from another, the one who reflects it is responsible for the other's influence. To make the heart reflect good qualities one must prepare and train it, for it is the good quality of heart that will keep away undesirable impressions and thoughts, so that the heart will only reflect good impressions and desirable influences. As a practice to purify the heart, repeat every morning and every evening, "My thoughtful self! Reproach no one, hold a grudge against no one, bear malice against no one; be wise, tolerant, considerate, polite, and kind to all."

As the cleansing of a metal object produces a shine on it, so does the cleansing of the heart, especially its cleansing from feelings that produce humiliation. When a person thinks, "I have been wrong by acting in a certain way, by saying a certain thing, or by having thought something that should not have crossed my mind," he loses so to speak a radiance that even beams out through his countenance and that is called in Persian *aab-e ruh,* meaning, "the radiance of the soul." Every person shows from his expression his condition of heart. Therefore innocence of expression is a sign of purity of heart. A person may be clever, learned, qualified, most able; he may be strong physically or even mentally, he may be wealthy or of high rank, but none of these outside things helps him to retain that glow of the countenance which depends only upon the purity of the heart.

Many know and some say that the eyes can tell one everything that is in the heart of man, but fewer there are who know the cause behind this. The eyes are like a thermometer in the center in the head, which is focused on the center of the heart. Every impression that the heart bears, beautiful or ugly, is mirrored upon the center of the head, and so it is reflected accordingly in man's visage, especially in his eyes, which express the most.

There are many clever people, but so few there are who

may be called wise. The clever ones plot and plan one against another and exchange evil thoughts between themselves. So the deceitful and treacherous, intoxicated by their interest in life, cover their eyes with the cover of selfishness, thus keeping the heart from showing out its light, which alone illuminates the path of every achievement in life.

It might seem hard work to empty one's heart of all bad impressions and all feelings, of all bitterness and evil thoughts, and yet it is not nearly so hard as the task of earning one's daily bread. Work in one's everyday life takes most of the day; emptying the heart of all undesirable things takes but a few moments' silence. It is the desire to erase from the heart every undesirable impression that enables one in time to purify one's heart.

Innocence is the real purity, according to the mystic, for innocence is the sign of purity of heart. The intuitive faculties play a greater part in the life of the innocent. People call them simple ones, but nevertheless innocence often proves more beneficial in life than worldly cleverness. The innocent are oftener blessed by Providence than the worldly-wise who are always trying to get the best of everyone and to seize every opportunity that may seem in any way advantageous.

It is not easy for a clever person to try and become innocent. Innocence is something natural that manifests with the blooming of the heart. It is the sign of the thriving of a spiritual personality. If one can develop anything it is only this, that one may abstain from trying to be clever, and know that a selfish and clever person, with all his qualifications of getting the best of another, sooner or later comes across a person cleverer than he. Often a clever person finds his own chain tied around his legs.

No one has arrived at a higher degree of spirituality without being innocent. Innocence does not mean not knowing; it only means knowing and yet not knowing. A stupid person must not be confused with an innocent person, for the former is blind, whereas the latter only closes his eyes when he wants to. It is really the wise who become innocent on arriving at a stage of perfection in wisdom. There are two kinds of persons who show childlike simplicity in their lives: the silly one who shows childish traits, and the wise one who shows innocence.

He alone is capable of removing from the heart of another doubt, deceit, fear, or malice whose heart is already pure from these things or who at least can empty his heart of them. There is a weakness of the heart and there is strength of the heart. The heart's weakness is caused by things it contains that enfeeble it, such as doubt, deceit, fear, and malice. Their absence produces that purity of heart which in itself is a power. This power can be increased by faith, hope, and righteousness.

Purity of the heart causes its expansion, and lack of purity makes it narrow. The mystic poet of Hyderabad, Asaf, says, "If the heart is large, it can be the largest of all things." Besides, it is purity alone that opens the doors of the heart. All that hinders that purity stands as a closed door of the heart.

The pure-hearted may seem to be thinking, saying, or doing simple things, and yet there is a beauty and charm in all they do, for there is nothing more attractive than light itself. All that is other than light depends upon light to show out its beauty; light is beauty in itself. Purity of heart is the only condition that allows the inner stream to rise. The pure-hearted see more deeply, though they say little. There is no pretense about them. What they know they know; what they don't know they don't know. The pure ones make all pure, for to them all is pure. Their presence makes everyone pure. As pure water is the best tonic, so is contact with the pure-hearted person. When one is able to accomplish this in the spiritual path, there is not much that then remains to be accomplished.

A tendency is generally seen in those treading the spiritual path to feel discouraged at having bad impressions of their own faults and shortcomings upon their hearts. They begin to feel that they are too unworthy to have anything to do with things of a sacred nature. But in spite of all the virtue humility has in it, this is a great error. When one acknowledges something wrong in oneself, one gives that wrong a soul out of one's own spirit, and by withdrawing from all that is good and beautiful, spiritual and sacred, instead of developing the spirit of rejecting all errors, in time one becomes a receptacle of what is wrong. One goes on disapproving and yet collecting errors, so producing within oneself perpetual conflict. When man becomes helpless before his infirmities he becomes a slave to his errors, and feels within himself an obedient servant to his adversary.

The greater the purity developed in the heart, the greater becomes the power of man. As great is his power within himself, so great becomes his power over others. A hair's breadth can divide power from weakness, though they appear to have as wide a gulf between them as there is between land and sky.

*Chapter 4.*

# THE SECRET OF LIFE: MAN'S ATTITUDE

Man's attitude is the secret of life, for it is upon his attitude that success and failure depend. Both man's rise and fall depend upon his attitude. By attitude I mean that impulse which is like a battery behind the mechanism of thought. It is not man's thought that is his attitude, it is something behind the thought pushing it to the fore; and according to the strength of that impulse the thought becomes realized. Behind every word one speaks, the attitude is the most important factor in bringing what one says to its successful accomplishment.

There are three different aspects of this subject which one should observe. One aspect is one's attitude towards oneself: whether one treats oneself as a friend or as an enemy, whether one is in harmony with oneself or in disharmony. Not everyone is in harmony with himself, and not everyone treats himself as a friend, although he may think he does. For man is generally his own enemy. He does not know it, but he proves it in his doings. One reads in the Qur'an, "Verily, man is foolish and cruel." Foolish because he does not even know his own interest, and cruel because he very often proves to be his own enemy. Apart from cruelty to others, man begins by being cruel to himself, and that cruelty is the cause of foolishness. Man may consider himself very practical and clever, yet he often proves to be his own enemy.

As Sa'adi says, "My cleverness, very often thou provest to be my worst enemy." Worldly cleverness without faith and strength and trust is usually nothing but a delusion. It is the development of trust in the heart, the development of faith, that first gives a man a friendly attitude toward himself, and he becomes his own friend by bringing his external being into harmony with his inner being. For it is when the inner being seeks one thing and the external being does something else that there is disharmony in the self. When the higher self desires to go one way and the lower self another way, then there is disharmony, the result of which is like a volcanic eruption. The two parts of his own being, which should unite in love, clash, and the result is fire. What causes people to commit suicide? What brings illness and depression and despair? Very often it is the conflict that exists within oneself. Therefore the attitude towards oneself must first be friendly, kindly, and harmonious. Even in spiritual matters one should not go against oneself. I remember that when beginning to get interested in spiritual matters I once asked my teacher, "Murshid, do you approve of my staying up most of the night for my vigils?" "Whom do you torture?" said my murshid, "Yourself? Is God pleased with it?" I had not another word to say.

When one thinks about one's dealings with friends, with relatives, with those with whom one comes in contact in everyday life, one will see that one attracts them or repulses them according to one's attitude. Whether a person is in business, in commerce, or in any other walk of life, he either repulses or attracts others, and on that depends his success or failure in life. The secret of magnetism depends on whether one considers oneself to be a friend or an enemy, a stranger. To him who considers everyone to be a stranger, even a friend is a stranger, while to him who considers everyone to be a friend, even a stranger is a friend. If one is afraid of someone who may harm one, then one inspires that person to do harm. If one distrusts someone and thinks that one day that person will deceive one, he will certainly be inspired to do so; but if one has trust, the power of that trust may some day turn even an enemy into a friend.

Honesty and dishonesty are reflected in the same way in everything one does. If the attitude is not right, then this wrong attitude is reflected upon whatever work one does or whomever one sees, and that person will respond in the same way. Therefore right- and wrongdoing is not only a religious teaching, something forced upon people; it is a scientific and logical truth. For with a wrong attitude nothing right can be accomplished, and with the right attitude nothing can go wrong, even if there are difficulties.

There is hidden in our heart a wonderful power. It is a divine power, a sacred power, and it can be developed and cherished by keeping our attitude right. No doubt this is not always easy. The influence of this life on earth, so full of changes, of temptations and of falsehood, continually upsets the steadiness of our attitude. Nevertheless strength still lies in the steadiness of the attitude, and any lack of steadiness is the cause of every failure and disappointment. There is a Hindustani saying, "A steady attitude secures success," and when we enter the spiritual realm the same rule applies. It is not the prayer that a man says, it is not the house where he prays, it is not the faith that he claims, it is the attitude that counts in religion. It is just like the ticket one is asked to show at a railway barrier. One is not asked what position one has, what property or what ancestors. No, they say, "Ticket please!" and if one has it one is admitted. That ticket is man's attitude. In order to enter into the spiritual spheres this right attitude is needed, and it shortens the path.

Now the question is how to know the right attitude from the wrong. To know the right attitude from the wrong is as easy as seeing things when the eyes are open. When one does not realize the attitude is wrong it means that at that time one closes one's eyes. The eyes do not fail one; one closes them. Man does not like to admit his wrong attitude to himself; he is afraid of his own faults. But the person who looks his own error in the eye, the person who criticizes himself, has no time to criticize others. It is that person who will prove to be wise. But human nature is generally such that one does something quite different. Everyone seems to be most interested in criticizing others. If one would criticize oneself, one would find endless faults, however saintly or wise one might be; there is no end of faults in a human being. And the consciousness of correcting one's faults, of making oneself better, of taking hold of the right attitude, is the only secret of success, and by it one attains to that goal which is the object of every soul.

The attitude should be first to seek God within; and after seeking God within, then to see Him outside. In the story of Alladdin in the Thousand and One Nights we read that Aladdin went to look for a lantern. That lantern is the divine light within, and it is very difficult to find. Once a person has found it, the next thing is to throw that light on the outer life, in order to find God both within and without. Prayer, night vigil, any form of worship—all these things are helpful. But if a person is not inclined to make peace with his brother, to harmonize with his fellow men, to seek to please those around him, then he has not performed his religious duties. For what can a person give to God, who is perfect? His goodness? His goodness is very little. His prayers? How many times will he pray? The whole day he spends for himself. If he prays two or three times, it is not much. If a man can do anything to please God, it is only to please His creatures, to seek their pleasure. There cannot be a better prayer and a greater religion than being conscientious in regard to the feelings of other people, being ready to serve them, to please them in every way, to forgive them, to tolerate them. And if when doing wrong one would realize that one was doing wrong to God, and in doing right that one was doing right to God, then one's attitude would be right.

The end and the sum total of all mysticism, philosophy, and meditation, of everything one learns and develops, is to be a better servant to humanity. Everything, from the beginning to the end, in the spiritual path is a training to enable one to serve mankind better, and if one does not follow the spiritual path with that intention, one will find in the end that one has accomplished nothing. There are many who seek wonderworking or great power to accomplish things. They may perhaps try and gain some power or other, but their soul will never be satisfied. The true satisfaction of the soul is in honest, humble service to another. If there were two people before me, one with great power of wonderworking, who could perform miracles, and another humble and kind and gentle and willing to do anything he could for his fellow men, I would prefer this last. I would say, "The first is wonderful; but the other is a sage."

The soul of man is goodness itself, if only he begins to love goodness. This is not something that is acquired; it springs up of itself. Right attitude towards God is a direct response to God. For His voice is continually coming as an answer to every call. The ears of the heart should be open and focused on that source whence the voice is coming. When that is done, the teacher within is found; then there is continual guidance, and one is guided to the extent that one keeps close to it. Then one needs no other guidance.

Attitude forms a channel for effort, and a right attitude makes a channel for a right effort. The world is the place of tests and trials. If one did not live in the world one would have no chance of doing good or bad. Even if one lived a very spiritual life in the wilderness it would do no good to anybody, not even to oneself, for one would not have gone through the tests and trials of the world. One can neither praise the life of a hermit nor condemn it. If he is happy it is good. Everyone knows his own life, and if he is happy he will give happiness to others also.

Sometimes a person is born to live a hermit's life. In living that life he will not find any torture or trouble. Let him live it: in that way he will prove to be his own friend. At the second step he takes he will be a friend of another. If someone asked me if the hermit's life is ideal, I would say it may be ideal for him, but you need not follow it. Is a hermit's life selfish, then? If we observe life it is very difficult to say who is selfish and who is not. The life of a hermit is not a life that one should sacrifice everything in order to follow. I would be the last to recommend it to anyone. But if one followed it for one's own pleasure and found happiness in it, I would not prevent it; for a Sufi maintains from first to last the freedom of the soul.

*Chapter 5.*

# HARMONY

Harmony is that which makes beauty; beauty in itself has no meaning. An object that is called beautiful at one time or place may be not beautiful at another. And so it is with thought, speech, and action. That which is called beautiful is only so at a certain time and under certain conditions that make it beautiful. So if one could give a true definition of beauty it would be harmony. Harmony in a combination of colors, harmony in the drawing of a design or a line, that is what is called beauty. And a word, a thought, a feeling, or an action which creates harmony is productive of beauty.

Whence comes the tendency towards harmony and whence comes the tendency towards inharmony? The natural tendency of every soul is towards harmony, and the tendency towards inharmony is an unnatural state of mind or affairs; the very fact that it is not natural makes it devoid of beauty. The psychology of man is such that he responds both to harmony and inharmony. He cannot help it, because he is naturally so made; mentally and physically he responds to all that comes to him, whether it be harmonious or inharmonious.

The teaching of Christ, "Resist not evil," is a hint not to respond to inharmony. For instance a word of kindness or sympathy or an action of love and affection finds response; but a word of insult, an action of revolt or of hatred, creates a response too, and that response creates still more inharmony in the world. By giving way to inharmony one allows inharmony to multiply. Where does all the great unrest and discord that one now sees pervading the world come from? It seems that it comes from the ignorance of this fact: that inharmony creates inharmony, and that inharmony will multiply. If a person is insulted, his natural tendency is to reply by insulting the other person still more. In this way he gets the momentary satisfaction of having given a good answer, but he has responded to that power which came from the other, and these two powers, being negative and positive, create more inharmony.

"Resist not evil" does not mean to take evil into oneself. It only means do not return the inharmony that comes to you, as a person playing tennis would send back the ball with his racket. But at the same time it does not suggest that one should receive the ball with open hands.

The tendency towards harmony may be likened to a rock in the sea: through wind and storm the rock stands firm; waves come at it with all their force, and yet it still stands bearing it all, letting the waves beat against it. By fighting inharmony one increases it; by not fighting it one refrains from adding fuel to the fire, which would otherwise increase and cause destruction. But no doubt the wiser we become, the more difficulties we have to face in life, because every kind of inharmony will be directed towards us for the very reason that we will not fight it. We should realize, however, that all these difficulties have helped to destroy this inharmony that would otherwise have multiplied. This is not without its advantages, for every time we stand firm where there is inharmony we increase our strength, though outwardly it may seem a defeat. But one who is conscious of the increase of his power will never admit that it is a defeat, and after a while the person against whom one has stood firm will realize that it was actually his own defeat.

The Sufi avoids all unrhythmic actions; he keeps the rhythm of his speech under the control of patience, not speaking a word before the right time, not giving an answer until the question is finished. A contradictory word he considers to be a discord unless spoken in a debate, and even at such times he tries to resolve it into a consonant chord. A contradictory tendency in a man finally develops into a passion, until he will contradict even his own idea if it happens to be pronounced by another. The Sufi in order to keep harmony even modulates his speech from one key to another; in other words he falls in with another person's idea by looking at the subject from the speaker's point of view instead of his own. He makes a basis for every conversation with an appropriate introduction, thus preparing the ears of the listener for a perfect response. He watches his every movement and expression, as well as those of others, trying to form a consonant chord of harmony between himself and another.

The attainment of harmony in life takes longer to acquire and more careful study than does the training of the ear and the cultivation of the voice, although it is acquired in the same manner as the knowledge of music. To the ear of the Sufi every word spoken is like a note which is true when harmonious and false when inharmonious. He makes the scale of his speech either major, minor, or chromatic, as the occasion demands; and his words, either sharp, flat, or natural, are in accord with the law of harmony.

Life in the world has a constantly jarring effect, and the finer we become the more trying it will be to us. And the time comes when the more sincere and full of good will, the more kind and sympathetic a person is, the worse life becomes for him. If he is discouraged by it he goes under, but if he keeps his courage he will find in the end that it was not disadvantageous, for his power will someday increase to that stage, to that degree at which his presence, his word,

The Buddha

and his action will control the thoughts and feelings and actions of others. Then his rhythm will become powerful and will cause the rhythm of everybody else to follow it. This is what is called in the East the quality of the master mind.

But in order to stand firm against the inharmony that comes from without, one must first practice standing firm against all that comes from within, from one's own self. For one's own self is more difficult to control than other people, and when one is not able to control oneself and one has failed, it is most difficult to stand firm against the inharmony outside.

What is it that causes inharmony in oneself? Weakness. Physical weakness or mental weakness, but it is always weakness. Very often, therefore, one finds that bodily illness causes disharmony and inharmonious tendencies. Besides, there are many diseases of the mind that the scientists of today have not yet discovered. Sometimes people are considered sane whose minds are in fact ill, and as not enough attention is paid to the defects which are inherent in the diseases of the mind, man has never had a chance to notice them in himself. He is continually finding fault with others; whether he works in an office, somewhere in a good position, at home, or anywhere else, he causes inharmony. Nobody realizes this, for to be treated as insane one must first be recognized as insane.

The cause of every discomfort and of every failure is inharmony, and the most useful thing one can impart in education today is the sense of harmony. To develop harmony in children and to bring it to their notice will not be as difficult as it appears; what is needed is to point out to the young the different aspects of harmony in all the various affairs of life.

*Chapter 6.*

# EXALTATION

There is a verse in the Bible: "It is the spirit that quickeneth, the flesh profiteth nothing." So what we call living is subtle; what is dead is coarse. In other words, what is dense is coarse, and what is fine is subtle.

It is true as the Hindus say that there was a golden age, then a silver age, a copper age, and an iron age. Certainly we are in the iron age. Never before in any period of history has there been such grossness and denseness as mankind shows today. And this has come about by the law of gravitation. When the consciousness is absorbed in gross matter, then a person gravitates towards the earth. When the consciousness is released from gross matter, then it soars towards heaven.

I do not mean to say that people were not gross two or three thousand years ago. But when we study traditions we find that they were also very fine and subtle in perception, more so than we are today. Our contact with the earth and earthly things has made us more rigid; they were more placid. And if we want proof of this we have only to study ancient languages such as Sanskrit, Zend, Persian, or

Hebrew and to see the manuscripts of ancient times and the way they explain things. Maybe they are quite strange to our present-day mentality and perception, yet their fineness is beyond words. And it seems we are going from bad to worse and are becoming coarser every day. If we only realized how far we are removed from what may be called fine perception!

When a person tries to understand subtle things by mathematical calculations alone, he has come into the dense sphere. He does not want to become fine; he wants to make the spirit, which is the finest thing, gross and intelligible. Therefore it is of the greatest importance for spiritual attainment to develop fine perception. I have seen people go into a trance or dive into a deep meditation and yet lack fine perception, and then it is of no value. They are not really spiritual. A really spiritual person must have a mentality like liquid, not like a rock. A mentality that is moving, not crude and dense.

This question has also a metaphysical side to it. There are two experiences in life: one realm of experience is sensation, the other realm is exaltation. It is by these two experiences that one tries to experience happiness. But what is experienced by sensation or in the form of sensation is not necessarily happiness, it is pleasure. It might give the appearance of happiness for a moment, but it is only a suggestion of happiness.

Exaltation is something that the mystic experiences. Those who are not mystics experience it also, but they do not know what it is; they cannot distinguish between sensation and exaltation. Sometimes exaltation may be the outcome of sensation. It is possible, but at the same time exaltation that depends upon sensation is not an independent exaltation.

There are different grades of exaltation. To the Sufi, the soul is a current that joins the physical body to the source. The art of repose naturally makes it easier for the soul to experience freedom, inspiration, power, because it is then loosened from the grip of the physical body. As Rumi says in the *Masnavi,* man is a captive on earth: his body and his mind are his prison bars, and the soul is unconsciously craving to experience once again the freedom that originally belonged to it. The Platonic idea about reaching the higher source is the same: that by exaltation the soul so to speak rises above the fast hold of the physical body; it may be only for a few moments, but it experiences in those moments a freedom that man has never experienced before.

A moment of exaltation is a different experience at every level. The supreme exaltation is hinted at in the Bible: "Be ye perfect even as your Father in heaven is perfect." Many religious people will say that it is impossible for man to be perfect, but it is said in the Bible just the same. At all times the knowers and seers have understood that there is a stage at which, by touching a particular phase of existence, one feels raised above the limitations of life and is given that power and peace and freedom, that light and life, which belong to the source of all beings. In other words, in that moment of supreme exaltation one is not only united with the source of all beings, but dissolved in it. For the source is one's self.

The source is greater than we can put into words. We can try to conceive it by comparing it with a seed, which is the source of the flower—the leaves, the stem, the branches, and the fragrance—while if we take the seed alone we do not see all those things in it, yet they were there all the time. On the other hand we cannot really compare even the seed with the source, for the seed depends upon the sun and water and earth for its growth, whereas the ultimate source does not depend upon anything. It is all that is strong and powerful. It is beyond words and beyond our limited conception even to think of the source, except that when we get greater inspiration, peace, joy, and magnetism, we appreciate things much better. In this way we may understand a little how great the source must be. The greater we are, the closer we reach to that source. As the great Indian poet Khusrau says,

"When I become Thou and Thou becomest me, neither canst Thou say that I am different, nor canst Thou say that Thou are different."

The different grades of exaltation are as the different notes in music. As we distinguish lower and higher notes, so it is with the different grades of the experience of exaltation. Even reading a beautiful poem can produce exaltation; good music gives exaltation, and a feeling of great joy does so too. It all breaks up congestion; there are fine cells of the nerves that become free, and the body experiences relaxation.

There is a difference between sensation and exaltation, but when we come to words, there is always confusion. One can say that exaltation is the fusion of all sensation; but if one says that through sensation exaltation is experienced, it is true also.

As much as we need sensation in life to make our experience of life concrete, so much or even more do we need exaltation in order to live life fully. The lower creation, such as birds and beasts, also has glimpses of exaltation. They not only rejoice in grazing and in finding seeds, in making nests or in playing in the air, in singing and in running about in the forest, there are also moments when even birds and beasts feel exaltation. And if we go into this subject more deeply we shall understand what we read in a most wonderful verse of Islamic tradition: "There are moments when even rocks become exalted, and trees fall into ecstasy." If that be true, then man, who is created to complete the experience that any living being can have, must experience exaltation as much as he experiences sensation.

What I mean by sensation is the impression one has of line and color; the preference one has for softness in structure; the appreciation one has of fragrance and perfume; the enjoyment one gains by tasting sweet and sour and pungent; the joy one experiences in hearing poetry, singing, and music. All these experiences are manifest in the realm of sensation. The world of sensation is one world; the world of exaltation is another. These two worlds are made for man to experience in order to live life on earth fully. And yet, with this possibility and opportunity in life, man continues to live a life of sensation, forgetting that there is another life as well, a life that can be experienced here on earth, and that completes life's experience.

There is a physical aspect of exaltation that comes as a reaction or result of having seen the immensity of space, having looked at the wide horizon, or having seen the clear sky, the moonlit night, and nature at dawn. Looking at the rising sun, watching the setting sun, looking at the horizon from the sea, being in the midst of nature, looking at the world from the top of a mountain, all these experiences—even such an experience as watching the little smiles of an innocent infant—these experiences lift one up and give one a feeling which one cannot call sensation: it is exaltation.

A higher aspect of exaltation is a moral exaltation: when we are sorry for having said or done something unpleasant; when we have asked forgiveness and humbled ourselves before someone towards whom we were inconsiderate. We have humbled our pride then. Or when we have felt a deep gratitude to someone who has done something for us; when we have felt love, sympathy, devotion which seem endless and which seem so great that our heart cannot accommodate them; when we have felt so much pity for someone that we have forgotten ourselves; when we have found a profound happiness in rendering a humble service to someone in need; when we have said a prayer that has come from the bottom of our heart; when we have realized our own limitation and smallness in comparison with the greatness of God. All these experiences lift man up.

The moment we have these experiences, we are not living on earth but in another world. The joy of such experiences is very great, and yet they can be gained without paying anything, whereas sensations cost something. We have to go to the theatre, to all kinds of entertainments; all these cost more than they are worth. But exaltation, which is beyond price, comes of itself, as soon as we have shown an inclination towards it. It is only a matter of changing our attitude.

Once I visited a great sage in Bengal. I said to him, "What a blessed life is yours, that gives pleasure and happiness to so many souls." But he answered, "How privileged I am myself that a thousand times more pleasure and happiness come to me."

Exaltation is a purifying process. A moment's exaltation can purify the evil of many years, because it is like bathing in the Ganges, as Hindus say. This is symbolical: exaltation is the Ganges, and if we bathe in it we are purified from all sins. It does not take much to make us exalted: a kind attitude, a sympathetic trend of mind, and exaltation is already there. If we were to notice it, we would find that when our eyes shed tears in sympathy with another, we are already exalted; our soul has bathed in the spiritual Ganges. Exaltation comes by forgetting self and by destroying selfishness. But remember, we can never claim to be unselfish; however unselfish we may be, we are selfish just the same. However, we can be wisely selfish; and if we are to be selfish, it is just as well to be so wisely. This is the same thing as what we call unselfishness, and it is profitable to be wisely instead of being foolishly selfish, because the former gains and the latter loses.

The third aspect of exaltation comes by touching the reason of reasons and by realizing the essence of wisdom; by feeling the profound depth of one's heart, by widening one's outlook on life; by broadening one's conception, by deepening one's sympathies, and by soaring upwards to those spheres where spiritual exaltation manifests. Today a person of common sense or a person who is called practical is in the habit of laughing at the idea that someone could have visions or experiences of ecstasy, that someone could go into what is called a trance. But this is nothing to be surprised at, nothing to laugh at. All these things are laughable, however, when done by the undeserving; and it is mostly such who make these claims and look for approbation from others for their experiences. Those who really experience these

Whirling

things do not need to tell people that they had this or that experience: their own joy is their reward. No one else should recognize it; the less others know about it the better.

Why must we show ourselves to be different from others? It is only vanity, and the greater our vanity the less progress we make along the spiritual path. The worst thing on the spiritual path is to try and show oneself to be different from others. Those who are really evolved are glad to act as everyone else acts. To novelists it seems beautiful to describe masters as living in caves of the Himalayas or moving about in the forest somewhere where one cannot go and find them, always keeping aloof and apart so that no one can reach them. But every soul has a divine spark, and therefore if there is any higher stage of human evolution it is for human beings, not for those outside the human world. If masters are outside the human world, there is no relation between us and them.

The great spiritual souls have lived in the world, in the midst of the world, and proved to be the greatest masters. Imagine the life of Abraham, of Moses, of Jesus Christ, and again the life of Muhammad—in war and battles, and yet as exclusive and remote, as spiritual as anyone could be. Picture Krishna, in Kurukshetra fighting in the battle, giving a world scripture. If they had all lived in mountain caves we would not have been benefited by them. What is the use of those holy ones who never experience from morning till evening the tests and trials of the dense world, where at every move there are a thousand temptations, a thousand problems? What can those who are outside the world do for us who are exposed to a thousand difficulties at every moment of our life? And these difficulties are increasing. With the evolution of the world life is becoming heavier, more difficult. No, the mastery, the holiness, the evolution must be shown here on earth. It is very easy to be evolved in the seventh heaven. But exaltation experienced and imparted to others here on the earth is exaltation which is more worthwhile.

As to the grossness and subtlety of human nature, the heroes, kings, masters, prophets—those who have won the heart of humanity—have been fine in perception and in character, they have not been gross. Their fineness was simple: there was always a simple side to it, but at the same time it was subtle, which made it beautiful. A person who can say without saying and who can do without doing is a subtle person, and that subtlety is worth appreciating. The one who sees and does not see, knows and does not know, the one who experiences and does not experience at the same time, the one who is living and yet dead, that is the soul who experiences life fully.

*Chapter 7.*

# THE LIVING HEART

Has God a consciousness of the whole creation besides the consciousness He has of separate beings? This may be explained in this way: if one's body suffers through pain from a sting or anything, every part of it is conscious of the pain that it has; it is not the afflicted part only that is conscious of it. One's whole consciousness shares in the pain. This means that the entire consciousness of a person experiences the same pain that a part of his body experiences; and sometimes an illness in a part of the body has an effect upon the whole body. No doubt the part that is affected by illness may show the sign of illness, while the other parts of the body may not show the sign, yet in some measure they are affected and suffer through it. If God is all and in all, then He experiences life not only through all forms and through all entities separately, but also collectively, as the pain of one organ is experienced by the whole body.

We see that our life is full of impressions that we receive consciously or unconsciously, and from these we derive either benefit or disadvantage. We learn from this that if we had the power to receive or to reject reflections, we would

Mother Krishnabai with Papa Ramdas

become the masters of life. Now the question is how to learn this; how can we manage to receive impressions that are beneficial, and also to reject those that we do not wish to receive?

The first and most essential thing is to make the heart a living heart by purifying it from all undesirable impressions, by clearing it of fixed thoughts and beliefs, and then by giving it a life. That life is within itself, and it is love. When the heart is so prepared, then by means of concentration one must learn how to focus it; for it is not everyone who knows how to focus his heart to receive a certain reflection. A poet, a musician, a writer, a thinker unconsciously focuses his mind on the work of someone who has lived before him, and by focusing on the work of a great personality he comes in contact with that personality and derives benefit from it, very often without knowing the secret. A young musician may be thinking of Bach or Beethoven or Wagner. By focusing his mind on their particular work he derives, without knowing it, a reflection of the spirit of Wagner or Beethoven, which is a great help to his work; and he expresses in his work the reflection that he receives.

This teaches us that as we go on in the path of spiritual attainment we arrive at a stage when we are able to focus our mind, our heart on God. And there we not only receive the reflection of one personality, but the reflections of all personalities. Then we see not in the form of a drop, but in the form of an ocean. There we have the perfect reflection, if we can only focus our heart on God.

Why is it that among simple and illiterate people a belief in God is to be found, and among the most intellectual there seems to be a lack of that belief? The answer is that the intellectual ones have their reason; they will not believe in what they do not see. If methods such as those of the old faiths and beliefs were prescribed—of worshipping God by worshipping the sun or a sacred tree or a sacred animal, or worshipping God before a shrine, an altar, or an image of some ideal—the intellectual one today would say, "This is something that I have made; this is something that I have known." It is an object, not a person; and in this way the intellectual person seems to be lost. The unintellectual ones have their belief in God and they stay there; they do not go any further, nor are they benefited by their belief.

But the process that the wise consider best for the seeker after truth to adopt is the process of first idealizing God and then realizing God. In other words: first make God, and God will make you. As you read in the *Gayan*, "Make God a reality, and God will make you the truth."

This may be understood by a story. There was an artist who was devoted to her art; nothing else in the world had any attraction for her. She had a studio, and whenever she had a moment to spare her first thought was to go to that studio and to work on a statue she was making. People could not understand her, for it is not everybody who is devoted to one thing like this. For a time a person interests himself in art, at other times in something else, at other times in the home, at other times in the theatre. But she did not mind; she went every day to her studio and spent most of her time in making this work of art, the only work of art that she made in her life. The more the work progressed, the more she began to feel delighted with it, attracted by that beauty to which she was devoting her time. It began to manifest to her eyes, and she began to communicate with that beauty. It was no longer a statue for her, it was a living being. The moment the statue was finished she could not believe her eyes that it had been made by her. She forgot the work that she had put into this statue and the time that it had taken, the thought, the enthusiasm. She became absorbed in its beauty. The world did not exist for her; it was this beauty that was produced before her. She could not believe for a moment that this could be a dead statue. She saw there a living beauty, more living than anything else in the world; inspiring and revealing. She felt exalted by the beauty of the statue.

She was so overcome by the impression that this statue

made on her that she knelt down before this perfect vision of beauty, with all humility, and asked the statue to speak, forgetting entirely that it was her own work. And as God is in all things and all beings, as God Himself is all beauty that there is, as God answers from everywhere if the heart is ready to listen to that answer, and as God is ready to communicate with the soul who is awakened to the beauty of God, there came a voice from the statue: "If you love me, there is only one condition, and that is to take this bowl of poison from my hand. If you wish me to be living, you no more will live. Is it acceptable?" "Yes," she said, "You are beauty, you are the beloved, you are the one to whom I give all my thought, my admiration, my worship; even my life I will give to you." "Then take this bowl of poison," said the statue, "that you may no longer be." For her it was nectar to feel, "I shall now be free from being. That beauty will be, the beauty that I have worshipped and admired will remain. I no longer need be." She took the bowl of poison, and fell dead. The statue lifted her and kissed her by giving her its own life, the life of beauty and sacredness, the life which is everlasting and eternal.

This story is an allegory of the worship of God. God is made first. The artists who made God were the prophets, the teachers who have come from time to time. When the world was not evolved enough they made God of rock; when the world was a little more advanced they gave God words. In praise of God they pictured the image of God, and they gave to humanity a high conception of God by making a throne for Him. Instead of making it in stone, they made it in the heart of man.

When this reflection of God, who is all beauty, majesty, and excellence, is fully reflected in a person, then naturally he is focused on God. And from this phenomenon that which arises out of the heart of the worshipper is the love and light, the beauty and power which belong to God. It is therefore that one seeks God in the godly.

# PART II

## SELF-CONTROL:

## THE MORAL OF RENUNCIATION

*Chapter 8.*

# THE STRUGGLE OF LIFE

No one can deny the fact that life in the world is one continual struggle. The one who does not know the struggle of life is either an immature soul or a soul who has risen above the life of this world. The object of a human being in this world is to attain to the perfection of humanity, and therefore it is necessary that man should go through what we call the struggle of life.

As long as an infant is innocent he is happy; he knows nothing of the struggle of life. The late nizam of Hyderabad, who was also a great mystic, wrote, "What were those days, when my eyes had not seen sorrow! My heart had no desire and life had no misery." This is the first stage. Thence we come to the maturity of the intelligence, and then we see that no one can be trusted, neither the friend nor the relation. None can stand the test when it comes; all are false and none is true. At first a person believes that this is directed specially against him. A dervish once wrote these lines on the wall of the mosque where he had spent the night: "The world believes in the ideal of God, yet knows not whether He is friend or foe."

The waves of the sea go up and down; the atom believes that they rise and fall for it. It thinks, "The wave raises me, so it is favorable to me," or "It lowers me, so it is unfavorable." In the same way man thinks a friend is favorable or unfavorable to him, but then he realizes that this is the nature of the world. In all of us there is the nafs, the ego, and every ego fights against the others. There is a sword in every hand, both in that of the friend and in that of the enemy. The friend kisses before he strikes; there is no other difference. And then one realizes that nothing else can be expected of the world.

The great Indian poet Tulsidas has said, "Everyone does and says as much as he has understood." Why should a man blame another for what he cannot understand? If he has no more understanding, from where can the poor man borrow it? Then a person begins to realize that whatever comes, he should take it calmly. If an insult comes he takes it calmly; if a good word comes he accepts it with thanks; if a bad word comes he takes that quietly. If it is a bad word he is only thankful that it is not a blow; if it is a blow he is thankful that it is not worse. He is ready to give his time and his services to all, to the deserving and the undeserving alike, for he sees in all the manifestation of God. He sees God in every form: in the highest, in the lowest, in the most beautiful, in the most worthless.

The Sufi says that if God is separate from the universe, he would rather worship a God who can be seen, who can be heard, who can be tasted, who can be felt by the heart and perceived by the soul. He worships the God who is before him. He sees the God who is in everything.

Christ said, "I and the Father are one." That does not mean that Christ laid claim to godhood for his own person. It is what the dervishes call *naminaust,* which means all is He and He is all. There is not an atom in the universe that He is not. We must recognize Him, we must respect Him in every face, even in the face of our enemy, of the most worthless. Knowing that all is God by reading a few books on philosophy is not enough; our piety and our spirituality are valueless if we do only this. To read a religious book and feel pious is not enough. To go to some religious place and be pleased that we are religious is not enough. To give to charity and be conceited, believing that we have done something great, is not enough. We must give our services and our time to the deserving and undeserving alike, and we must be thankful to God that He has enabled us to give.

For this is the only opportunity we have of giving. This life is short, and we shall never have the same opportunity to give, to serve, to do something for others. In the Sermon on the Mount it is said, "Whosoever shall smite thee on thy right cheek, turn to him the other also." Someone may say or think that he should hit back; but a Sufi would not hit back. Why? Because he does not want twenty blows instead of one.

It is said that if a man asks you for your coat, you should give him your cloak also. Why? Because neither the cloak nor the coat are yours. If someone thinks, "This is mine, I should keep it, I should guard it," he will always be watching his goods. If they are yours, whose were they before? Whose will they be after you? Someone will take them after you, and all that you value so much will be in the hands of others.

Then it is said that if someone asks you to go with him one mile, you should go with him two miles. That means if someone makes use of our services, let us not think, "Why should I, such an important person, serve another, give my time to another?" Let us give our services more liberally than we are asked to do. Let us give service, give our time; but when the time for receiving comes, do not let us expect to receive anything. Let us not expect our friend to be as we are to him; that will never be possible. We must then practice renunciation.

We must practice virtue because we like it; do good because we like to do it and not for any return; expect no kindness or appreciation; if we do, it will become a trade.

This is the right way for the world in general, and the only way of becoming happy. Its moral is called the moral of renunciation.

There are two different attitudes that people adopt while going through this struggle of life. One struggles along bravely through life; the other becomes disappointed, heart-broken, before arriving at his destination. As soon as a person loses the courage to go through the struggle of life, the burden of the whole world falls upon his head. But he who goes on struggling through life, he alone makes his way. The one whose patience is exhausted, the one who has fallen in this struggle is trodden upon by those who walk through life. Even bravery and courage are not sufficient to go through the struggle of life: there is something else that must be studied and understood.

One must study the nature of life; one must understand the psychology of this struggle. In order to understand this struggle one must see that there are three sides to it: struggle with oneself, struggle with others, and struggle with circumstances. One person may be capable of struggling with himself, but that is not sufficient. Another is able to struggle with others, but even that is not sufficient. A third person may answer the demands of circumstance, but this is not enough either; what is needed is that all three should be studied and learned, and one must be able to manage the struggle in all three directions.

The question is, where should one begin and where should one end? Generally one starts by struggling with others, and then one struggles all through life, and never finishes. The one who is somewhat wiser struggles with conditions, and perhaps he accomplishes things a little better. But the one who struggles with himself first is the wisest, for once he has struggled with himself, which is the most difficult struggle, the other struggles will become easy for him. Struggling with oneself is like singing without an accompaniment. Struggling with others is the definition of war; struggling with oneself is the definition of peace. In the beginning, outwardly, it might seem that it is cruel to have to struggle with oneself, especially when one is in the right. But the one who has penetrated deeper into life will find that the struggle with oneself is the most profitable in the end.

What is the nature of the struggle with oneself? It has three aspects. The first is to make one's thought, speech, and action answer the demands of one's own ideal, while at the same time giving expression to all the impulses and desires that belong to one's natural being. The next aspect of the struggle with oneself is to fit in with others, with their various ideas and demands. For this a person has to make himself as narrow or as wide as the place that he is asked to fill, which is a delicate matter, difficult for all to comprehend and to practice. The third aspect of the struggle with oneself is to give accommodation—large or small, as the demand may be—to others in one's own life, in one's own heart.

When we consider the question of the struggle with others there are also three things to think about, of which the first is how to control and govern people and activities that happen to be our duty, our responsibility. Another aspect is to learn how to allow ourselves to be used by others in various situations in life; to what extent we should allow others to make use of our time, our energy, our work, or our patience, and where to draw the line. And the third aspect to consider is how to fit in with the standards and conceptions of different personalities who are at various stages of evolution.

Regarding the third aspect of this struggle, there are conditions that can be avoided, and there are conditions before which one is helpless. And again there are conditions that could be avoided, and yet one does not find in oneself the capability, the power, or the means to change them. If one studies these questions of life and meditates in order that inspiration and light may fall on them, that one may understand how to struggle through life, one certainly will find help and arrive at a stage where one finds life easier.

The Sufi looks upon the struggle as unavoidable, as a

struggle through which he has to go. He sees from his mystical point of view that the more he takes notice of the struggle the more the struggle will expand, and the less he makes of it the better he will be able to pass through it. When he looks at the world, what does he see? He sees everybody with their hands before their eyes, looking only at their own struggles, which are as big as their own palm. He thinks, "Shall I also sit down like this and look at my struggles? That will not answer the question." His work therefore is to engage in the struggle of others, to console them, to strengthen them, to give them a hand. Through that his own struggle dissolves, and this makes him free to go forward.

How does the Sufi struggle? He struggles with power, with understanding, with open eyes, and with patience. He does not look at a loss; what is lost is lost. He does not think of the pain of yesterday; yesterday is gone for him. Only if a memory is pleasant does he keep it before him, for it is helpful on his way. He takes both the admiration and the hatred coming from around him with smiles. He believes that both these things form a rhythm with the rhythm of a certain music: one and two, the strong accent and the weak accent. Praise cannot be without blame, nor can blame be without praise. He keeps the torch of wisdom before him, because he believes that the present is the echo of the past, and that the future will be the reflection of the present. It is not sufficient to think only of the present moment; one should also think where it comes from and where it goes. Every thought that comes to the Sufi's mind, every impulse, every word he speaks, is to him like a seed, a seed that falls in this soil of life and takes root. In this way he finds that nothing is lost: every good deed, every little act of kindness, of love done to anybody will someday rise as a plant and bear fruit.

The Sufi does not consider life as different from business, but he sees how real business can be achieved in the best manner. The symbol of the mystics of China was a branch laden with fruit in their hand. What does this mean? It means that the purpose of life is to arrive at that stage where every moment becomes fruitful. And what does fruitful mean? Does it mean fruits for oneself? No, trees do not bear fruit for themselves, but for others. True profit is not that profit which one makes for oneself, true profit is that which one makes for others. After attaining all that one wants to attain, be it earthly or heavenly, what is the result of it all? The result is only this, that all that one has attained, that one has acquired, whether earthly or heavenly, one can place before others. *Propkar,* which in the language of the Vedanta means working for the benefit of others, is the only fruit of life.

*Chapter 9.*

# THE WISDOM OF THE WARRIOR: WILL POWER

In this continual battle of life, the one who stands firm through it all comes out victorious in the end. Even with all power and understanding, if one gives up through lack of hope and courage, one has failed. What brings bad luck in this life, in this battle, is a pessimistic attitude and what helps man to conquer in the battle of life, however difficult, is an optimistic attitude.

There are some in this world who look at life with a pessimistic view, thinking that it is clever to see the dark side of things. To some extent it is beneficial to see the difficult side also, but the psychological law is such that once the spirit is impressed with the difficulty of the situation it loses its hope and courage. Once a person asked me if I looked at life with a pessimistic attitude or if I was an optimist. I said, "An optimist with open eyes." Optimism is good as long as the eyes are open, but once the eyes are closed then optimism can be dangerous.

In this battle drill is necessary. And that drill is control over one's physical organs and over the faculties of the mind. For if one is not prepared for this battle, however courageous and optimistic one may be, one cannot succeed. Another thing is to know something about this warfare: to know when to retreat and when to advance. If one does not know how to retreat and wishes always to advance, one will continually be in danger and will become a victim of life's battle. There are many people who in the intoxication of life's battle go on fighting; in the end they will meet with failure. Young people, strong and hopeful, who have had fewer difficulties, may think of nothing else but battling against all that stands in their way. They do not know that it is not always wise to advance. What is necessary is first to fortify one's position, and then to advance. One can see the same thing in friendship, in business, or in one's profession. A person who does not understand the secret of the law of warfare cannot succeed.

Besides, one must protect one's own on all sides. Very often what one does in the intoxication of the battle is to go on and on, without protecting what belongs to one. How many people in the courts, in law cases, for perhaps a very little thing, go on and on spending money! In the end the loss is greater than the success. Again, how many in this world will perhaps lose more than they gain, only because of their fancy or pride! There are times when one must give in, there are times when one must relax things somewhat, and there are times when one must hold fast the reins of life. There are moments when one must be persistent, and there are moments when one must be easy.

Life is such an intoxication that although everybody thinks that he is w orking in his own interest, hardly one among thousands is really doing so. The reason is that people become so absorbed in what they are trying to get that they become intoxicated by it, and they lose the track that leads to real success. Very often in order to get one particular benefit people sacrifice many other benefits because they do not think of them. The thing to do is to look all around, not only in one direction. It is easy to be powerful, it is easy to be good, but it is difficult to be wise—and it is the wise who are truly victorious in life. The success of those who possess power or of those who perhaps have goodness has its limitations. One would be surprised if one knew how many people bring about their failures themselves. There is hardly one person in a hundred who really works for his true advantage, although everyone thinks that he does.

The nature of life is illusive. Under a gain a loss is hidden; under a loss a gain is hidden. Living in this life of illusion, it is very difficult for man to realize what is really good for him. Even with a wise person, much of his wisdom is demanded by life and by its battle. One cannot be gentle enough, one cannot be sufficiently kind; the more one gives to life, the more life asks of one. There again is a battle.

No doubt the wise gain most in the end, although they have many apparent losses. Where ordinary people will not give in, the wise will give in a hundred times. This shows that their success is very often hidden in apparent failure. But when one compares the success of the wise with that of ordinary people, the success of the wise is much greater.

In this battle a battery is needed, and that battery is the power of will. In this battle of life arms are needed, and these arms are the thoughts and actions that work psychologically towards success. For instance a person says to himself every morning, "Everybody is against me, nobody likes me, everything is wrong, everywhere is injustice, all is failure for me, there is no hope." When he goes out he takes that influence with him. Before he arrives anywhere, at his business, profession, or whatever he does, he has sent his influence before him, and he meets with all wrongs and all failure; nothing seems worthwhile, there is coldness everywhere. And there is another person who knows what human nature is, who knows that one has to meet with selfishness and inconsideration everywhere. But what does he think of it all? He thinks it is like a lot of drunken people, all falling upon each other, fighting each other, offending each other. Naturally a sober person who is thoughtful will not trouble with those

Courtesy of Self-Realization Fellowship.

Sri Yukteswar

who are drunk. He will help them, but he will not take seriously what they say or do. In this world of drunkenness a person who is drunk naturally has to fight more than he who is sober, for the latter will always avoid it. He will tolerate, he will give in, he will understand; for he knows that the others are drunk, and he cannot expect better from them.

Besides this, the wise know a secret, and that secret is that human nature is imitative. For instance, a proud person will always revive the tendency of pride in his surroundings; before a humble person even a proud man will become humble, for the humble one revivifies the humbleness in him. From this one can see that in life's battle one can fight the proud with pride but also with humility, and sometimes gain by it.

From the point of view of the wise human nature is childish. If one stands in the crowd and looks at it as a spectator, one will see a lot of children playing together. They are playing and fighting and snatching things out of each other's hands, and they are bothering about very unimportant things. One finds their thoughts small and unimportant, and so is their pursuit through life. The reason for life's battle is often very small when it is looked at in the light of wisdom. This shows that the knowledge of life does not always come by battling, it comes by throwing light upon it. He is not a warrior who becomes impatient immediately, who loses his temper suddenly, who has no control over his impulses, who is ready to give up hope and courage. The true warrior is he who can endure, who has a great capacity for tolerance, who has depth enough in his heart to assimilate all things, whose mind reaches far enough to understand all things, whose very desire is to understand others and to help them understand.

One may ask,"How can one distinguish between the wisdom of the warrior and lack of courage in the battle of life?" Everything is distinguished by its result. There is a well-known saying that all is well that ends well. If at the end of the battle the one who was apparently defeated has really conquered, doubtless it was through wisdom and not through lack of courage. Very often apparent courage leads to nothing but disappointment in the end. Bravery is one thing; the knowledge of warfare is another. The one who is brave is not always victorious. The one who is victorious knows and understands; he knows the law of life.

What is sensitiveness? Sensitiveness is life itself; and as life has both its good and evil sides, so has sensitiveness. If one expects to have all life's experiences, these will have to come through sensitiveness. However, sensitiveness must be kept in order if one wants to know, understand, and appreciate all that is beautiful, and not to attract all the depression, sorrows, sadness, and woes of the earth. Once a person has become so sensitive as to be offended with everybody, feeling that everybody is against him, trying to wrong him, he is abusing his sensitiveness. He must be wise as well as sensitive. He must realize before being sensitive that in this world he is among children, among drunken men, and he should take everything, wherever it comes from, as he would take the actions of children and drunken people. Then sensitiveness can be beneficial.

If together with sensitiveness one has not developed one's will power, it is certainly dangerous. No one can be spiritually developed without being sensitive; there is no doubt that sensitiveness is a human development. But if it is not used rightly it has a great many disadvantages. A sensitive person can lose courage and hope much sooner than another. A sensitive person can make friends quickly, but he can abandon his friends quickly too. A sensitive person is ready to take offence and to take everything to heart, and life can become unbearable for him. Yet if a person is not sensitive he is not fully alive. Therefore one should be sensitive, but not exaggeratedly so. The abuse of sensitiveness means yielding to every impression and every impulse that attacks one.

There must be a balance between sensitiveness and will

power. Will power should enable one to endure all influences, all conditions, all attacks that one meets from morning till night. Sensitiveness should enable one to feel life, to appreciate it, and to live in the beauty of life. It is true that by the cultivation of will power one sometimes persuades oneself wrongly; there is that danger but there is danger in everything. There is even danger in being healthy but that does not mean that one must be ill. One must acquire a balance between power and wisdom. If power is working without the light of wisdom behind it, it will always fail, because power will prove to be blind in the end. What is the use of the wise person who has no power of action, no power of thought? This shows that wisdom directs, but that one accomplishes by power; that is why both are necessary for the battle of life.

What is most advisable in life is to be sensitive enough to feel life and its beauty and to appreciate it, but at the same time to consider that one's soul is divine, and that all else is foreign to it; that all things that belong to the earth are foreign to one's soul. They should not touch one's soul. When objects come before the eyes they come into the vision of the eyes; when they are gone the eyes are clear. Therefore one's mind should retain nothing but all that is beautiful. For one can search for God in His beauty; all else should be forgotten. By practicing this every day, by forgetting all that is disagreeable, that is ugly, and remembering only what is beautiful and gives happiness, one will attract to oneself all the happiness that is in store.

*Chapter 10.*

# THE CULMINATION OF THE EGO

Not only has the human race evolved as time has passed, age after age, but an individual also evolves in his lifetime. In other words, humanity evolves gradually during a world's lifetime, while an individual, if he evolves at all, does so during his life. It is possible that the human race may take an opposite course: instead of evolving it may go back. So it is with individuals too, but a person who is really evolving will not go back. If he did go back some steps he would feel uneasy and discontented, and he would go forward again. Perhaps he might go back a hundred times, but then a hundred times he would go forward again, for a person who has once experienced the joy and happiness of evolution will not be content with going back; feeling the discomfort of it, he will go on.

No doubt the rhythm of every person's evolution is different. One can read in the *Vadan* that one soul creeps, another soul walks, another soul runs, and another soul flies; and yet they live on the same earth, under the same sun, and they are all called human beings. How strange it is that at the present time a new spirit has awakened in humanity, and one does not recognize the evolution of personality any longer! What one does distinguish is nationality; whatever country one enters, the first thing they ask for is one's passport. It does not matter what evolution one has, and it does not matter what one's soul is experiencing; as long as one has a passport that distinguishes one as the subject of this or that country, that is the important thing. Very often people make a great virtue of saying, "I am as good as you." But imagine the insolence of it! The better one is, the less one considers oneself to be. The one who is really better could not say, "I am as good as you." This means that the consciousness of the present-day man is inferior; he says, "I am as good as you," because unconsciously he feels inferior in his mind.

Whose fault is it? One might say it is the fault of nations, of races, of education, and one might give many other excuses. But it is the spirit of the times. It is no one's fault; yet at the same time it is not necessary to go through a condition in a kind of intoxication; it is better to awaken to the knowledge of that condition. It is better to become acquainted with the real condition of humanity today. When we study human nature from a metaphysical point of view, we see that the origin of human nature is the same as the origin of all other things, and the central theme of that origin is intolerance. Without reason, man's first feeling is that another must not exist. Later that feeling becomes modified, and man becomes more sympathetic, more harmonious and considerate; but the first feeling he has is that another should not exist.

Where does this feeling come from? In reality there is one life and there is one being. This world of variety is made of one Being: it is the manifestation of the One. But at the same time in this world of variety, in this manifestation, the one Being loses that consciousness of being one, and there arises the consciousness of being many. In that way one being comes to stand against another being. Friendship, sympathy, harmony, attachment, devotion, all these come afterwards as man evolves, but they are not his first tendencies. The first

Moula Bakhsh

tendency is a kind of jarring influence. For instance, how happy one feels when one is sitting in a train alone, but as soon as another person enters, one thinks that this is a great crime! One would rather he had gone to another compartment and left one alone. It is a natural feeling when one is in a restaurant eating at a table alone, and a stranger comes to sit at the same table. He may be an angelic person, but as soon as he comes, one thinks, "Why? Have they not got any more tables?" And this feeling comes even to harmonious people; I am not speaking of the inharmonious ones. Is there then anything to be surprised at if in the history of the world there have been so many wars and battles? And for what? For nothing. Man is more fond of war than of peace. He likes peace after a war, but if he had loved peace before the war there would never have been a war.

What is the soul? If there is any explanation that can be given of the soul, it is the feeling of "I am." The feeling of one's existence, this is the soul; that part of one's being which feels that one exists. And what is the ego? Ego is what is gathered around the soul, and that is the knowledge of oneself. When a person says or feels, "I exist," that is the feeling of the soul. But he goes further and says, "I exist as what? I exist as a physical body, as hands, as feet, as a head, as a tall person, as a short person, as a thin person, as a stout person." It is that feeling of being a tangible and visible being, it is that knowledge surrounding the soul that makes the ego, the *nafs*. There are many friends in this world and there are many enemies, but the best friend and at the same time the worst enemy is our own ego. It is our best friend when it becomes a friend, but first of all it is the worst enemy. Every offence a person takes at something, every insult that a person feels, every impulse to do something— it all comes from the nafs.

The ego is like a rose, and also like the thorns that surround the rose. It takes the place of the thorns when it is not cultivated, and it becomes a rose when it is refined. The way to make it refined is to humble oneself and to crush one's desires. It is by the process of crucifixion that a person refines the ego. It is a hard grain, and it must be ground till it becomes a fine powder, out of which a paste is made.

When the ego remains in the condition of a thorn, more thorns come, and more and more, till it increases its thorns to such an extent that everyone who touches that person is dissatisfied. We all have friends to whom we should be most grateful if they would keep away from us. We love them, we like them, but we would be very glad if they would keep away. What is it? It is the thorns that hurt.

In what way do these thorns manifest? They manifest in the form of words, of actions, of desires, in the form of manner. Why does one feel annoyed with certain people in life even before they have uttered one word? Because the thorn is pricking. Perhaps that person will say, "But I have not said anything, I have not done anything, "but he does not know that he has thorns. There are perhaps so many that even before he utters one word, before he moves, his presence pricks us. It is a natural outcome of the ego. Either the ego develops thorns or it develops into a rose, and when it develops into a rose then everyone is attracted to it because of its beautiful petals, its delicacy, its fragrance, its color, its softness, its structure. Everything about it is attractive, appealing, and healing.

For every soul there are four stages to pass through in order to come to the culmination of the ego, which means to reach the stage of the rose. In the first stage a person is rough, thoughtless, and inconsiderate. He is interested in what he wants and in what he likes; as such he is naturally blind to the needs and wants of others. In the second stage a person is decent and good as long as his interests are concerned. As long as he can get his wish fulfilled he is pleasant and kind and good and harmonious, but if he cannot have his way, then he becomes rough and crude and changes completely. There is a third stage, when someone is more concerned with another person's wish and desire and less with himself, when his whole heart is seeking for what he can do for another. In his thought the other person comes first and he comes afterwards. That is the beginning of turning into a rose. It is only a rosebud, but then in the fourth stage this rosebud blooms in the person who entirely forgets himself in doing kind deeds for others.

In Sufi terms the crushing of the ego is called *nafs kushi*. How do we grind it? We grind it by sometimes taking ourselves to task. When the self says, "Oh, no. I must not be treated like this," then we say, "What does it matter?" When the self says, "He ought to have done this; she ought to have said that," we say, "What does it matter, either this way or that way? Every person is what he is; you cannot change him, but you can change yourself." That is the grinding.

When a thorn shows itself and you grind it as soon as you notice it, that same thorn by being crushed will turn into a rose, for the thorn also belongs to the rosebush. When a person says, "I will not occupy this position; I will not eat this; I hate it; I despise it; I cannot bear it; I cannot look at it; I cannot endure it; I cannot stand it," these are all little thorns. A person may not know it, but they are thorns, and when they are crushed, then the rose comes out of them. How easy it is for people to say they want to know about mysticism and occultism. If there were an even bigger name, they would like to take an interest in that, and they believe that by reading books one can understand it, by taking lessons one can learn it, or by doing certain practices one can know it. But it is the everyday life that teaches us from morning till night. Every moment of the day and night we are up against something that our nafs rebels against; and if we took that opportunity to crush it, to put it down, in some years' time our personality would become a rose.

Is .it then always wrong to be what is called an egoist? There are many kinds of egoists. There are good points and there are bad points in an egoistic person. The egoist is selfish, and selfish people can produce cruelty and dishonesty. But there is another side to it, and that is pride and

independence and indifference, which give him content-
ment. Besides, when the real egoist, whose ego stands before
him like a statue of rock, watches the ego, then after some
time that ego becomes a living being. It comes to life and
becomes the very being that one is seeking. Therefore the
right egoist is right and the wrong egoist is wrong.

For whom shall we build a throne of soft cusions? For our
own vanity's sake, thinking that we are better than others?
No, for the pleasure of others, and not for our vanity. As
soon as the question arises, "Am I not better than others, am
I not more spiritual or wiser than others?" then there is "I."
That is wrong. What does it matter what we are as long as
we are able to give pleasure to others, to make life easy for
others? For this is the world of woes; there is no end to our
troubles. From the king to the pauper, from the richest to the
poorest, there are endless troubles hanging over the head of
every individual. If we can be of some little use to anybody,
we can more easily learn what mysticism is, for the only real
mysticism is when a person realizes that he pleases God by
pleasing mankind.

It is only in this way that we can crush our ego. Every time
that we notice its pinprick, every time that its thorns appear
before our eyes, we should crush it and say, "What are you?
Are you not thorns; are you not the cause of unhappiness
for others and myself as well? I do not want to see my own
being in such a form, in the form of thorns! I want my being
to be turned into a rose, that I may bring happiness, pleasure,
and comfort to others." If there is anything needed in
spiritual teaching, in seeking truth, in self-realization, it is
the refinement of the ego. For the same ego that begins by
being our worst enemy will in the end, if developed and
cultivated and refined, become our best friend.

"Know thyself and thou wilt know God," said the great
Sufi philosopher Ali. To know the self is the most difficult
thing in the world, because what man can perceive first is
only a part of the self, a limited part. When man asks himself, "What is it in me that is I?" he finds his body and his

mind, and in both he finds himself limited and apart from others. It is this conception of his being that makes man realize himself as an individual.

If man dived deep enough within himself he would reach a point of his ego where it lives an unlimited life. It is that realization that brings man to the real understanding of life, and as long as he has not realized his unlimited ego he lives a life of limitation. When a person in this illusion says "I," in reality it is a false claim. Therefore everyone has a false claim of "I" except some who have arrived at a real understanding of truth.

This false claim is the nafs, and the annihilation of this false self is the aim of the sage. But no doubt to annihilate this false ego is more difficult than anything else in the world, and it is this path of annihilation that is the path of the saints and sages.

# Chapter 11.

# CHARACTER BUILDING

The will power plays a great part in character building. The will power becomes feeble when a person yields to every little tendency, inclination, and fancy he has; but when a person fights against every little fancy and tendency and inclination he learns to fight with himself, and in this way he develops will power. When once a person's inclinations, fancies, and tendencies have grown stronger than his will power, he experiences in his life several enemies existing in his own self, and he finds it difficult to combat them. For inclinations, fancies, and tendencies, when powerful, do not let will power work against them. If there is any such thing as self-denial, it is this practice; and by this practice in time one attains to a power that may be called mastery over oneself.

In small things of everyday life one neglects this consideration because one thinks, "These are *my* tendencies, *my* fancies, *my* inclinations, and by respecting them I respect myself; by considering them I consider myself." But one forgets that what one calls *my* is not oneself, it is what wills that is oneself. Therefore in the Christian prayer it is said,

"Thy will be done," which means, "Thy will when it works through me"; in other words, "my will, which is Thy Will, be done." it is this illusion of confusing one's possession with oneself that creates all illusion and keeps man from self-realization.

Life is a continual battle. Man struggles with things that are outside him, and so he gives a chance to the foes who exist in his own being. Therefore the first thing necessary in life is to make peace for the time being with the outside world, in order to prepare for the war that is to be fought within oneself. Once peace is made within, one will gain by that sufficient strength and power to use through the struggle of life within and without.

Self-pity is the worst poverty. When a person says, "I am . . ." with pity, before he has said anything more he has diminished himself to half of what he is; and what is said further diminishes him totally. Nothing more of him is left afterwards. There is so much in the world that we can pity and that it would be right for us to take pity upon, but if we have no time free from our own self we cannot give our mind to others in the world. Life is one long journey, and the further behind we have left ourself, the further we have progressed towards the goal. Verily, when the false self is lost, the true self is discovered.

In character building it is most necessary that one should learn how to face the world, the world where one meets with sorrows and troubles and pleasures and pains. It is very difficult for one to hide them from the world, and at the same time a wise person is not meant to show all he feels, nor to show at every moment what he feels. The ordinary person reacts like a machine in answer to every outer influence and inner impulse, and in this way he very often cannot keep to the law of the music of life.

Life to a wise person is music, and in that symphony he has to play a certain part. If one were feeling so low that one's heart was sounding a lower pitch, and the demand of life at that moment was that one should voice a higher pitch, then one would feel that one had failed in that music in which one was meant to play one's part fittingly. This is the test by which one can distinguish the old soul and the child soul. The child soul will give way to every feeling; the old soul will strike the higher note in spite of every difficulty.

There are moments when laughter must be kept back, and there are times when tears must be withheld. Those who have arrived at the stage where they can act efficiently the part that they are meant to act in this life's drama even have power over the expression of their face; they can even turn their tears into smiles, or their smiles into tears. One may ask, "Is it not hypocrisy not to be natural?" But he who has control over his nature is the more natural; not only is he natural, he is the master of nature, while the one who lacks power over nature, in spite of his naturalness, is weak.

Also, it must be understood that real civilization means the art of life. What is that art? It is knowing the music of life. Once a soul has awakened to the continual music of life, that soul will consider it as his responsibility, as his duty, to play his part in outer life, even if it be contrary to his inner condition for the moment. One must know at every moment in one's daily life what life demands of one, what it asks of one, and how one shall answer the demand of one's life. This requires one to be awakened fully to life's conditions. One must have insight into human nature, and one must be able to know one's own condition fully. If one says, "I am as I am; if I am sad, I am sad; if I am glad, I am glad," that will not do. Even the earth will not bear the person who will not answer life's demands. The sky will not tolerate that person, and the sphere will not accommodate him who is not ready to give what life demands of him. If this is true, then it is best when duty is easily done and willingly done.

In the orchestra there is a conductor and there are many who play music, and every player of an instrument has to fulfill his part in the performance. If he does not do it right, it is his fault. The conductor will not listen if he says he did not do it properly because he was sad or because he was too glad. The conductor of the orchestra is not concerned with his sadness or his gladness, he is concerned with the part that the particular musician must play in the whole symphony. This is the nature of our lives. The further we advance in our part in this orchestra, the more efficiently we perform our part in life's symphony. In order to be able to have this control over oneself, what is necessary? We must have control over our inner self, because every outward manifestation is nothing but a reaction of the inner condition. Therefore the first control that one has to gain is over one's own self, one's inner self, which is done by strengthening the will and also by understanding life better.

For the person who walks in the path of God the only struggle is a constant battle with the ego. It is the ego that forms the cover on the light of the soul, and the light hidden under the ego is the "light hidden under a bushel." Man's sense of justice, his logic, his reason, his intelligence, his affection, all are covered by the ego. If he judges anyone it is from the point of view of his own interest; if he reasons his selfish mind produces the result; in his affections he puts self first; his intelligence is darkened by self. This is the condition of the average man. In proportion as man takes away the covering from the soul, so much juster, truer, more sincere, more loving does he become. Selfishness develops the sense of self-interest, and very often a person may gain earthly prosperity because of it. But as all things in this world are subject to change, death, and decay, he remains in the end empty-handed; while the unselfish man, who has perhaps been debarred from earthly goods by his lack of the sense of self-interest, at least remains possessed of his sense of reason and is rich in the equalities of love, justice, and intelligence.

The whole tragedy of life is in losing sight of one's natural self, and the greatest gain in life is coming into touch with one's real self. The real self is covered by many covers of ego. Those that predominate above all others are hunger and passion; beneath these are pride and vanity. One must learn to discriminate between what is natural and what is unnatural, what is necessary and what is unnecessary, what brings happiness and what brings sorrow. No doubt it is difficult for many to discriminate between right and wrong, but by standing face-to-face with one's ego and recognizing it as someone who is ready to make war against one and by keeping one's strength of will as an unsheathed sword, one protects oneself from one's greatest enemy, which is one's own ego. And a time comes in life when one can say, "My worst enemy has been within myself."

There are three different stages through which the ego develops and reaches the ideal state. The first step is called *ammara* by the Sufis, and in this the ego is satisfied by the satisfaction of the passions and the appetites.

From this animal stage the ego may rise to a higher stage, which is man's ego, and that stage is the gratification of vanity. This ego is termed by Sufis *lawwama,* and this stage in the beginning causes a person to act in every way that is likely to cause harm and to be hurtful and unjust to others. This continues until he learns to understand the true nature of vanity, since all good as well as all evil is born of vanity. When vanity ceases to cause man to do evil, he has reached the human stage. But when vanity causes man to do good the ego becomes humane, using this word in the oriental sense in which it means more than human, as it is derived from the two words *hu,* divine, and *manas,* mind.

The first lesson that the ego must learn in order to develop into the humane state is that of pride in the form of self-respect. As man has the inclination to have good clothes and good ornaments in order to appear in the eyes of others what he considers beautiful, so he must feel the same inclination towards the building of personality by the ornamentation of every action and manner in the way he considers good and beautiful.

*Chapter 12.*

# CHECKING THE PHYSICAL EGO

The ego is divided into three parts, the physical ego, the mental ego, and the spiritual ego. The mental ego is the cover of the spiritual ego, and the physical ego is a cover over the mental ego. The ego indeed is one, but these are the three different aspects of the ego.

The physical ego is nurtured by the gratification of the bodily appetites. One sees that after a meal or some refreshing drink a feeling of stimulation arises, and no doubt it covers with an additional cover the "I" within. And therefore there is a difference between sleep and meditation. Although both produce rest, yet one rest is produced by stimulation of the body, and the other rest is produced without it. There have been cases of meditative people sleeping only two or three hours out of the twenty-four without becoming ill. A person who can sleep well shows the sign of health, and yet is subject to any illness. The gratification of every appetite is a momentary stimulation and rest to the body, but this momentary satisfaction creates a further appetite, and every experience in the satisfaction of the appetites gives a desire for more satisfaction. Thus the ego, the cover over one's mental and spiritual being, becomes thicker and thicker until it closes all light from within. There are some who eat in order to live, but there are many who live in order to eat. The body is an instrument for the experience by the soul of the external world, but if the whole life be devoted to the instrument, then the person for whom the instrument exists is deprived of his experience in life.

The blindness that the physical ego causes can be clearly seen among the lower creatures by the lion's inclination to fight with another lion, the dog's inclination to watch the bone off of which it has already eaten the flesh, which it still does not want another dog to touch. This same physical ego gives man pride in his strength, in his beauty, in his power, in his possessions. If there is a spark of light, in time it must expand into a shining star; and when there is the slightest darkness, that darkness must expand and put the whole life in a mist. In the intoxication of the physical ego man becomes so interested only in the satisfaction of his appetites that he can readily harm or injure or hurt not only his enemy but his dearest friend. As a drunken man does not know what he says or does, so a person blinded by his physical ego is intoxicated and can easily say or do things regardless of the pleasure, comfort, happiness, harmony, or peace of others.

In the satisfaction of bodily appetites there are two things: necessity and avidity. A satisfaction that is necessary for existence is one thing, and ever-increasing joy in the satisfaction of bodily appetites is another thing. When man acts without regard to this, in either way—in satisfying the appetites or in abstaining from satisfaction—he makes a mistake. In order to train the ego it is not necessary that cruelty be done to nature. Discrimination is needed to understand how far we should satisfy the appetites and in what degree we should refrain from being addicted to such satisfactions.

Intense desire for bodily satisfaction has a bad influence on one's mentality, the psychical action of which works unfavorably on oneself and one's surroundings. It produces jealousy, envy, greed in one's nature; and if the thought currents are strong, it produces psychically poisonous effects. There is a belief in the East that is known by the name of *nazr,* a belief that any food or drink can have a poisonous effect upon the one who eats or drinks it if it has been exposed to an evil eye. This superstition is known in almost all parts of the East in some form or other, and the psychical idea behind it is that the intense feeling of envy produces a thought current that must surely spread its poison, causing harm to the one against whom the feeling works.

In order to train the ego it is necessary that one should distinguish what is the right of the ego and what is not its right. The ego has a tendency to want what it needs and also what it does not need. The first is its natural appetite, and the second is greed. The ego has a tendency to want more and more of what it likes, regardless of right and justice and regardless of the aftereffect. For instance, a person may eat and drink more and more until this makes him ill. Every kind of gratification of desire or appetite gives a tendency to want more.

Then there is the desire for a change of experience, and when a person gives in to it, it never ends. An excess of desire in appetites or passions always produces an intoxication in man, and it increases to such an extent that the limited means that man has become insufficient to gratify his desires. Therefore, to satisfy his desires he wants more than what is his own; he wants what belongs to other people. When this begins, naturally injustice begins. When he cannot get what he wants, then there is pain and disappointment.

When a person gratifies his desires more than other people, the others who see this want to take away the gratification he has. One naturally expects a thinker to understand this and to relieve his ego of all that is unnecessary. The training of the ego is this, to eat to live and not to live to eat, and so with all things one desires. The nature of desire is such that nothing will satisfy it forever, and sometimes the pleasure of a moment costs more than it is worth. When one's eyes are closed to this, one takes the momentary pleasure regardless of what will come after.

The training of the ego is not necessarily a sad life of renunciation, nor is it necessarily the life of a hermit. The training is to be wise in life, to understand what we desire, why we desire it, and what effect will follow; what we can afford and what we cannot afford. It is also to understand desire from the point of view of justice, to know whether it is right and just. If the ego is given way to in the very least in the excess of its desires, it becomes master of one's self. Therefore in training the ego even the slightest thing must be avoided that may in time master us. The ideal life is the life of balance, not necessarily the life of renunciation. But renunciation must be practiced if it is necessary for balance. Verily, balance is the real life.

When we consider the whole unrest of the present time in the world, we find that it is caused by the physical ego. The wars and revolutions seem to have the desire for comfort and pleasure and for more earthly gain behind them. Since the happiness of the world depends upon the moral standard of the majority, it is upon the education of human nature and the psychical law of happiness that the peace of the world depends.

*Chapter 13.*

# VANITY: THE PLANT OF DESIRE

The whole of manifestation is the expression of that spirit of the Logos which in Sufi terms is called *kibria.* Through every being this spirit is manifested in the form of vanity, pride, or conceit. Vanity expressed crudely is called pride. Had it not been for this spirit working in every being as the central theme of life, no good or bad would have existed in the world, nor would there have been great or small. All virtues and every evil are the off-spring of this spirit. The art of personality is to cut off the rough edges of this spirit of vanity, which hurts and disturbs those one meets in life. The more a person says "I," the more he disturbs the minds of his listeners.

Many times people are trained in politeness and are taught a polished language and manner, yet if this spirit of vanity is pronounced it will creep up, in spite of all good manners and beautiful language, and express itself in a person's thought, speech, or action, calling aloud, "I am, I am!" If a person be speechless, his vanity will leap out in the expression of his glance. It is the hardest thing to suppress and to control. For adepts the struggle in life is not so great with the passions and emotions, which sooner or later, by more or less effort, can be controlled, but with vanity, which is always growing. If one cuts down its stem then one cannot live, for it is the very self, it is the I, the ego, the soul, or God within; it cannot be denied its existence. But struggling with it beautifies it more and more, and makes more and more tolerable that which in its crude form is intolerable.

Vanity may be likened to a magic plant. If one sees it growing in the garden as a thorny plant and cuts it down, it will grow in another place in the same garden as a fruit tree. And when one cuts it down again, in another place in the same garden it will spring up as a bush of fragrant roses. It exists just the same, but in a more beautiful form, which gives happiness to those who touch it. The art of personality therefore does not teach the rooting out of the seed of vanity, which cannot be rooted out as long as man lives; but its crude outer garb may be destroyed in order that, after dying several deaths, it may be manifested as the plant of desires.

The first form of the ego is that which the body helps to form, and the next is that which is formed by the mind. This aspect of the ego lives for vanity, which causes a person to do good and also to do evil. Its desire is always the satisfaction of its pride, and when this increases, in the end it results in tyranny and cruelty. A person expects others to see him as he thinks he is, and often his selfishness is excessive and it is impossible for others to admire him as much as he wants. One wishes to be admired for his clothes, his jewels, his possessions, his greatness and position; and when this desire increases it makes a person blind and he loses sight of right and justice. It is natural that the desire for things that gratify the vanity should have no end; it increases continually. The tendency to look at others, to view them with hatred and prejudice, to consider them inferior to oneself— all such tendencies come from this ego.

There are even cases when people spend money in order to insult another: to make someone bow before him, to make him give way, to put him in a position of inferiority, to make him appear contemptible. The desire for the satisfaction of vanity reaches such a point that a person would give his life for the satisfaction of his vanity. Often someone shows generosity not for the sake of kindness but to satisfy his vanity.

The more vanity a person has the less sympathy he has for others, for all his attention is given to his own satisfaction and he is blind toward others. This ego so to speak restricts life, because it limits a person. Coldness, pride, jealousy, all come from this ego. There is nothing so displeasing to the surroundings as conceit in whatever form, and what is the use of an opinion that is pleasing to us and unpleasing to all our surroundings?

In reality a person's true satisfaction comes from the opinion that others have of him, not from his own opinion of himself. There is nothing more repellent than a thorny ego. The outward manner cannot hide an ego that is not soft, even if the manner is very humble. It shows itself suddenly, unconsciously, in a word or an action that jars upon another.

The training of this ego requires more care than the training of the other ego, for it is a more difficult and subtler matter to be aware of the desires of the mind and to weigh them than to be aware of and to weigh the desires of the body. No doubt vanity is natural to the ego, and the ego is natural to every human being. But there are desires of the mind that are necessary and there are desires of the mind that are not necessary. The more one controls the ego, the more one allows the virtues and merits that are in one's heart to manifest. This ego gives a false idea of greatness, but its effacement results in true greatness.

There is a tendency in man to think a great deal about what others think of him, and in some natures this tendency develops quickly. This develops in him self-consciousness, which is the root of several defects of man: it enfeebles man physically and mentally and makes him dependent upon the opinion of others. He lives so to speak in the good opinion of others, and he is as dead when they have a bad opinion of him.

This tendency makes a person sensitive, often hypersensitive. It often reaches such a point that at every word he speaks he looks around for approval, and in the same way every new movement he makes is calculated to produce an effect. This makes his body and his mind both heavy and burdensome to his soul. It develops in nature that weakness which in ordinary words is called touchiness: taking offense at every little thing. And the nature of many people is such that they enjoy bringing out any weakness that may be in a person. It becomes a pastime or pleasure to such people, and the life of one who is sensitive is made so difficult that he has no rest at home or abroad. Everyone seems to him to be wicked, everyone's presence seems to have a jarring effect upon him, and he seeks to be exclusive and to find a seclusion which life does not permit of his finding. If he happens to be in a position where he has to speak or sing or perform in any way, he fails to do his best, and when he meets people he cannot stand a criticism or reply to a jest. The presence of others has the effect of a weight upon the soul. The desire of the sensitive person is always to be in hiding—keeping away from people, looking at others with nervousness, dislike, or fear. Such a person, however great his virtues or merits, is always incapable of free expression of his gift.

Man has the desire to do good and to refrain from doing evil because this feeds his vanity. Among one thousand good and virtuous people there is scarcely one who does good and refrains from evil because that is his natural inclination.

The majority of those engaged in art, science, religion, or politics are conscious all the time of the opinions of others, and they can only work upon the lines they are following if appreciation comes from some quarter. The least antagonism or opposition which comes discourages them and often kills their desire. Among thousands there is one great soul that can keep firm and strong in his purpose through life, unshaken and unweakened by opposition from any side. It is that person who wins in the end and accomplishes things that are worthwhile.

In the lives of all the great souls who have accomplished wonderful deeds in life, you will surely find this mystery hidden. These souls have not learned it; it happens to be their nature. The thinker will see in this a philosophy that teaches that it is the ego that chains man's feet, keeping him from progress in all paths of life. The ego not only makes man self-conscious, but it makes him a coward and then renders him helpless. He is timid because he sees his own limitations, and he is helpless because everything stronger overpowers him and he confines his being within a certain limit. Besides all the other disadvantages that self-consciousness brings with it, there is above all else one thing it does: it prevents man from realizing that the thought of self keeps him away from God. In the heart of man there is room for one only, either for himself or for God.

*Chapter 14.*

# THE PURIFICATION AND TRAINING OF THE EGO

The human ego has two sides to its nature. One side strives for its nature's demands, and that side of the ego may be classed as the animal ego. But there is another side that manifests when the ego shows its agitation for no other reason than intolerance. This feeling is a kind of blindness, or intoxication, and it arises from an excess of energy coming out from the soul quite unrestrained; it covers, so to speak, the light of the soul, as smoke may cover the light that comes from a flame. In order to allow the divine spirit to guide one's life, one must clear the soul of its smoke part, leaving only the flame to illuminate one's life.

It is the nature of the ego during its period of ignorance that all that is very beautiful or powerful and all that is below the standard of its ideal agitates it. This sensitiveness may increase to such an extent that all that does not bring any comfort or joy or happiness to the ego may become repugnant to it. It is this ignorant stage of the ego that in the Sanskrit language is called by the wise *ahamkara*. The whole method that the wise have taught in any age and in any part of the world has been for recognizing and understanding this ignorance, which is the primary nature of the ego, and then for purifying one's ego from this by gentleness, by humility, by self-control, by tolerance, and by forgiveness.

Man can dissimulate this ignorance, but that is not enough; often outward manner may become a mask over something ugly hidden behind it. There is only one thing that can free the ego from this ignorance, and this is the love of God, the contemplation of God, and the knowledge of God. Love of God comes from belief in God. Belief is the first thing necessary, but belief needs support. It can be kept up by the belief of others surrounding one or by learning or study that will strengthen it. But he to whom the love of humanity is unknown can never know the love of God: as you can see the painter in his picture, the poet in his poem, the musician in his music, so in humanity you can see God.

It is a science and an art to understand the nature of the human ego and to train it. One can understand its nature by a study of human nature, but one can learn the way of training it by training one's own ego. Man can train his ego by being patient with all around him that has a jarring effect upon him, for every jar upon the soul irritates the ego. When man expresses his irritation he develops a disagreeable nature; when he controls it and does not express it, then he becomes crushed inwardly. The idea is to rise above all such irritations.

The very nature of life has a jarring effect, which every sensitive soul can feel. If a person wishes to keep away from all jarring influences he had better not try to live, for life is a continual jarring. Life is motion, and it is the nature of motion to strike against something. Strength is not what is required to stand against the jarring influences of life. There is no wall of stone or of iron that can always stand against the waves of the ocean, but a small piece of wood, little and light, can always rise and fall with the waves, yet stay always above them, uninjured and safe. The lighter and the littler man's ego becomes, the more power of endurance it has. It is two strong egos that strike against one another. The little ego, the light ego, just skips over when the powerful wave of a strong ego comes, allowing the latter to knock itself against a stronger wall that may throw it over.

The art of dealing with egos of different grades of evolution is to learn gentleness, tolerance, and forgiveness, which all come from charity of heart. When a person stands on the same plane as the other then he is subject to the influence of another ego, but if he rises above it then every influence of the other ego falls flat. There is a poem in Hindustani, the verse of Ghalib, "The world seems to me like a children's playground. How unceasingly busy the infants seem with their toys!" Verily, the secret of peace is hidden under the cover of the ego.

In order to learn forgiveness man must learn tolerance first. There are people whom man cannot forgive. It is not that he must not forgive, but it is difficult to forgive, beyond his power, and in that case the first thing he can do is to forget. The first step towards forgiveness is to forget. It is true that the finer the person is the more he is subject to being hurt by the smallest disturbance that can produce irritation and inharmony in the atmosphere. A person who gives and takes hurt is capable of living an easy and comfortable life in the world, but life is difficult for the fine person, for he cannot give back what he receives in the way of hurt, and he can feel it more than an average person. Many seek protection from all hurting influences by building some wall around themselves, but the canopy over the earth is so high that a wall cannot be built high enough. The only thing one can do is live in the midst of all inharmonious influences, to strengthen the will power and to bear all things, yet keeping a fineness of character and a nobleness of manner, together with an ever-living heart. To become cold with the coldness of the world is weakness, and to become broken by the hardness of the world is feebleness, but to live in the world and yet to keep above the world is like walking on water. There are two essential duties for the person of wisdom and love: to keep the love in his nature ever increasing and expanding, and to strengthen the will so that the heart may not be easily broken. Balance is ideal in life: man must be fine and yet strong; man must be loving and yet powerful.

There is no better way of training the ego than denying it what it wants for the satisfaction of its vanity. Spirituality may be called a capacity; plainly explained it may be called a depth. In some people there is naturally this capacity; this depth, and in some it may be made. In order to collect rainwater people dig the ground and make a capacity for the water to collect. So in order to receive the spiritual life and light one must open a capacity within oneself. The egoist has no capacity, for it is his ego that makes the heart so to speak solid, giving no accommodation to the essence of God. The more one denies the demands of the ego that satisfy its vanity, the more capacity one makes to be filled by the life of God. It is painful sometimes, and it often seems hard, to deny all that the ego demands, but it always results in great satisfaction.

When the will is able to rule one's life and not one's bodily appetites or mental fancies, then there is the reign of the Golden Age, as the Hindus say: there is no injustice, and there is no reward. When man finds disturbance in his life, a lack of harmony in the external world, he must take refuge in the reign within, which is the kingdom of God. To a Sufi this body is the temple of God, and the heart is His shrine. As long as man keeps God away from His temple, from His shrine, his limited ego reigns, and that reign is called by the Hindus the Iron Age. A person who has not opened his heart to God for Him to abide in may yet be a good person, but as his life will be involved in the activities of the world, his ego will turn from bad to worse, culminating in the worst state of mind. It is that condition of mind which is personified in the religious term "Satan."

In order to learn to realize "I am not, but God is," one must first deny oneself for one's fellow man. Respecting another, enduring a person or an action that is uncongenial to oneself, tolerating all, overlooking the faults and covering the weakness that one finds in one's fellow men, being ready to forgive—all these things are the first lessons in self-denial.

*Chapter 15.*

# SELF–EFFACEMENT

The only difference between spiritual attainment and the continual struggle of life is that in worldly life one struggles in another direction. In worldly life, be it in business or politics or industry or whatever one's life's path, if a person proves to be lacking in that power which enables him to struggle along, he meets nothing but failure. He may be a good person, a saintly person, a spiritual person, but that does not count. It is for this reason that many in the world lose faith in goodness and in spirituality when they see that this goodness does not seem to count in life. It is absurd for a spiritual person to say that by spirituality, goodness, and piety one's worldly struggle will be helped. One should have the inspiration and power to answer life's demands in life's struggle. The seeker on the spiritual path should not forget that floating in the air is no good; standing on the earth is the first thing necessary. There are many who dream, who live in the air, but that does not answer our purpose. When they complain that they are doing spiritual work yet are in bad circumstances, they forget that the language of these paths is different, the law of these paths is different. That is why I distinguish between these two paths, in order to make it clear that the one has little to do with the other. This does not mean that the wicked person will succeed or that success is gained by evil; if it were so, it would only be a mortal success. Nevertheless one would not blame the spirit for failure in worldly things, for worldly things belong to another inspiration; if it were not so all great sages would be millionaires.

The worldly struggle is outward struggle. The struggle on the spiritual path is inward struggle. No sooner does one take the spiritual direction than the first enemy one meets is one's own self. What does the self do? It is most mischievous. When one says one wants to fight it, it says, "I am yourself. Do you want to fight me?" And when it brings failure, it is clever enough to put the blame on someone else.

Do all those who have failed in life accuse themselves? No, they always accuse another person. When they have gained something they say, "I have done it." When they have lost something they say, "This person got in my way." With little and big things, it is all the same. The self does not admit faults; it always puts the blame on others. Its vanity, its pride, its smallness, and its egotistical tendency, which is continually active, keep one blind.

I remember a Persian verse made by my murshid which relates to the self: "When I feel that now I can make peace with myself, it finds time to prepare another attack." That is our condition. We think that our little faults, since they are small, are of no consequence, or we do not even think of them at all. But every little fault is a flag for the little self, for its own dominion. In this way battling makes man the sovereign of the kingdom of God. Very few can realize the great power in battling with and conquering the self.

But what does man generally do? He says, "My poor self, it has to withstand the conflicts of this world; should I also battle with this self?" So he surrenders his kingdom to his little self, depriving himself of the divine power that is in the heart of man. There is in man a false self and a real self. The real self contains the eternal; the false self contains the mortal. The real self has wisdom; the false self has ignorance. The real self can rise to perfection; the false self ends in limitation. The real self has all good, the false self is productive of all evil. One can see both in oneself: God and the other one. By conquering the other one, one realizes God. This other power has been called Satan; but is it a power? In reality it is not. It is and it is not: it is a shadow. We see shadow, and yet it is nothing. We should realize that this false self has no existence of its own. As soon as the soul has risen above the false self, it begins to realize its nobility.

But then there is the practical aspect. How does the false self show? What form has it? It rises up in support of its own interest. It defends itself from the attacks of others. It feels exclusive towards everyone. It knows itself as an entity separate from friend and foe. It concerns itself with all that is transitory; it is blind to the future, and ignorant of the past. It manifests in the form of self-pity. It expresses itself in the form of vengeance. It lives by feeding upon bitterness, and its life is always spent in obscurity. Its condition is restlessness and discontent. It has a continual appetite for all that is there; it is never satisfied. It has no trust in anyone, no thought for anyone, no consideration for anyone. It lacks conscientiousness and therefore manners. The little self thinks only of its own advantage and its own comfort. Giving to others, giving to those around it is dreadful to the self, for it knows no sacrifice. Renunciation for it is worse than death. That is the little self.

When we blame another person, when we dislike somebody, we overlook the same element in ourselves. There is no soul in the world who can say, "I have not this in me." If only he were just! For mostly it is the unjust person who blames another. The more just we become, the more silent will we be in all circumstances. If outwardly we see faults in others, inwardly there is the sum total within ourselves. For instance the little child cannot help loving. If a thief comes, the child wants to love him and smiles at him. Why is it? Because a thief is not awakened in the child. The child is from heaven, the thief from the earth. There is no place for him there; that is why he is no thief to the child. We accept something because we already have it in us. If we consider our knowledge, a thousand things we seem to have experienced, we find that other people have told us most of them and we believed them at once. As soon as a person tells us about someone wicked, we think, "Now we know, we can be quite sure about it." But when a person comes along and says, "I have seen a most wonderful thing; this man is so good," everyone thinks, "Is it really true? Is it possible to be as good as that? Is there not anything bad in him?" Goodness is unnatural to many people.

One might ask whether the spiritual path is a tyranny over oneself. No, for it is by treading it that one molds one's character, that one makes one's personality. In this is all religion. When a person begins to think, "I must not bring harm to or hurt anyone I meet, worthy or unworthy, friend or foe," only then does he begin his work in the spiritual direction. Spirituality is not wonderworking. Spirituality is attained by right attitude.

Where is the shrine of God? It is in the heart of man. As soon as one begins to consider the feelings of another, one begins to worship God. One might say that it is difficult to please everyone. No doubt it is. It is more difficult still if one has in oneself the inclination to please everyone.

There is a story of a murshid who was going with his mureeds to visit a village. He was keeping a fast, and the mureeds also had taken a vow of fasting. They arrived at a peasant's home where there was great enthusiasm and happiness, and where a dinner was arranged for them. When they were invited to the table, the murshid went and sat down, but the mureeds did not dare because they had taken a vow of fasting. Yet they would not mention it to the murshid. They thought, "Murshid is forgetful; Murshid has forgotten the vow." After dinner was over and they went out the pupils asked at last, "Did you not forget the vow of fasting?" "No," was the murshid's answer, "I had not forgotten. But I preferred to break the fast rather than the heart of that man who with all his enthusiasm had prepared the food."

The thirst for life makes us overlook little opportunities of doing good. Every moment of life brings an opportunity for being conscious of human feeling—in prosperity, in adversity, in all conditions. It costs very little; only a little thought is necessary. A person may be good but at the same time not be conscientious about little things. There is no greater religion than love. God is love, and the best form of love is to be conscientious regarding the feelings of those with whom we come in contact in everyday life.

The further one goes, the more difficulties there are; one finds greater faults in oneself as one advances along the spiritual path. This is not because the number of faults has increased, but the sense has become so keen that one regards differently faults that formerly one would not have noticed. It is like a musician: the more he advances and the better he plays, the more faults he notices. He who does not notice his faults is in reality becoming worse. There is no end to one's faults. To think of them makes one humble.

To say, "God is in me," before one has realized this other, metaphysical aspect of truth, is not humble but profane. God is in the depth of the heart, but to know this is of no use when the doors of the heart are not open. It is the realization of one's innumerable faults that makes one humble and effaces the little self from one's consciousness, and it is in the effacement of the self that real spiritual attainment lies.

By a keen outlook on life we find that what disturbs us most in life is the jarring effect of the ego of another person. Those who know the right manner of developing personality know that the first lesson in life is to efface that ego as much as possible. Christ says, "Blessed are the poor in spirit." That poorness in spirit is the softening of the ego. When the ego is softened in a person, then there is a

Courtesy of Office Central de Lisieux, Editions du Carmel de Lisieux, 51 rue du Carmel, 14100 Lisieux, France.

Saint Thérèse of Lisieux

charm in the thought, speech, and action of that person. Sometimes after going through a disillusionment, suffering torture, a person shows some charm in his personality, and that charm comes from the softening of his ego. But any virtue that develops naturally, forced by life or circumstances, is not virtue in the same sense as that which has been developed by one's own effort. Every beautiful action, thought, or speech is derived from effacing the self or ego. For instance, every manner or courtesy comes from holding the reins of the ego. Beauty of speech always depends on the same effacement of the self, and so it is with thought.

As soon as the ego expresses itself without control it hurts the ego of another person. Family feuds in ancient times, and now wars, all come from the same source, the ego. Those whose contact brings us comfort, ease, peace, always have softened ego. It is vanity or pride that hardens the ego, and it is love and light that soften it. The greater the person, the finer the ego. No example can be better than that of Christ washing the feet of his disciples.

What builds man's ego is every kind of gratification of the ego, and what breaks it is patience and renunciation. The question whether it would be advisable to destroy the ego, since others take advantage of a refined person, is answered by saying that it is not necessary that one should work against the ego, but one must control it.

Nobody in life has such power of enslaving a person as his own ego. Man is, in fact, from the divine essence; and being so, he has the right to be king in his own life, which is his kingdom. By the gratification of the ego man falls from kingship to slavery, and in the end his own life becomes a burden to him. In order to gain his kingdom he must destroy the illusion that in satisfying his ego he shows his power. In reality he satisfies his enemy in satisfying his ego. A Persian poet says, "Each time I make peace with my enemy, he has the opportunity of preparing again for the struggle."

The great battle that the Sufis and sages and yogis fight is the battle with the ego. While the sage battles with his own ego, the ordinary man battles with other people's egos. The difference between the results of these two battles is that the victory and failure of the ordinary man are momentary, but the victory of the sage is eternal. The former when he has finished one battle must begin another; but the latter, once he has succeeded, is victorious.

Humility is the principal thing that must be learned in the path of training the ego. It is the constant effort of effacing the ego that prepares man for the greater journey. This principle of humility can be practiced by forgetting one's personality in every thought and action and in every dealing with another.

No doubt this is difficult and may not seem very practical in everyday life, though in the end it will prove to be the successful way, not only in one's spiritual life but in one's everyday affairs. The general tendency is to bring the personality forward, which builds a wall between two souls whose destiny and happiness lie in unity. In business, in the professions, in all aspects of life, it is necessary that one should unite with another in this unity in which the purpose of life is fulfilled.

There are two forms of effacing the self, which in other words may be called giving in. One way is by weakness, the other is by willingness. The former is a defect, the latter a virtue. One comes by lack of will, the other from charity of heart. Therefore in training the ego one must take care that one is not developing a weakness presuming it to be a virtue. The best way of dealing with the question is to let life take its natural course and at the same time to allow the conscience to keep before it the highest ideal. On one side life taking its natural course, and on the other side the conscience holding its highest ideal balancing it—this will make the journey easy.

The words of Christ that teach man to walk with another two miles if the other wants him to walk one prove the great importance of harmony in life. The idea in Christ's teaching of giving in is also expressive of harmonizing with the wishes of another person. No doubt in this discrimination is necessary. That harmony is advisable which develops into harmony and culminates in a greater harmony, not that which may seem in the beginning to be harmony but which would result in greater inharmony. In the training of ego, balance must be taken as the most important principle.

Jesus Christ says, "Blessed are the poor in spirit." Why is not the word ego used instead of spirit? Man's glance, expression, posture, and so forth all speak of his ego, and tell to what extent it is hard and to what extent soft. People seek to disguise the true nature of the ego by diplomatic language and by good manners, but these do not really hide the ego, which is expressing itself in everything they say and do. Every particle of man's body and every atom of man's mind is controlled by this ego. If there is anything that is meant by the word spirit as used above, it is this. The least word spoken against it rouses man's anger; praise tickles his vanity and goes to the heart of the ego.

The question arises "If this ego is the chief thing in man's development, why should we fight against it? Is it not the essence of man?" The answer is that there is the spirit of man and the spirit of God. These two are different and yet the same. Think of the sea and of the bubble—how vast the one, how small the other! How dare man claim that he is God! The emptiness in which the echo is noise is found only in a heart that can claim such greatness as that.

The true emptiness is filled by the divine light, and it is such a heart that in humility is turned to nothingness, so that the light shines out. Man's ego is a globe, and the spirit of God is the light. "Poor" is used by Christ in the sense of thin, and when the ego is poor or thin, the spirit of God shines out. "Rich in spirit" would mean thick, or dense, in the ego nature, which would stand as a wall against the divine light hidden in the heart.

*Chapter 16.*

# RESIGNATION

There are two distinct paths by which one attains to the spiritual goal, and one is quite contrary to the other. One is the path of resignation; the other is the path of struggle. No doubt in the path of struggle there is also resignation, and in the path of resignation there is also struggle. But generally the one who is treading the path of resignation has only one thought, to be resigned; whereas to the one who strikes the path of struggle, struggle is the main object. Both paths are essential; it is not possible to ignore one of them or to accept only one of them. People often think Sufism means being passive, but it is not so: it is being both active and passive. It is the knowledge of the secret of man's life on earth, of what he needs for his character, for his condition.

When we reflect upon these principles, we find that there are things in life to which we can only be resigned. It is easy to be resigned to things one cannot help, but if one has the power to struggle it is difficult to be resigned. The one who is resigned in easy conditions may not find it difficult, but he does not know what resignation means. For instance a man may have poor relations who want a part of his capital because they are in great need, but in spite of this he cannot resign to letting them have it. Yet when during the night thieves break into his house and leave with his whole fortune, he may resign himself very quickly to his loss. This kind of resignation is no virtue. To resign oneself means to do so even when one has the power to resist.

All the great ones have recognized the value of resignation and have taught it. One might think that resignation is unpractical and that this selfish world will take advantage of one. This is true, but the loss is small compared with the gain, if only the heart can sustain the loss. Yet if one is not contented with what has been done, it is better not to be resigned.

If one can be resigned, so much the better; but one should not force one's nature. A man once asked another to lend him his raincoat. It was immediately given, but at the same time the giver was very much annoyed that the other should have asked for it, and when he himself was obliged to go out in the rain he was vexed at having to get wet. It would have been much better for him to have said at once that he was sorry not to be able to lend the coat. Once having given it, however, he should not have begrudged it, but should have been glad to get wet having helped the other man. If he gave it he should have done so with his whole heart.

One who is really resigned does not show it. It is not easy. How many people in this world try to learn wonderful spiritual things! But this resignation which is such a simple thing is yet miraculous; this virtue is not only beautiful, it is a miracle. There is resignation in so many little things. We do not always recognize it, but it is there. Those around us may ask us to do something that we do not like. Perhaps they say something to us that we do not wish to take in silence; we want to answer back. Then there are the little pinpricks from all we meet in everyday life. If we were not resigned, we would feel irritated all the time. Therefore to be resigned is not weakness, it is a great strength. As one goes further, one finds that one can be resigned even to cold and heat, to places that are uncongenial—and all this resignation has a meaning, and we benefit by it. We should form a habit of being resigned; not having resigned ourselves to an experience means the loss of an opportunity.

There are two forces working: the collective power and the individual power. In Sufi terms the one is *kaza,* the other *qadr.* Very often the individual power will not surrender and consequently is crushed. For instance if a man is called upon to fight for his country but says that he will not join the army, he is helpless before the might of the whole nation, however fine his idealism may be. Here he must resign himself to the condition in which there is a conflict between a lesser and a greater power; in this case resignation is the only solution.

Of course everything must be understood rightly. Resignation preached foolishly is not profitable. A mureed who was learning the lesson of resignation from a murshid was once walking in the middle of the road engrossed in the thought of resignation when a mad elephant came from the other direction. A wise man told him to get out of the way, but he would not because he was trying to resign himself to the elephant, until he was roughly pushed aside by it. They brought him to his murshid who asked him how he came to be injured. He answered that he was practicing resignation. The murshid said, "But did nobody tell you to get out of the way?" "Yes," he answered, "but I would not listen." "But," said the murshid, "why did you not resign yourself to that person?" Often fine principles can be practiced to great disadvantage. Nevertheless, resignation has proved to be the path of the saints, because it develops patience in man. And what is patience? It is all the treasure there is. Nothing is more valuable, nothing a greater bliss than patience.

A story is told about the Prophet Muhammad. He was very ill; he had been suffering for many years. Through his trial his insight became clearer, but his suffering was so great that those around him could not stand it anymore, and so he had to seek refuge with God in the forest to spare them from seeing his pain. As his sight was keen and the ears of his heart were open, he heard a voice coming from the trees, "I am the medicine for your disease." The Prophet asked, "Has the time of my cure come?" The voice answered, "No." He said, "Why should I take you, then?" Later he had the same experience. Again he heard the voice, and when he asked if the time of his cure had come, this time the answer was yes. But the Prophet again said, "Why should I take you?" for he still could not resign himself.

When we think of an extreme ideal, we may wonder if it is not unpractical, especially at this time where there are so many treatments and so many mechanical things. But the thoughtful person will consider how many people have ruined their lives by going from one treatment to another, lacking the patience and resignation in which resides their complete cure. The remedy is not always the answer to the difficulty; often patience is the answer. It seems that man becomes more and more impatient every day, owing to this superficial life. There is hardly any resignation to little things, even though it is so much better to be resigned than to worry.

When we throw the mystical light upon this subject, we find that by being resigned we form a harmonious connection with the infinite. And how should we learn this? Should we do it by being resigned to God? No, that is a still greater lesson. The first lesson to learn is to resign oneself to the little difficulties in life, not to hit out at everything one comes up against. If one were able to manage this, one would not need to cultivate great power; even one's presence would be healing. Such a person is more precious than the branch of the rose, for that has many thorns but few flowers.

Resignation is the outcome of the soul's evolution, for it is the result of either love or wisdom. The truth of this can be seen in the lives of a child and a grown-up person. As soon as a child becomes attracted to an object, the only thing it knows is that it wants it, and if it is denied this object the child is dissatisfied. Yet as the child grows up and evolves in life it learns resignation. That is the difference between an unripe soul and a soul advanced on the path of wisdom; for the ripened soul shows in its nature the development of the power of resignation. Man certainly has a free will, but its power is very small in comparison with the all-powerful will of God, which manifests in the form of more powerful individuals, of conditions that cannot be changed, and in many other ways. Resignation does not mean giving something up; resignation means being contented to give it up. To be resigned means to find satisfaction in self-denial.

Self-denial cannot be a virtue when it is the result of helplessness and culminates in dissatisfaction. The nature of an unevolved ego is to resent everything that arises in life that hinders the accomplishment of a certain object; but when a person accepts being resigned in the face of a difficulty, and at the same time feels satisfaction, then even without having accomplished his object he has risen above it. In this way for the truly resigned soul even a defeat is really a success.

Resignation is a quality of the saintly souls. It is bitter in taste but sweet in result. Whatever a man's power and position in life may be, he always has to meet with a more powerful will, in whatever form it may manifest. In truth, this is the divine will. By opposing the divine will one may break oneself, but by resigning oneself to it one opens up a way. For resignation has the nature of water: if anything obstructs it, it takes another course; and yet it flows on, making its way so as to meet the ocean in the end. This is what the saintly souls do who tread the path of resignation and yet keep their own will alive. That will has the power to make its way. A person who is resigned by nature becomes in the end a consolation to himself and happiness for others.

Resignation is not necessarily weakness, laziness, cowardice, or lack of enthusiasm. Resignation is really the expression of mastery over one's self. The tendency to submit to the will of another or to certain conditions does not always work to the disadvantage of the resigned one. It may sometimes seem to be unprofitable, but in the end the benefit of such a virtue is realized. Lack of power of endurance is the cause of souls being unready to resign themselves, for they cannot endure their pain or sustain their loss. Those who are resigned practice resignation even in the small things of everyday life. They avoid using their power of will needlessly in every little thing they do. Resignation is passivity, and sometimes it seems to be a disadvantage in the life of an active person who has an object to accomplish. But a continual activity kept up by power and energy very often results in disaster. Every activity should be balanced by passivity. One should be active when it is time to be active, and become passive when conditions ask for passivity. It is in this manner that success in life is attained and that happiness, which is the quest of every soul, is gained.

The symbolical meaning of the story of Christ riding on a donkey on Palm Sunday is that the donkey, which has a cross on its back to indicate that it must bear all burdens, shows its resignation by submitting to the will of its master. That is the privilege of the one who serves: however humble, he will have the privilege of serving God.

*Chapter 17.*

# RENUNCIATION

Renunciation and asceticism are two different things. The Sufi's moral is renunciation, but it is not always the moral of the ascetic. The ascetic does not marry, he does not eat good food, he does not wear fine clothes or do anything that is enjoyable; while the Sufi thinks that everything in the world is for him, so that he need not leave the world with a wish unfulfilled. But he does not depend upon these things; he keeps himself free from them. He does not go to the mountains to be in solitude, he lives in the world. He goes to the mountains if he wishes to; still, the mountains cannot hold him for ever. It is much easier to be religious or spiritual in a cave of the mountains than in the world, but the Sufi has no need to run away from the world, for he has recognized and sees the face of his Beloved, the face of God, everywhere.

If a religious teacher were to say, "No, you must not hear music, you must not go to see a play, you must not watch dancing, you must not dance yourself," perhaps one in a thousand of his pupils would obey his words and go away into the wilderness. No doubt that pupil would find much more there to help him in his search for spirituality, but he would not have experienced the world, and so he would always remain exposed to temptation.

It is much more meritorious and much more difficult to live in the world—to have the responsibilities of life, to give attention to friends and relations, to serve friends and enemies—and yet to remain spiritual. To be troubled by one's surroundings, to be loaded with responsibilities, and to be exposed to opposition is much harder and greater than to be an ascetic in the jungle. Both courses have their dangers. If one leaves the world, the innate inclination to enjoy and to experience the world may at any moment draw one back, as it did the yogi Mahachandra, who was a great saint and had many chelas, and yet was taken away by the queen Mahila and made a king. He fell in a moment from the great height that he had reached by many years of hard perseverance. The yogi says that it is better to leave the world, but the Sufi chooses a life in the world with renunciation. He prefers to experience the world in the service of all while at the same time practicing renunciation.

Sacrifice is less than renunciation, though a sacrifice is a renunciation just the same; sacrifice is a lesson that the prophets and teachers taught in order that man should learn renunciation. The virtue of a sacrifice lies in the willingness with which it is made. Renunciation, however, is something that arises not as a principle but as a feeling.

Renunciation has an automatic action on the heart of man, an action that very few realize because very few arrive at that stage where they can renounce. By this action a spiritual spark is kindled in the soul, and when a person has arrived at that stage he has taken the first step on the path of spirituality. The spark produced by this action in the depths of the heart culminates in a flame, a torch in life; and this changes the whole outlook on life. The whole world seems changed, the same world in which one has lived and suffered and enjoyed and learned and unlearned—everything appears to change once renunciation is learned.

Renunciation is in fact the denial of the self and of that which could be of use to one. As all things in this world can be used and abused, so the principle of renunciation can be used and abused. Among the many wrong meanings people attach to self-denial the one that is most common is that it means denying oneself the pleasures and the happiness that the world can offer. If practicing renunciation as a principle were a good thing, then there would seem to be no purpose behind the whole of creation. The creation might well never have been manifested if renunciation had been the principle. Therefore renunciation in itself is neither virtue nor sin; it becomes a virtue or sin according to the use we make of it.

When one considers renunciation from the metaphysical point of view, one finds that this principle serves as a flight of stairs by which to rise above all things. It is the nature of life in the world that all the things we become attracted to in time become not only ties but burdens. Life is an eternal journey, and the more loaded with burdens one is, the harder the journey becomes. Think how the soul, whose constant desire is to go forward, is daily held back by ties and continually more burdened! As the soul goes on it finds its feet in chains. It wants to go forward, but at every step it is more distracted, so that it becomes more difficult to go on.

That is why all the thinkers and the wise who have come to the realization of life have used renunciation as a remedy. The picture that the sage gives of this is the fable of the dog and the loaf. A dog carrying a loaf in its mouth came to a pool; and when it saw its reflection in the water it thought that it was another dog; it howled and barked and lost its bread. The more we observe our errors in life, our petty desires, the more we find we are not far from the dog in the fable. Think of the national catastrophes of recent times, and how the material things of the world that are forever changing, that are not everlasting have been tugged at and fought for! This shows that man is blinded by material life and disregards the secret, hidden things behind that life.

When we try to reason out what we should renounce and how we should practice renunciation, we should remember that no virtue is a virtue if it is forced upon someone who is incapable of it. A person upon whom a virtue is forced, who is forced to renounce, cannot make the right renunciation. No virtue that gives pain is a virtue. If it gives pain, how can it be a virtue? A thing is called a virtue because it gives happiness; that which takes away happiness can never be a virtue. Renunciation is only rightly practiced by those who understand renunciation and are capable of practicing it. For instance, there may be a person with a loaf of bread who is traveling in a train and finds somebody who is hungry and in need of bread. He himself is hungry too, but he has only one piece of bread. If he thinks that it is his dharma to give it away and be starving, but is unhappy about this, he would do better not to give it away, for then it would be no virtue. If he did this once, he would certainly not do it again another time, as he suffered by it and the virtue brought him unhappiness. This virtue would never develop in his character. He alone is capable of renunciation who finds a greater satisfaction in seeing another eat his piece of bread than in eating it himself.

Only he whose heart is full of happiness after an act of renunciation should make a renunciation. This shows that renunciation is not something that can be learned or taught. It comes by itself as the soul develops, when the soul begins to see the true value of things. All that is valuable to others a seer begins to see differently. Thus the value of all the things that we consider precious or not precious is according to the way we look at them. For one person the renunciation of a penny is too much; for another that of everything he possesses is nothing. It depends on how we look at things. One rises above all that one renounces in life. Man remains the slave of anything that he has not renounced; of that which he has renounced he becomes king. This whole world can become a kingdom to a person who has renounced it.

Renunciation depends upon the evolution of the soul.

One who has not evolved spiritually cannot really renounce. Toys so precious to children mean nothing to the grown-up; it is easy to renounce them. And so it is for those who develop spiritually: for them all things are easy to renounce.

How can one progress in this path of renunciation? By becoming able to discriminate between two things. A person with the character of the dog in the fable cannot renounce. He loves both alternatives, but life is such that when there are two things before us we have to lose one of them. Man's discrimination must decide what to renounce and for what reason: whether to renounce heaven for the world or the world for heaven; wealth for honor or honor for wealth; whether to renounce things momentarily precious for everlasting things, or everlasting things for things momentarily precious. The nature of life is such that it always shows us two possibilities, and often it is very difficult to choose between them. Frequently one thing is at hand and the other further from our reach, and it is a puzzle which one to renounce or how to get the other. Also, we often lack the will power to renounce. It requires not only the power to discriminate between two things, but also the will power to do what we want to do. It is not an easy thing for a person to do in life what he wishes to do; life is difficult. Often we cannot renounce because our own self will not listen to us; and if we cannot even listen to ourselves, then how difficult it must be for others to listen to us!

Renunciation can be learned naturally. We must first train our sense of discrimination in order to distinguish between that which is more valuable and that which is less so. We can learn this by testing, just as real gold is tested against imitation gold: that which lasts for a short time and then turns black is imitation; that which always keeps its color is real. This shows that the value of things can be recognized by their constancy. We might ask if we should not recognize the value of things by their beauty. Indeed we should recognize them by their beauty, but we must also recognize beauty by its durability. Think of the difference in the price between a flower and a diamond! The flower, with all its fineness, beauty of color, and fragrance, falls short in comparison with the diamond. The sole reason is that the beauty of the flower will fade the next day, while that of the diamond will last. This shows a natural tendency; we do not need to learn it. We are always seeking for beauty, as well as for that which is lasting. If a friendship does not last, however beautiful it may be, what value has it? What value have position and honor that do not last? Man, however, is like a child, running after all that attracts him and always changing. But at the same time his soul seeks constancy.

In learning the lesson of renunciation we can only study our own nature, what our innermost being is yearning for, and try to follow what it tells us. Wisdom comes by this process of renunciation. Wisdom and renunciation go together; by renunciation man becomes wiser, and by being wise he becomes capable of renunciation. The whole trouble in the lives of people in their homes, in the nation, and in the world at large is always man's incapacity for renunciation.

Civilization itself is really only a developed sense of renunciation that manifests itself in our consideration for each other. Every act of courtesy, of politeness, shows renunciation. When a person offers his seat, or anything that is good, to another, it is renunciation. Civilization in its real sense is renunciation.

The highest and greatest goal that every soul has to reach is God. As everything needs renunciation, that highest goal needs the highest renunciation. But a forced renunciation, even for God, is not a proper nor a true renunciation. Proper renunciation one can only find in those who are capable of it. Think of the story in the Bible of Abraham sacrificing his son. Man today is apt to laugh at some of the ancient stories, reasoning according to his own point of view. But think how many fathers and mothers have given their children as a sacrifice in wartime for their nation, their people, or their honor! This shows that no sacrifice can be too great a sacrifice for one's ideal. There is only the difference of ideal: whether it is a material or a spiritual ideal, whether for earthly gain or for spiritual gain, whether for man or for God.

As long as renunciation is practiced for spiritual progress, so long it is the right way. But as soon as renunciation has become a principle, it is abused. Man, in fact, must be the master of life; he must use renunciation, not go under in renunciation. So it is with all virtues. When virtues control a man's life they become idols; and it is not idols that we should worship, it is the ideal behind the idol.

*Chapter 18.*

# SELF-CONTROL AND REACTION

Every circumstance, favorable or unfavorable, in which a person finds himself, and every person, agreeable or disagreeable, in whose presence he is, causes him to react. Upon this reaction depends the person's happiness and his spiritual progress. If he has control over this reaction, it means that he is progressing; if he has no control over it, it shows that he is going backward. When you take two people, a wise and a foolish one, the wise person reacts more intensely than the foolish one; also, a fine person naturally reacts more than a dense one, a just person more than an unjust one, and a spiritual person more than a materialist. Yet it is lack of mastery when one has no control over one's reactions. A person who is fine, spiritual, sensitive, wise, and just but who has no control over his reactions is incomplete. This shows that even becoming fine and just and spiritual is not sufficient; for all these qualities, though they make one finer and more sensitive, yet weaken one in the face of the disturbing influences of the crowd. And when this is the case one will not be perfect.

The balance of life lies in being as fine as a thread and as strong as a steel wire. If one does not show endurance and strength to withstand all the opposing and disturbing influences among which one always has to be in life, one certainly reveals weakness and lack of development. In the first place this reaction causes a person a certain amount of vanity. He believes he is better than the one who disturbs him, though he cannot with certainty say that he is stronger. When he cannot put up with conditions around him he may think that he is a superior person, but in reality the conditions are stronger than he. If we are born on earth, if we are destined to walk on the earth, we cannot dream of paradise while we have to stand firm in all the circumstances that the earth presents us with. When a person progresses towards spirituality he must bear in mind that together with his spiritual progress he must strengthen himself against disturbing influences. If not, he should know that however much he desires to make progress he will be pulled back against his will by conditions, by circumstances.

There are four different ways in which a person reacts: in deed, in speech, in thought, and in feeling. A deed produces a definite result, speech produces effect, thought produces atmosphere, and feeling produces conditions. Therefore no way in which a person reacts will be without effect. A reaction will be perceived quickly or slowly, but it must be perceived. Very often a reaction is not only agreeable to oneself, but to others also. A person who answers an insult by insulting the other stands on the same level of insult, the one who does not answer stands above it. In this way one can rise above things against which one reacts, if only one knows how to fly. It is flying above things instead of standing against them as a material person does. How can one call oneself spiritual if one cannot fly? That is the first condition of being spiritual.

The whole mechanism of this world is action and reaction, in the objective world as well as in the world of humanity. Only, in man there is the possibility of developing that spirit which is called the spirit of mastery, and that spirit is best developed by trying to gain control over one's reactions. Life offers us abundant occasions from morning till evening to practice this lesson. With every move, at every turn we make, we are faced with something agreeable or disagreeable, harmonious or inharmonious—either a condition or a person. If we react automatically we are no better than a machine and no different from thousands and millions of people who react so. The only way to find in ourselves a trace of that divine heritage which is mastery is by controlling our reactions against all influences. In theory it is simple and easy; in practice it is the most difficult thing there is to master. But when we think of its usefulness we shall find that there is nothing in the world that is more necessary and more important than this development. If there is any strength to be found in the world, that strength is within ourselves and the fact that we are able to control our reactions is the proof of this. Self-control preserves dignity, it maintains honor; it is this which sustains respect, and it is this which keeps people wise. It is easy to think but it is difficult to continue to be a thoughtful person.

Very often people have asked me if there is any practice, any study, anything that one can do in order to develop will power; and I have answered that yes, there are many practices and many ways, but the simplest and best practice that one can follow without being taught is to have one's reactions always in hand. Such expressions as, "I cannot endure," "I cannot stand," "I cannot sustain," "I cannot have patience," all mean to me, "I am weak." By speaking thus we only admit in other words that we are weak, and can there be anyone in the world who is a worse enemy to us than our own weakness? If the whole world were our friend, that one enemy, our weakness, would be enough to ruin our life; but once this enemy is conquered we can stand against all those who come into conflict with us.

Now the question is how one should set to work in the development of will power. One must take into consideration one's physical condition. The nervous system must be in proper condition. It is from nervousness that man goes from bad to worse; even a good person with good intentions may prove to be otherwise, for he may have good intentions but be unable to carry them out because his nerves are weak. What he needs is the habit of silence, of concentration, of meditation. A person who continually goes on talking or doing things and does not meditate for a while, who does not take a rest, cannot control his nervous system and keep it in order. If there is anything that can control the nervous system it is right breathing, and when that right breathing is done, together with a concentration of thought, then the nervous system is greatly fortified. There are many things that cause unhappiness, and these can often be avoided by keeping the nervous system in hand.

When we look at it from a higher point of view, the will can be developed by denying the impulses that sometimes arise suddenly and that clamor for an answer. What is called self-denial is really this: that one controls one's thoughts and wishes and desires and passions. But that does not mean retirement from life in the world; it only means taking one-self in hand.

It is never too soon to begin control, and it is never too late to improve it. If this kind of education is given from child-hood, wonderful results can be brought about. In ancient times in India (though one sees very little of it now), youths were trained in *asana,* a certain way of sitting, of walking, of standing; and by that they first achieved control over their muscles and nerves. It would be of immense value if educa-tion today adopted both the study of controlling reactions and the practice of it in sports and gymnastics. If a youth of twelve to sixteen years could learn to breathe clearly and rhythmically and deeply enough, that alone would be some-thing.

The control of reactions will always give a certain amount of pain, but at the same time it is by suffering that one will gain the power to rise above it. But of course if this is not understood rightly one might endanger oneself. There is a danger in both cases: on one side there is a pit, on the other side there is water. A person who, because he is afraid of getting hurt or being oppressed by someone, is always keeping his thoughts and feelings suppressed might if he had expressed them have become a very bad man; but by not having been able to express them he is ruined. Therefore one should develop one's discrimination in order to analyze one's reaction, to understand it before it is expressed. One should always ask oneself, "That which is in my hand now, shall I not throw it away? By throwing it away, shall I do something wrong? Where shall I throw it? Will it fall on my head? What will become of it?" A person should know what he has in his hand. If in order to avoid breaking another person's head he breaks his own head, he has done wrong too.

Then what should he do? Instead of throwing the impulses that come to him out automatically, he should first weigh them, analyze them, measure them and use them to the best advantage in life. A stone is not used only to break another person's head or to break one's own head, it is also used to build houses. Use everything where it will be most useful, where it will be of some advantage. All such things as passion and anger and irritation one looks upon as very bad, as evil; but if that evil were kept in hand it could be used for a good purpose, because it is a power, it is an energy. In other words evil, properly used, becomes a virtue; and virtue wrongly used becomes an evil. For instance, when a person is in a rage, or when he really feels like being angry, if he controls that thought and does not express it in words, that gives him great power. Otherwise the expression has a bad effect upon his nerves. His control of it has given him an extra strength that will remain with him. A person who has anger and control is to be preferred to the person who has neither.

Does not self-control take away spontaneity? Self-control gives a greater spontaneity. It develops thought power; it makes one think first about every impulse, which otherwise would have manifested automatically. In other words: hold the word between the lips before it drops out.

Is impulse before it is controlled wrong in itself, or is it good? When one thinks about the origin of impulse one goes in quite a different direction of thought. Then one has to think in what direction it is facing; also of the direction of the mind, whether it is in illumination or in darkness. The mind is sometimes illuminated, sometimes in darkness, and one should think about the condition of the mind at the time. There is another thing to be considered in this connection: a person may have good intentions and his mind may be focused on good ideas, and then another with evil intentions and wrong ideas may say or do something that automatically turns the mind of the first person to evil against his own will. There is the word of the Bible, "Resist not evil." Sometimes evil will come like fire thrown by a person into the mind of another. A fire then starts in that mind which had been without it, and in reaction it too expresses that fire. To resist evil is to send fire in answer to fire; in other words to partake of the fire that comes from another. But by not partaking of it one casts the fire out, and it falls on the person who threw it. The best thing is to go through every condition that life presents with patience, with understanding, with open eyes, and so try to rise above it with every little effort we can make.

The work that a Sufi considers to be his sacred task has nothing to do with any particular creed, nor has it to do with any particular religion; it is only this simple thing: to be in rhythm with life's conditions and to be in tune with the infinite. When one asks how one can arrive at being in accord with life instead of being frightened by life's conditions, the answer is by meeting them and observing them keenly, and then by trying to harmonize oneself for the time being with those conditions, while the next effort is to rise above them if they are adverse.

At this time the world's condition is such that it seems that the art of personality has been much neglected. Man, intoxicated with the life of cupidity and the competitive spirit, is held by the commercialism of the day, is kept busy in the acquirement of the needs of this everyday life, and the beauty that is the need of the soul is lost to view. Man's interest in all aspects of life—science, art, philosophy—remains incomplete in the absence of the art of personality. How rightly the distinction has been made in the English language between man and gentleman!

# PART III
# THE ART OF PERSONALITY

*Chapter 19.*

# OUR GOD PART AND OUR MAN PART

Not only in this age but also in past ages, the first thing realized by man has been his own limited existence formed of matter, which he called "I." This is not his fault; it is because religions have been interpreted with the intention of dominating the people, of holding them in the grasp of those who understood their meaning. The priests have only allowed people to understand very little, and all the rest they have kept for themselves. They have said, "You are ordinary beings. God is much too high for you to understand. We can communicate with Him, we can understand Him, but you must stay where you are."

All his life Buddha fought hard against this. When someone spoke to him of a spirit, of God, or made a show of a holy or spiritual life, he said, "I do not believe in it." But this was very extreme, for it led people into another error; it led them to say that there was no God, no spirit.

Another reason for this separation was that it has always been the tendency of those who had the same way of thought, the same belief or faith, to come together in one group, in one society, in order to have the encouragement of

127

each other's thought. By this they separated themselves from the rest of humanity.

The mystic has never believed with a blind belief. In fact he does not believe, he experiences. He experiences that he is himself the whole being. There is a verse of a Hindustani poet that says:

> Behind the human face God was hiding,
>     I did not know.
> I veiled my eyes and was separated from truth
>     I did not know.

It is a very beautiful verse, and it has a deep meaning.

All of us have our God part and our man part. Man is made of two things, spirit and substance. The spirit is the finer part and the substance is the grosser part: the finer part, the spirit, has turned into the grosser part. One part is the external, limited self that we see, and the other is the unlimited being.

Man's external self is composed of the five elements, but in reality man is much larger and extends much further than we generally believe. For instance, when someone stands before an audience he appears to be of a certain size; but when he speaks he is as large as the area to which his voice carries. Although a friend or a beloved may be thousands of miles away he will feel our attachment, our affection. The feeling originates here, but manifests over there; this shows that in our feelings we are larger still.

The breath goes still further; by the breath we can send our thoughts wherever we wish, and we are able to know the thought and the condition of every being. The thought of someone who wishes to accomplish a certain thing reaches out in order to prepare it. Man is like a telescope: at one end there is the man part, the limited existence, and at the other end there is the God part, the unlimited being. At one end we are so small; at the other we are so vast that we are the whole being.

If each of us is so great, as great as the whole being, we might ask how there can be room for so many of us. Are there then several whole beings? There are not. Through our ignorance we see many and make distinctions, saying, "This is I, that is you; this is a friend, that is an enemy; I like this one, that one I do not like." But in the hereafter all are connected, we are all the same.

Man has two natures, *farishtagi,* the angelic, and *hayvanat,* the animal. Hayvanat means man's body and that part of his nature which needs food, drink, sleep, and the satisfaction of all its passions. His anger and his jealousy are animal; also his fear of one who is stronger than himself and his envy of one who is better than he. In all these man is the same as the animals.

Farishtagi is the part of his nature that goes back to its source. It is not man's intelligence; the animals also have intelligence, though they cannot ask, "From where have I come? For what purpose am I here?" When man knows this, when he recognizes his origin, then he is a divine being. This angelic nature is his kindness, his love, his sympathy, and his desire for knowledge. A great Hindustani poet has said, "We created man for feeling; if not, for Our praise the angels were enough in heaven."

In his worship man, thinking that he glorifies God, in reality reduces God. We take a part and call it "I." We occupy this part and thereby deduct it from God. I remember that my murshid when he met with any difficulty used to say with a deep sigh, *"Bandagi becharegi,"* which means, "By coming here, He has become helpless."

What connection is there between Allah and *bandeh,* between God and man, and what connection is there between man and God? What we call "I" is formed by the impressions of the external world, the world of illusion, which have fallen upon the soul. An infant will never say "I." If it has something in its hand and one takes it away, it does not care. It does not distinguish between old and young. Whoever comes near to it, friend or enemy, is the same to the infant. The intellect that recognizes things by their distinctions and differences has deluded the soul.

We can see that that which we call "I" is not the true nature of our soul, because we are never really happy. Whatever we do, whatever we have, whatever power we possess, we can never be happy. We say that this or that makes us unhappy, but it is only the distance that makes us so; the soul is unhappy in its separation.

A person sees that his coat is grand and he thinks, "I am grand." It is not he who is grand, it is his coat. Whatever is before the soul, the soul recognizes as "I." But what is "I"? The coat is not I, because when the coat is taken off, the self remains. When we are not experiencing through the senses, the consciousness still remains.

The Sufi, by the inactivity of the senses, by different postures and practices, produces stillness. Then by the repetition of the name of God he merges his consciousness in the whole consciousness, in God. This has been understood by the Greek philosophers; it has also been understood by the Vedantists. The Sufi keeps to the adoration, the reverence that he has for God; he bows and prostrates himself before God, and he gives the beautiful name of Beloved to God. He understands that by saying, "This too is God," he glorifies God, he does not reduce Him. With all his humility, with all his devotion, he realizes his oneness with the highest Being.

It is difficult to separate God from man; in reality there is no separation. God's action and man's action are the same, only God's action is perfect and man's action is imperfect. We upon earth are dependent upon so many things. First of all we must eat. If he did not need to eat, man would not have to work; he could sit with his friends and think of God or of something else. Then he must sleep. And there are so many other necessities.

There is a verse of Zahir which says, "The seekers lost themselves before they sought Thee." And the great poet Amir says, "Do not say that man is God, for he is not God.

And do not say that man is separate from God, for he is not separate."

It is not difficult to have occult or psychic powers; to be virtuous is not difficult, nor to keep our life pure. But to be merciful, to be compassionate, to be human is difficult. God has many names: the Great, the Almighty, the Sovereign, but He is mostly called the Merciful and the Compassionate. In these qualities we are never perfect, and we never shall be. One should go into one's room at night and repent of what one has done, of all the thousand bad thoughts one has had of friends and enemies. A Persian poet says, "The whole secret of the two worlds is in these two words: with thy friends be loving, with thy enemies, courteous."

If we have understood this then this world is nothing; and if we have recognized that it is a passing thing, why not let others enjoy themselves while we look on? Why not let others put on a beautiful dress, while we look at it? Why not let others eat a good dinner while we watch or stay in the kitchen to cook it? Why not let others sit in a carriage and we pull it, instead of sitting in it ourselves and making others draw it? Keeping our life noble means being merciful and compassionate. But it is the tendency of everyone to take what is best from another; even in friendship there is that tendency. All are seeking their own enjoyment and want to leave the worst to another. But if one is a seeker of God one should take the opposite way, even if it is contrary to all the world.

There are three courses one may take in life: the first is renunciation; this is the way of the saints and the sages. It means following in the ideal and accepting whatever troubles and sorrows and ill treatment may result. The second is selfishness, which means being more selfish than the rest of the world. The third is greatest and the most difficult. It is having all the responsibilities, all the cares of life, friends and everything, and being as unselfish and as good as possible, and yet just selfish enough not to be trampled upon.

If a person is turning round in a circle, the first time he goes slowly, the second time he goes faster, the fourth time he goes faster still, and the fifth, sixth, seventh, or eighth time he will fall down. The first time he experiences the joy of turning, the second and third and fourth times he experiences it more and more, till at last he is drunk with it and falls down and experiences it to the full. This is what the universe has been doing, night and day, from the creation till now. In every activity there is an intoxication. Whatever we do we wish to do more and more, whatever the action may be. If a man is a patriot he will be more and more patriotic. A singer will sing more and more songs until he loses his voice. If a person gambles he will want to do it more and more. If a person has been drunk or drugged he will want more and more of whatever the drink or drugs may be.

Hafiz says, "Before sunrise the wine was poured out. The wine was borrowed from the eyes of Saki, the wine-giver." Saki is manifestation, which so intoxicates us that we believe that this is all that exists, until we have become so enslaved by it that we cannot free ourselves anymore.

*Chapter 20.*

# MAN, THE SEED OF GOD

There are various ideas and beliefs as to the relationship between God and man; and it is natural that there should be various beliefs, because every man has his own conception of God. There is no comparison between God and man, for man, being limited, can be compared with another being, but God, being perfect, is beyond comparison. The prophets and masters in all ages have tried their best to give man some idea of God's being; but it has always been difficult, for it is impossible to define God in words. It is like trying to put the ocean into a bottle. However large the bottle, it can never accommodate the ocean. The words that we use in our everyday language are the names of limited forms, and we give God, who is above name and form, a name for our convenience. If there is any possibility of understanding God and His being, it is only possible through finding the relationship between man and God. The reason for calling man the seed of God is that this picture gives, to some extent, an idea of the relationship that exists between man and God.

There is a root, there is a stem, there are branches, there are leaves, and there comes a flower; but in the heart of the flower there is something that tells the history of the whole plant. One might say that it is for the sake of the flower that the plant was created, but in point of fact it is the seed in the heart of the flower that continues the species of that plant. That seed is the secret of the plant, and it is its source and goal. It is that seed that was the beginning; it is from that seed that the root came; then the seedling emerged, and so it became a plant. After that the seed disappeared but after the coming of the leaves and branches and the flowers it appeared again, not as one seed, but as many seeds, in multiplicity; and yet it was the same. Towards what goal, for what result did this happen? In order that the seed should come again as the result of the whole plant.

To the man of simple belief, who believes only in his particular idea, there is no relationship between God and man; but for the man who wishes to understand this relationship, the proof of it is to be found in everything. This is the idea that is spoken of in the Bible, where it is said that God created man in His own image. It is the same as if the seed out of which the plant comes were to say, "Out of my own image I have created the seed that will come forth from the heart of the flower. I shall appear as many, although in the beginning I am one grain."

This idea again explains to us why it is said that man was created in God's image when the whole of manifestation, the whole of creation has come from God. The leaf, the branch, and the stem have all come out of the seed, but they are the image of the seed. The image of the seed is the seed itself. Not only this: the essence of the seed is in the seed. Of course there is some energy, some power, some color, some fragrance in the flower, in the leaves, and in the stem; but at the same time all the properties that belong to the stem, flower, petals, and leaves are to be found in the seed.

This shows us that man is the culmination of the whole of creation, and that in him the whole universe is manifested. The mineral kingdom, the vegetable kingdom, and the animal kingdom are to be found in the being, in the spirit of man. This not only means that the different properties such as mineral and vegetable are to be found in the physical body that is made for man, but his mind and his heart also show all the different qualities. The heart is like either a fertile soil or a barren desert: it shows love or lack of love, the productive faculty or destructiveness.

There are different kinds of stones: there are precious stones and there are pebbles and rocks; but among human hearts there is a still greater variety. Think of those whose thoughts and feelings have proved to be more precious than anything that the world can offer: the poets, the artists, the inventors, the thinkers, the philosophers, the servants of humanity, the inspirers of man, the benefactors of mankind. No wealth, no precious stone whether diamond or ruby can be compared with these; and yet it has the same quality. Then there are rock-like hearts: one may knock against them and break oneself, and still they will not move. The heart has a wax-like quality, or it has the quality of the stone. There are melting hearts and there are hearts that will never melt. Is there anything in nature that is not found in man? Is there not in his feeling, in his thoughts, in his qualities, the aspect of running water, of a fertile soil, and of fruitful trees? Is there not in the heart of man the image of the plant and of fragrant flowers? But the flowers that come from the human heart live longer; their fragrance will spread through the whole world, and their color will be seen by all people. How delicious are the fruits that human hearts can bear! They immortalize souls and lift them up.

There are on the other hand mentalities in which nothing springs up except the desire to hurt and harm their fellow-men, producing poison through their fruits and flowers, hurting others by thought, speech, or action; and they can hurt more than thorns. There are some whose feelings and thoughts are like gold and silver, and there are others whose thoughts are just like iron and steel. The variety that one can see in human nature is so vast that all the objects that one can obtain from this earth cannot equal it.

Man not only shows in his nature, in his qualities, in his body, in his thought and feeling the heritage of this earth, but also that of heaven. Man is subjected to the influence of the planets, of the sun, of the moon, of heat and cold, of air and water and fire, and of all the different elements of which this whole cosmic system is composed. All these elements are to be found in his thoughts, in his feelings, in his body. One can find a person with warmth representing fire; another person who is cold represents water. There are human beings who in their thought and feeling represent the air element; their quickness, their restlessness, show the air element in them.

Does not man represent the sun and moon in his positive and negative character? Does not duality of sex show this? In every man and in every woman there are both the sun quality and the moon quality, and it is these two opposite qualities that give balance to the character. When one quality is predominant and the other is completely missing then there is a lack of balance somewhere.

If one pursues the thought of mysticism still further, one finds that not only is all visible manifestation present in man, but also all that is invisible. If the angels, fairies, ghosts, elementals, or any other of man's imaginings can be found anywhere, it is in human nature. Angels at all times have been pictured in the image of man.

If all that exists in the world and in heaven is to be found in man, then what remains? God Himself has said in the scriptures that He made man in His own image. In other words, "If you wish to see Me, I am to be found in man." How thoughtless it is, then, on the part of man when, absorbed in his high ideals, he begins to condemn man, to look down upon man! However low and weak and sinful a man may be, there is yet the possibility of his rising higher than anything else in the whole of manifestation, whether on earth or in heaven; nothing else can reach the height that man is destined to reach. Therefore the point of view of the mystics and the thinkers of all ages has always been reflected in their manner, which was a respectful attitude to all men.

In the example of the life of Jesus Christ one can see what compassion, what forgiveness, what tolerance, what understanding the master showed when a sinner was brought before him. A man who shows contempt towards his fellow men may be called religious or pious, but he can never be called truly spiritual or wise, whatever be his condition. The man who has no respect for mankind has no attitude of worship towards God. The one who has not recognized the image of God in man has not seen the Artist who made this creation; he has deprived himself of that vision which is most sacred and most holy. A person who thinks that man is earthly does not know where his soul comes from. The soul comes from above; it is in the soul of man that God is reflected. A man who feels hatred and contempt, whatever be his belief, faith, or religion, has not understood the secret of all religions, which is in the heart of man. And certainly, however, good, however virtuous a person may be, however tolerant or forgiving, if at the same time he does not recognize God in man, he has not touched religion.

There is, however, another side to the question. As man evolves, so he finds the limitations, the errors, and the infirmities of human nature; and so it becomes difficult for him to live in the world and to face all that comes. Also, it becomes very difficult for man to be fine, to be good and kind and sensitive, and yet at the same time to be tolerant. The tendency comes to push everything away, and to keep oneself away from everybody else. But the purpose of being born on earth is not that, it is to find that perfection which is within oneself. However good and kind a man may be, if he has not found the purpose for which he was born on earth he has not fulfilled the object of life.

There are as many different aspects of that purpose as there are people in the world; but behind all of them there is one purpose, which may be called the purpose of the whole creation. That purpose is accomplished when the architect builds a house that he has designed and he enters it and sees how well it is made; that purpose is accomplished when a play is produced and the producer watches it—that is the fulfillment of his purpose. Every man seems to have his own purpose, but all these purposes are nothing but steps to the one and only purpose that is the purpose of God. If our small desires are granted today, tomorrow there is another wish; and whatever be the desire, when it is granted there is next day another desire. This shows that the whole of humanity is directed towards one desire, the desire that is God's object: the fuller experience of life within and without, the fuller knowledge of life above and below. It is the widening of the outlook: that it may become so wide that in the soul, which is vaster than the world, all may be reflected; that the sight may become so keen that it may probe the depths of the earth and the highest of the heavens. In this lies the fulfillment of the soul and the soul who will not make every possible effort and every sacrifice for its attainment has not understood religion. What is the Sufi Message? It is the esoteric training, practicing and working throughout life towards that attainment which is the fulfullment of the purpose of God.

*Chapter 21.*

# THE PRIVILEGE OF BEING HUMAN

Character is, so to speak, a picture with lines and colors that we make within ourselves. It is wonderful to see how the tendency of character building already springs up in childhood, just as one sees in a bird the instinct of building a nest. A child begins by noticing all kinds of things in grown-up people, and then it adopts whatever it likes most and whatever attracts it. By this we understand that when a person is absorbed in himself he has no time for character building, for he has no time to think of others. For instance, if even the greatest actors do not forget themselves on the stage, they cannot act. The musician, if he cannot forget himself while playing, cannot play well. As with everything else, the whole task of building oneself depends entirely on forgetting oneself. This is the key to the whole of life. I have met people distinguished in art, science, philosophy, religion, in all fields, and found that they had all reached greatness by means of this quality, the quality of forgetting themselves. And again I have seen people with great qualities who could not bring out the best in their lives because they did not possess this one quality.

I remember a vina player, a very wonderful musician, who used to play and study many hours a day, but whenever he had to play before an audience he became self-conscious. The first thought that came to him was himself; and when that happened all the impressions of the people there would fall upon him. Generally he would then take his vina, cover it up, and run away. On the other hand I have heard Sarah Bernhardt simply recite the Marseillaise, that was all. But when she appeared on the stage and recited this poem, she would win every heart in the audience, for at that time—it was during the war—she was France. What enabled her to be France was her concentration, her way of forgetting herself.

Character building is much greater and more important than the building of a house, a city, a nation, or an empire. One might ask why it is so important, as it is only the building of our insignificant self, while many have built an edifice or even a nation and they are gone and there is no memory of them left. The Taj Mahal is one of the most wonderful buildings in the world. Those who see it—artists, architects—have a great admiration for it, but that is all. No one cares who made it; no one's heart is moved on account of the builder.

To this day the Hindus repeat, early in the morning, "Ram, Ram"; the Buddhists call on the Lord Buddha and the Christians on Christ. Why? Only because of the personalities of these holy ones, the magnetism that was theirs. The words of Christ spoken so many hundreds of years ago are remembered today simply because of his personality. It is not spirituality alone: there have been many *majdhubs* who were very spiritual. They were united with God, but they have gone and no one remembers them. It is not piety: there are many pious people sitting in the mosques and churches telling their rosaries. Their piety is for themselves; they cannot move the world. So if it is not spirituality and not piety, what is it then? It is the development of humanity in us.

This development concerns our intelligence, our heart, and our mind. It concerns the intelligence because if we have love but no intelligence to know the pleasure of the beloved, then we can be a great lover but our love will be of no avail. It concerns the heart because if we have intelligence but no feeling, no sympathy, we may speak very politely, we may be very polished in manner, but if there is bitterness within, if we do not feel what we say, it would be better if we had not said anything. It concerns the mind because if we have intelligence and feeling but no thoughtfulness, no sense of what is appropriate, we are ignorant. One may be well acquainted with European manners and decorum, but if one is sent to the court of an eastern king, one will be at a loss. Or a person may know all the etiquette of an Indian court, but if he comes to Europe he knows nothing about western ways.

It is a great privilege to be human so that we can develop our humanity and be human in mind, in reality as well as in form. The privilege consists in being man, who is the ideal of God.

It is not the rock, which does not know whether a king, a beggar, a holy man, or a wicked person stands upon it, it is not the angels, who have no heart to feel with and for another, who only feel the praise of God and praise Him: it is man who has been given a heart.

A Hindustani poet says, "To become a nabi, saint, prophet, ghawth, qutub is very difficult. What shall I tell you of the struggles of their life, since it is even difficult for man to become human?" Indeed, to attain to spiritual grades is very difficult. We should first try to become human. To become an angel is not very difficult; to be material is very easy; but to live in the world, in all the difficulties and struggles of the world, and to be human at the same time, is very difficult. If we become that, then we become the miniature of God on earth.

*Chapter 22.*

# THE HEART

From a mystical point of view personality is formed around the heart. For a materialist the heart is the piece of flesh hidden in the breast, but for the mystic the heart is the center of the person around which the personality is formed. Consciously or unconsciously man loves the word "heart," and if we were to ask a poet to leave that word out and write his poems without using it, he would never satisfy himself or others. Few people think of this; yet the poets who have most appealed to humanity have used the word heart most. For what is man? Man is his heart. A dead heart means a dead man; a living heart a living man.

People look for wonderworking and surprises, for phenomena of all kinds. Yet the greatest phenomenon, the greatest surprise, and the greatest wonder are to be found in one's heart. If there is anything that can tune man to the highest pitch, that can tune the strings of his soul to the right note, it is only the tuning of the heart. The one who has not reached his heart has not reached God. People may be relations, friends, partners, collaborators and yet be quite separate; nearness in space does not make people real friends. There is only one way of coming near to one's friends, and that is by way of the heart. If there is anything that is the most wonderful in heaven and on earth, it is the heart. If a miracle is to be found anywhere, it is in the heart. For when God has tuned the heart, what is there that is not to be found in it?

The Nizam of Hyderabad once wrote, "If one only knew how large the heart is! It accommodates heaven and earth, all the sea and all the land." The greatness or smallness of people does not depend on outer things. Whatever rank or position a person has, if his heart is not great he cannot be great; and if his heart is great he remains great under all circumstances. It is the heart that makes one great or small.

Hearts can be of different kinds: there is the golden heart, the silver heart, the copper heart, the iron heart. The golden heart shows its color and its beauty; it is precious, and at the same time it is soft. The silver heart shows inferior qualities compared with the golden heart, yet coins are made of silver; it is useful. Of the copper heart pennies are made, and pennies too are useful in everyday life: they are even more used than gold and silver coins. Copper is strong and hard, and it needs many hammerings to shape it and make something out of it. Then there is the iron heart, which must be put into the fire before anything can be done with it. When the iron becomes hot in the glowing fire, then we can make something out of it, but the blacksmith must be always ready: as soon as the fire begins to glow, he must start at once. If he lets it go, it will turn cold in a moment.

Besides these aspects there is the heart of rock and the heart of wax. The heart of rock must be broken; it must be cut; nothing reaches it. Cold, heat, fire, sun, or water has little effect upon the heart of rock. But when the heart is of wax, it melts as soon as the sun falls upon it, and when it is heated one can mold it any way one likes. Then there is the heart of paper that flies like a kite in the wind: to the north, to the south, to the east, to the west. One can control it as long as the string is strong enough to hold it, but when there is no wind it drops down.

Are these examples sufficient? No, there are innumerable

hearts, each differing in quality, and once we begin to distinguish the qualities of the heart, we begin to see miracles, living phenomena, every moment of our life. Is there anything that can be compared with the heart? It dies and lives again; it is torn and mended again; it is broken and made whole; it can rise and it can fall, and after falling it can rise again, and after rising it can fall again instantly. There is one heart that can creep, another that can walk, another that can run, another that can fly, and yet we cannot limit the action of the heart. We cannot imagine how the heart can be illuminated and darkened in a moment! It is a maze we enter, and when we are inside we can never get out. The heart can be confusion and it can be paradise, it can be heaven itself. And if we ask where we can see the soul manifest to view, it is in the heart. Where is paradise, where is heaven, where is love, and where is God? We can answer each of these questions by saying "In the heart of man."

Imagine how wonderful, and at the same time how obscure! If we call the heart the spark of fire, then we can see its different aspects as sympathy in the form of heat, as longing in the form of fire, as affection in the form of glowing, as devotion in the form of flame, as passion in the form of smoke that blinds one's eyes. That which gives one courage to stand firm in the battlefield, to struggle through life, to endure all that comes, that which strengthens one to have patience, what is it? It is the heart. If the heart fails, one falls; if the heart rises, one rises.

When the heart is directed towards one ideal, one object, one point it develops: when the heart is going from one point to another it is weakened, for then the fire element of the heart dies. The little spark is brought to a blaze when one blows upon it, and yet the fire is put out by blowing. Why? Because man's blowing is directing the air to one single spot, but the wind blowing all around extinguishes the fire.

When a person says, "I love everybody," one can be sure he loves nobody; but when he says, "I love my mother, my father, my son, my daughter, my friend, or my beloved," then he has taken the first step on the path of love. But no one in the world can claim to love and at the same time know love. The moment one knows what love is one loses the claim. Before one can say, "I love," one must be able to show it by jumping into the fire and losing oneself in it.

A Hindu poet says, "The first initiation in the order of lovers is to become nothing." Another poet says, "O Love, you have taught me first the lesson, which many learn at the end!" When someone says, "If you will be good to me I will be kind to you. I will respect you," it is a business proposition. And when a person says, "I wish someone loved me," he is very mistaken, for he will never be loved; he may wait for eternity. Love never asks to be loved. Love is more independent than anything, and it is love that makes one independent.

There is a love that is like an infant: it must be taken in one's arms; it cannot stand; if it is not taken up it cries. It is not mature; it is not developed; it is not yet love. Then there is love that is like a child that has not yet learned to walk. It has to hold on to a table or chair to steady itself; that love too is undeveloped. But there is love that stands on its own feet and walks alone; that is independent love, and one can depend upon it.

Love shows its quality by constancy. Where there is no constancy there is no love. People have wrongly understood the meaning of love: the real meaning is life itself. The feeling that one is alive, that feeling itself is love.

Then what is love? Love is God and God is love. As long as one is involved in selfish thoughts and actions one does not understand love. Love is sacrifice, love is service. Love shows itself in regard for the pleasure and displeasure of the beloved. That love can be seen in all aspects of life, once it is understood. Love for those who depend upon one, for those with whom one comes in contact in every aspect of life, love for one's country, for one's race, for humanity—it can extend even to love for every little creature, for the smallest insect that lives. Thus the drop of water becomes the ocean; thus can limited man expand through love. The more sympathy expands, the further it reaches heavenward, until man becomes as great as the Absolute.

Instead of teaching the lesson of indifference, Sufis have taught the lesson of love and sympathy, and have called it the cultivation of the heart. In Sufi terminology this is called *suluk,* which means the divine manner, the loving manner. When a refined manner is directed by the heart quality, it becomes a loving manner, the manner of God, and all such attributes as gentleness, tolerance, kindness, forgiveness, mercy, and compassion spring from it. The great teachers and prophets did not become what they were by their miracles, their wonderworking; what was most apparent in them was the loving manner.

Read the lives of the prophets. Look at the way Jesus Christ had with all those who came to him. When the sinners who were condemned and expelled from society were brought to the master he raised them up with his compassion. He was on the side of the accused ones. The fishermen who were with the master never understood him, and even the most educated could not. Yet the master lived with them and won their hearts in the end by his loving manner. Think of the Prophet Muhammad, whose most beloved daughter was killed by an Arab before his eyes. When the Arab said, "I did not do it on purpose; will you forgive me?" the Prophet forgave him instantly. When he became a conqueror and judge, his enemies, who had ill-treated him and turned him out of the country, were brought before him in rows and asked him, "What will you do to us?" The Prophet said, "You are my brothers. God will forgive you." Think also of the compassion of Buddha towards even the smallest insect.

For attainment on the spiritual path study is secondary and magical powers are unimportant. The first and most important principle is the cultivation of the heart quality, and there is only one way to cultivate this quality: to become more and more selfless at each step that we take. For what prevents the loving manner is the thought of self; the more we think of ourself, the less we think of others, until at the end of the journey our self meets us like a giant, a giant who will prove to be the stronger. But if with the first step we take on the spiritual path we struggle with this giant, we can only conquer him by the power of love.

Love is the stream which when it has risen up falls again like a fountain, each drop forming a virtue. Virtues taught in books have not the same power, but virtues springing naturally from the spring of love in the depth of the heart are love itself. There is a Hindu saying, "No matter how much wealth you have, if you do not have the treasure of virtue, it is of no use." True riches are the ever-increasing fountain of love, from which all virtue comes.

*Chapter 23.*

# THE UNDERSTANDING OF THE HEART

There are people who look at life with their brain, or their head as they call it, and there are others who look at life with their heart. Between these two points of view there is a vast difference; so much difference that something that one sees on the earth, the other sees in heaven; something that one sees as small, the other sees as great; something that one sees as limited, the other sees as unlimited. These two types of people become opposite poles. No one will admit that he looks at things with his head; everyone will say that he looks at life with his heart. But if one only knew what it is to look at life from the heart! The most evolved person in the world will only go as far as to say, "I have not yet learned to look at life from the heart; I would like to know how to do it; I would like to learn it."

One might say that emotional and devotional people are flying in the clouds, and that those who act with reason and logic are standing on the earth. This is true. But in the first place angels ride on clouds, and if the soul has an angelic quality the clouds are its sphere, not the earth. One may ask where then is the place for practicality in life. But what is practicality, as one calls it, and all that one is so careful about? How long does it last; what is it worth? No doubt it is true that man is born on earth to bear the weight of his physical body and its needs—a roof over his head, a piece of bread to sustain him. But if man believes that this is all there is to think about, he is making a great mistake, devoting all his life to what he calls practicality and never thinking of the heavenly treasure that is hidden in the heart of man.

The heart of man is like water. Either it is frozen, and then it is snow or ice, or it is water, and then it is liquid. When it is frozen it has turned into a crystal; when it is liquid it is in a condition to flow, and it is natural for water to be running. Then there are two principal kinds of water, salt water and sweet water. The sea, which is quite contented with itself, indifferent to all, has salt water because it is independent of all else. It gives health, happiness, and pleasure to those who are near it, because it asks nothing from anyone. It rises and falls within itself, it is independent, it is immense; and in that way it shows perfection. But with that independent perfection its water is not sweet. The ascetic who has closed his heart with the perfection of God and with the realization of truth is like the sea: independent, indifferent to all things. His presence heals people, his contact gives them joy and peace, and yet his personality is uninteresting to others, as is the salt water of the sea.

When the sea is calm it is a pleasure to travel on it, and when the sea is rough there is no worse illness than seasickness. And it is through its tranquility and calmness and peace that the powerful mind, the mind of a soul that has touched perfection, opens itself to everyone, as the sea lays itself before those who journey on it with open heart. Ships and boats pass over it; those who journey enjoy traveling on the sea. But when the sea is disturbed by wind and storm it is also perfect in its annoyance; it can shake the boats and steamers. In the same way the mind of the sage can have an effect upon all things in nature: it can cause volcanic eruptions, it can cause disasters, revolutions, all manner of things, when once its tranquility is disturbed. Aware of this quality of the heart and knowing the great powers possessed by a man who has touched divine perfection, people in the East give careful regard to the pleasure or displeasure of the sage. They believe that to annoy a sage is like annoying the whole of nature; to disturb his tranquility means to shake the whole universe. Compared with this a storm on the sea is a very small thing; the heart that has touched perfection, if once upset, can upset the whole universe.

The water of the river is sweet. It is sweet because it is attracted to the sea, it is longing to reach the sea. The river represents the loving quality, a quality that is seeking for the object it loves. A heart that loves God and His perfection may be likened to the river that seeks the sea. That is why the personality of the seeker is more pleasant than the personality of the one who is contented with what he knows.

There is little danger in traveling on the river. There is great joy in swimming in the river, and along its banks there is fine scenery to look at. And so it is with the personality that is like the river; that continual flowing of the feeling of sympathy means that the sympathy is living. As the river helps the trees and plants and the earth along it, so it is with the kind, sympathetic person whose feeling is liquid. Every- where he goes he takes with him that influence which nourishes, which helps souls to flourish and to progress.

One sometimes finds a little stream. It is not a river, it is only a small running stream; but it is even more beautiful to look at. It expresses modesty, fineness of character, beauty, for its water is pure. The little stream expresses the nature of an innocent heart, the heart that cannot be pre- vented from being sympathetic and loving by any experi- ences of the world that make water turn bitter. Bitter experiences have not touched it, and it remains pure and clear. It inspires poets, it uplifts the composer, it quenches the thirst of the thirsty, it is an ideal subject for the painter to paint. With its modesty it has purity, and with its purity it has life.

There is also the water of the small pool. It is sometimes muddy, sometimes dirty because of its narrowness, its smallness. In the same way the narrow heart always has mud in it. Because it is narrow and because it is not deep enough, all the elements of the earth enter it and take away its purity.

Again, there is the water of the large pool, where water lilies grow, where fish swim, where the sun is reflected, and where the moonlight produces a beautiful vision. One would like to sit and look at it, because it expresses to everyone who can see it the liquid nature of the heart, the heart that is not frozen, the heart that is like water. It is still, it is calm. Sitting by its side can make one's heart tranquil, and because of its stillness one can see one's reflection in it.

Spring water is most healing and most inspiring, because it comes from above and runs downhill. That is the character of the inspired mind. The heart that like a spring pours out water in the form of inspiration, in poetry or music or some other form, has beauty; it has a healing quality. It can take away all the worries and anxieties and difficulties and troubles of those who come to it, like the water of the spring; it not only inspires but it heals.

There is also the fountain that rises and falls in so many drops. This is manmade, in the same way that personality also is manmade. When man has made a personality of himself, then the feeling that rises from the heart through that personality is like a fountain. Each drop falling from it takes the form of a virtue.

Then the water that rises from the sea towards the sky in the form of vapor represents the aspiration of the heart. The heart that aspires upward, that wishes to reach upward shows the quality of vapor. It is the heart of the devotee, of the one who is always conscious of seeking the higher ideal, touching the higher principles. That heart of inspiration forms itself as clouds and pours down just like the rain, bringing celestial beauty in the form of art or poetry or music, or of anything that is good and beautiful.

There are hearts that have been exposed to fire for a long, long time, and there comes a sulphury water from them, purifying and healing; for it has gone through fire, it has gone through suffering, and therefore it heals those who suffer.

There are hearts with many different qualities, like water with different chemical substances: those who have suffered, those to whom life has taught patience, those who have contemplated. They all represent one or another of the water that heals, and so do their personalities. People who have had deep experiences of any kind—of suffering, of agony, of love, of hate, of solitude, of association, of success, of failure—all have a particular quality, a quality that has a special use for others. When a person realizes this, he will come to the conclusion that whatever has been his life's destiny, his heart has prepared a chemical substance through sorrow and pain or through joy and pleasure, a chemical substance that is intended for a certain purpose, for the use of humanity, and that he can only give it out if he can keep his heart awakened and open. Once it is closed, once it is frozen, man is no longer living. It does not matter what he has gone through, for even the worst poison can be of some use. There is no person, however wicked, who is of no use, if only he realizes that the first condition for being useful to humanity is to keep his heart open.

As to spiritual attainment, it is something that we can never absorb through the head; it can only be received through the heart. Let two persons listen to the teachings of a teacher, one with his heart and the other with his head. The latter will be thinking, "Is it so or is it not so?" or, "How is it, if it is so? How can it be; and if it is, why is it?" There is never an end to the "why?" But another person will listen with his heart, and while both logic and reason are at his disposal they are not troubling him. His heart is open, he listens, and the quality of the heart is such that whatever falls upon an open heart becomes instantly revealed. When one says, "I cannot understand you," it is just like saying, "I have my heart closed to you"; there is no other reason for not understanding another person. But when one can say that one has understood it all, it means one's heart was open; that is the reason why one has understood it.

Thus understanding does not depend upon the head, it depends upon the heart. By the help of the head one can make it more clear; it becomes intelligible, and one can express it better. But to begin with it must come from the heart, not from the head. Besides, a person who only uses his head says, "It must be so because I think it is so," whereas the person who has the heart quality says, "It is so because I believe it to be so." That is the difference. In one person there is a doubt; in the other there is conviction.

There is in Arabic a word that is very difficult to translate, *iman.* It is not exactly faith or belief; the nearest equivalent one can find for it is conviction, a conviction that cannot be changed by anything, a conviction that does not come from outside. One always seeks for conviction, but nothing and nobody convinces. Conviction is something that comes from one's own heart, and it stands above faith and belief, for belief is the beginning of that same thing of which faith is the development and conviction the culmination.

Spiritual attainment is nothing but conviction. A man may think, "Perhaps it is so." He may think about the best doctrines or about the highest ideas that there are, but he will still think, "It is so, perhaps." There is always perhaps attached to it. But then there is another person who cannot use the word perhaps because he does not think about it. He cannot say, "It may be so," when he knows that it is so. When a person arrives at the stage when the knowledge of reality becomes a conviction, then there is nothing in the world that will change it. If there is anything to attain to, it is that conviction which one can never find in the outside world; it must rise from the depths of one's own heart.

*Chapter 24.*

# THE TUNING OF THE HEART (1)

No one in this world may be called loveless; at the same time, everyone is not necessarily full of love. Either the fire is burnt out and the heart has turned to ashes, or the heart has a spark of love in its depths just as the stone has a spark of fire that hardly ever shows itself. One may ask if it is not a weakness to be sympathetic, as it is the sympathetic person who gives in, and the one without sympathy holds on to himself. But sometimes the one who gives in is more powerful than the one who thinks that he should not give in. Very often a person does not give in owing to fear, doubt, or lack of confidence in himself, and often it is the brave and courageous who give in. It is not always a weakness, although in some cases it may be so.

Sentiment is often underestimated when it is compared with reason. This is a mistake, for where there is real sentiment it is much stronger, much more powerful than reasoning. The one who goes from one reason to another and then again to another reason is often found to be very weak. Besides, the person of reason has no magnetism, he has only reason. He can argue, discuss, talk too much, but he does not

154

attract. The person of sentiment has strong magnetism; he can attract without words because he has something living in him. In the person of sentiment is to be found the divine element, the heart quality.

Someone came to the great poet of Persia Jami and asked him if he would take him as a pupil and teach him spiritual truth. Jami asked, "Have you ever loved in your life?" He said, "No, never." Jami said, "Go and love first. Let your heart be tuned, let it be melted first. Then come to me and I will show you the spiritual path."

Sympathy is the main quality to be cultivated in order to develop the spiritual faculty. But if one would ask me what I mean by sympathy, it is something I cannot explain. All such words are different names, different aspects of one and the same thing. What is called sympathy, kindness, mercy, goodness, pity, compassion, gentleness, humility, appreciation, gratefulness, service, is in reality love. And what is love? Love is God.

Someone will say, "Yes, once I was very friendly and loving," and if you ask him, "Why not today?" he will answer, "I was digging and I found only mud." But wherever you dig there is water. One need only dig deep enough, until one has found water. If one does not dig till one finds water one only gets mud. Those who are disappointed in human nature and those who allow their hearts to become cold because of this have lost a great deal. Somebody once said to me, "I have lost my friend, and since then I have lost sympathy for human nature." I said, "Your first loss was not so great, but I pity you for your second loss. It was then that you should have kept your sympathy."

There are five different aspirations the wise may have in their search for spirituality: seeking for knowledge, seeking for life, seeking for happiness, seeking for peace, and seeking for an ideal. All these five can only be sought in one's own heart, and then only when the heart is tuned to a certain pitch.

One may say, "I seek for knowledge," but there are two

kinds of knowledge. One kind of knowledge is that of names and forms, in other words, the knowledge of facts. But there is a difference between a fact and truth. In our everyday language we often confuse these two words, and we say truth for fact and fact for truth. In order to attain to higher knowledge we should not try to gain it in the same way as we try to gain outer knowledge of names and forms. The outer knowledge we gain by learning; the inner knowledge we gain by unlearning. We can only gain the inner knowledge when the heart is tuned to its proper pitch. Criminals, those who are repulsive, and all those who are working towards their own defeat, one will mostly find to be devoid of heart quality. It is because of the lack of heart quality that all the inclinations come that drag a person downward. However highly a man may be qualified or however intelligent, whatever his profession, it does not matter; if the heart quality is lacking a person will go down. The ultimate result is that this person goes downward and not upward. It cannot be otherwise.

The inner knowledge is beyond words, and to try to put it into words is like trying to put the sea in a bottle. It is impossible. It is something that we can only realize of ourselves, and then only when we have tuned our heart to the proper pitch. How can anybody explain what a high note means? One cannot explain it; we must sing ourselves and find out what a high note is. When we produce it ourselves we know what it means. Thus inner knowledge should be acquired by the tuning of the heart, in order that the heart itself knows what it is. Many have tried to describe the inner knowledge by saying they are one with God, or a part of God, or that they are God. But all these are insolent terms. Why try to put something into words that cannot be expressed? Apart from inner knowledge, can even a deep sentiment such as gratefulness, sympathy, admiration, respect, be put into words? Words would only limit these sentiments.

The power that the heart quality has is immense. The hen, when it is taking care of its young ones, will not hesitate to fight an elephant in defence of its chicks. The heart full of love for its young gives the hen such power that it does not even see the size of the elephant. Its confidence in its own power is greater than the strength of the elephant.

Those who have accomplished great things, those who have held their life cheap for a high ideal, have not thought about it with their brains; their hearts have felt it. It is the heart quality that gives courage and bravery, not the brain. Therefore if one wants to seek for the divine power of the Almighty God, it should be sought for in one's own heart.

We also confuse pleasure and happiness. Sometimes we say pleasure for happiness, or happiness for pleasure. In reality very few in this world know what happiness means. Pleasure is the shadow of happiness, for pleasure depends upon things outside ourselves; happiness comes from within ourselves. Happiness belongs to the heart quality; pleasure to the outer world. The distance between pleasure and happiness is as vast as that between earth and heaven. As long as the heart is not tuned to its proper pitch one will not be happy. That inner smile which shows itself in a man's expression, in his atmosphere, belongs to happiness. If position were taken away and wealth were lost in the outer life, that inner happiness would not be taken away. And the smiling of the heart depends upon the tuning of the heart; the heart must be tuned to that pitch where it is living.

The fourth aspiration is peace. Peace is the longing of our soul, but not necessarily for rest or comfort; it is far greater than that. Peace is something that relieves every atom of our body and mind from stress. It is a kind of upliftment. It cannot be compared with any earthly experience; it it like being raised to the higher spheres, for it is there that a person really experiences peace. And where does it come from? It comes from the same tuning of the heart.

The fifth aspiration is the ideal. Again it is the heart quality that is necessary for the ideal; if one has no heart then the brain cannot make an ideal. It is the heart that tries to reach it. Christ said, "Seek ye first the kingdom of God, and all these things shall be added unto you." By getting in tune with the God ideal one will become so attuned that one will find a way open to the heart of every person one meets and a connection with every condition and with every object, thereby realizing at-one-ment with the Absolute.

Thus the five different aspects of spiritual attainment are all attained by the tuning of the heart. What is this tuning of the heart in reality? When a string of the violin is loose it does not give the sound it is meant to give, and therefore it does not fulfill the purpose for which it was put on the violin. It can only be used for that purpose when one has tuned it to the right pitch. The same condition is needed with the heart. It must have a certain awakening, a certain amount of life in it, that can only be brought about by sympathy. When that sympathy is not there, then the heart is like a loose string on a violin.

Many will object, "But does not our heart depend also upon our everyday environment, on the circumstances of life? If the environment is not agreeable, how can we make it right?" Indeed, the first stage of our development depends upon environment and circumstances; but there is nothing in this world that we cannot try to improve. There are many things that we can help and improve, if we would only try. Sometimes it is difficult, but often we think it is difficult while it is not really so. The greatest difficulty is loss of patience. When patience is exhausted things cannot be made better, and then they remain in the same condition; but when one really wants to make one's environment better and sacrifice all one can in order to do so, then one can. Too often one expects more from others than they are able to give, and that makes one helpless and dependent. Once a person has become so independent that without the help of others he can keep his feelings untouched, he becomes like the sun, that burns without oil. In that it differs from lamps that burn with oil, for when the oil is finished then their light goes out.

The relationship between the heart and the conditions of the outside world is such that it is the condition of the heart that influences one's life's affairs. When the heart is out of tune everything goes wrong; it makes the whole atmosphere out of tune. Once a lady said to me, "I have had bad luck this week. I lose or break many things; everything tears and gets destroyed." I said, "There is something wrong with yourself. You yourself are out of tune; especially this week something has upset your rhythm." And on thinking this over, she found out that it was so.

The more keenly one studies life, the more one will find that the heart has an influence on both failure and success, on rise and fall, on favorable and unfavorable conditions in life. No sooner has the heart been tuned than conditions in life become better and ill luck is averted; wrong reasoning, people becoming tired and disappointed with one another, things going wrong, losses—all these things disappear as soon as the heart is tuned. It is difficult enough to keep a delicate instrument like the violin tuned, and the heart is incomparably more delicate; it is the instrument on which the soul, the spirit plays. It is on the model of the heart that the harp we know has been made, and the ancient artists have put a harp or a lute in the hands of the angels. Symbolically the angels mean heart, the heart quality.

The reason why the heart influences our life is that the heart is like the seed out of which has grown the plant that we call ourself. Thought, speech, and action, like fruits and flowers, are the effect of the heart; what the heart produces is the same as that which was already in it. For instance, a person cannot conceal his feelings all the time. He may play at being a friend, he may play at being brave. But whatever he plays at he is able to maintain for a certain time and no longer, for what is in the heart must come out sometime or other in the form of actions or words, from the lips, in the expression, or as atmosphere. The heart never fails to express itself in some form. What does it express? What it possesses, what it is. A person may be our bitter enemy and for a long time try to hide it, but in some form or other it will come out. A person may be our friend but wish to show indifference, but his love will leap out. If a person has something against us or if he has admiration for us, it cannot remain hidden. He will close his lips, not showing anything in his actions and never saying it, but even through his eyes it will come out; it will show through the expression; it will manifest through the atmosphere. The heart will speak louder than words.

Our heart is also closely related to the people we meet, to such an extent that in industry, business, professions, science, politics, and domestic life, in every aspect of life, the people we meet are affected and influenced by the condition of our heart. If the heart is out of tune, let a man be in his office, the factory, his home, among friends, in a club, in society, whatever he says or does not say or whatever he does, his very presence will upset the atmosphere. Therefore the secret of magnetism, the mystery of attraction in a person, is solved by the study of the heart. Very often we are uncomfortable in the presence of someone, or someone's presence attracts us without that person having said one word. We may feel as if we had always known a person, as if we had always been friends though we had never seen him before. If we are in tune, we tune others also; but if a person's heart is not in tune, then everyone in his presence also gets out of tune. That is the mystery of attraction and repulsion.

Very often we will see that people attract one day and perhaps the week after or a month or a year later, there is repulsion. The reason why that person attracted for the moment was that his heart was in tune; but then after some time his heart got out of tune again. It is because of this that a person who was once attracted may feel repulsion another time; and because he does not know the reason he will always blame the other. Human nature is such that man sees himself last. Especially if it comes to blame he never thinks of himself; he first blames the other.

If we go still deeper into this subject, then we shall find that not only with human beings, but even with nature, with the atmosphere, with the weather, with the climate, there is also the tuning of the heart. Even flowers feel it. Many people can keep flowers in their hand for a long time, while with others, no sooner have they touched a flower than it fades. The fading of the flower means that it becomes out of tune. There are stories of sages in the East who, after having left a place of rest and peace where they had been staying—perhaps under the shade of a tree or in a village— came back after ten years and found the place in a bad state; but the moment they returned it became fertile again and flourished. What does it mean? That they were in tune.

When we begin to think more about human nature and study it more, we shall find that there is no creature as selfish as man can be. With all his intelligence and goodness and kindness, the most unjust and inconsiderate creature is man; inconsiderate about the feelings of his fellow men, towards a relative who depends on him or someone who waits upon him, who cares for him, or towards someone who relies upon his word. Man has always *his* motive, *his* convenience, *his* joy, *his* object before him; all else he sets aside. But he is the victim of his own inconsiderateness, though he does not know that it is really the cause of all failure, ill luck, difficulties, problems, or anything else he has to face.

There are so many debts to pay in life. Not only money, but there are obligations to those around us, obligations to those who justly or unjustly, foolishly or wisely expect something from us—thought, consideration, love, service— our obligations towards friends and acquaintances, obliga- tions towards strangers. Today the life we live keeps our minds so much at work that every day we become less and less considerate, less and less thoughtful. Thus the unknown influences which come upon us and bring about changes in our life are such that we blame this or that person or the stars and planets and other things; but in reality it all belongs to the realm of the heart. As soon as we realize this, we con- sider our relationships to others. Our duty, our interest, our virtue in the world is to be thoughtful, to be considerate about every word we say, every thought we think, every feeling we have, considering what influence it will have upon someone else and whether it will bring him pleasure. If there is any religion or spirituality, it is in this.

There is a still higher stage of our development, and that is the attitude of going forth and sympathizing with all we meet. This comes by understanding; the more understanding we have of human nature, the more sympathetic we become. Even for those who do not deserve it we should have sympathy. In this way sympathy, which is symbolically like water, spreads in time; it will expand like the water of the ocean. It becomes an everlasting spring that rises and falls. In order to teach this, the wise of India turned the river Ganges and the river Jumna into places of pilgrimage and called them sacred. These rivers rise in the same place at the top of the Himalayas, and from there they divide and descend, becoming larger streams. The place where they join, near Allahabad, is a place of pilgrimage. Those who go there are purified from all sin.

Its symbology is this, that the water that rises from the top of the Himalayas is like a spring of love coming from the heart. That which rises from the heart is the first place of pilgrimage. Then it goes on like holy rivers Ganges and Jumna, and the place where these rivers meet is called *Sungam,* which means sympathy. And where the river reaches the sea it is called the unity with God. It is a beautiful picture of life that one can observe in this symbolic form. If we interpreted it rightly we could have the sacred pilgrimage to the Ganges here and everywhere; the sacred river is the sympathy coming out of our own heart, and the reaching towards God is the perfection, the spiritual attainment.

*Chapter 25.*

# THE TUNING OF THE HEART (2)

Spirituality is not necessarily intellectuality nor orthodoxy nor asceticism. Orthodoxy, ascetism, and intellectual pursuit after truth are all the various ways people have taken in order to reach the spiritual goal. But the way is not the goal. If there can be a definition of spirituality, it is the tuning of the heart.

In this material age of ours heart quality is totally forgotten, and great importance is given to reason and logic. When we argue with a person, he wants us to argue with reason; we must be logical. Sentiment and idealism have no place. It is because of this that humanity is getting further and further away from spiritual attainment. The chief and the best quality is ignored; and by being ignored that quality becomes dead. If a poet happens to live in a village where no one understands poetry, if an artist lives in a town where no one cares for his pictures, if an inventive genius has no opportunity of bringing his inventions out, their faculties and talents become blunted, and finally they die. The same happens to the heart quality: if it is not taken notice of, if it has no opportunity to develop, if it is ignored, then this quality becomes blunted, and in the end it dies. As it is expressed in a song, "The light of a whole life dies when love is done." What remains? There is no sign of life; what remains is intellectuality expressing itself by the power of egoism. It is difficult to live in the world because selfishness is ever on the increase.

There is a certain fineness that belongs to human nature, a certain nobleness, a certain delicacy, a certain manner. And all these become blunted when the heart quality is left undeveloped.

I have been traveling for many years, seeing people engaged in the pursuit of truth, and to my very great disappointment I have found many who, although interested in higher things, are yet arguing and discussing. "Do you believe what I believe?" or, "My belief is better than your belief," always intellectually. We do not need to use so much intellect in seeking God, in attaining spirituality, for this does not come through intellect; it comes by the tuning of the heart.

People will say that this may be so, but that all the same there are many emotional and affectionate people. But emotional people are not always loving people. Maybe they are outwardly, but very often the more emotional people are, the less loving; for one day their love is on the rise, next day it drops. They are just moved by emotions like clouds. One day the sky is clear; next day it is covered over. One cannot depend upon emotions. That is not love. It is the feeling nature that should be developed, the sympathetic nature.

Besides there exists, especially in the western world, a false conception of the strength of personality. Many have understood this wrongly, and under the guise of strength they want to harden their hearts. Many think that for a person to be touched or moved by anything is not natural or normal. On the contrary, if a person is not touched or moved it is not natural; he is then still in the mineral kingdom and not yet in the human kingdom. To be human and not to be touched or moved by something touching, appeal-

Courtesy of Samuel Weiser, Inc.

Ramana Maharshi

ing, only means that the eyes of the heart are closed and its ears blocked; that the heart is not living. It is the wrong understanding of a high principle. The principle is that man must be feeling yet at the same time so strong that however much feeling he has he should have enough strength to hide it. It does not mean he must not have feeling; a person without feeling is without life.

However much one studies psychology, theoretically or practically, one will not attain to spirituality. Spirituality does not belong to intellectuality; it has nothing to do with it. In connection with spirituality, intellectuality is only useful insofar as an intellectual person can better express spiritual inspiration.

One might ask if it is not natural to attain spirituality. Does it not come without any effort on our part? And if it is not natural, then what is the use of attaining spirituality? The answer is that spirituality is not only for human beings but also for the lower creation, for every being; not spirituality in the sense in which we usually understand it, but in the sense of being tuned to one's natural pitch. Even birds have their moments of exaltation. At the setting or the rising of the sun, the breaking of dawn, in moonlight, there come times when birds and animals feel exalted. They sing and dance and sit on the branches of the trees in exaltation. Every day they feel this exquisite joy. And if we go still further, if we have eyes to see life in those forms in which others do not see it, in the rock or the tree, we find that there are times when even the trees are in a complete state of ecstasy. Those who live naturally, who open the doors of their hearts, whose souls are in contact with nature, find nature singing, dancing, communicating. It is not only a legend, a story of the past, that saints used to speak with the trees. It is an actual fact, and is the same today as in the past. Souls are always of the same nature. They are the same, only we have become unbelievers, we have no confidence in life. We have become material, we have closed out eyes to what is before us. Souls can become saints and sages today just as in the past. Are the stars not the same as ever? They communicate also today with the one who is able to understand them. But we have turned our back on nature; we live in an artificial world. Not only have we become material, we have become matter itself.

Sufis in all ages, mystics of India, Persia, and Egypt, have considered the awakening of the heart quality to be the principal thing in life. For all the virtues that the priest can teach and prescribe, all the virtues that one is told to practice in life, come naturally when the heart opens. One need not learn virtue; virtue becomes one's own. Virtues that are taught, how long do they last? If there is any virtue it must come by itself; spirituality is natural. And if animals and birds can feel spiritual exaltation, why not we? But we do not live a natural life. We have tried in our civilization to be as far removed from nature and natural life as possible, breathing an artificial atmosphere contrary to climatic influences, eating food that we have manufactured, turning it into something quite different from what nature had made it.

The most important question is how to make the best of our life, how to make the best of this opportunity which is passing by us. Every moment lost is incomparably more valuable than the loss of money. As man comes to realize this, he will more and more come to the conclusion that while he thought that he was progressing, he has really been moving around in the same maze. If only he had found the door, that door which is called by the wise spiritual attainment! However well-educated one may be, however much one has collected or accomplished, however much power and position one has gained, none of this will be lasting; there is only one thing that is everlasting, and that is spiritual attainment. Without this there will always be dissatisfaction, and uncomfortable feeling. No knowledge, power, position, or wealth can give that satisfaction which spiritual attainment can give.

There is nothing more easy and nothing more difficult in

the world: difficult because we have made it difficult; easy because in reality it is the easiest thing possible. All other things one has to buy and pay for. We have even to pay for our water. But for spiritual attainment we do not need to pay any tax. It is ours, it is ourself; it is the discovering of ourself. Yet what one values is what one gets with difficulty. Man loves complexity so much; he makes something big and complicated and says, "This is valuable." If it is simple he thinks that it has no value. That is why the ancient people, knowing human nature, told a person when he said he wanted spiritual attainment, "Very well; for ten years go around the temple, walk around it a hundred times every evening. And go to the Ganges. Then you will get inspiration." That is what should be done with people who will not be satisfied with a simple explanation of the truth, who want complexity.

What is necessary is to develop a sympathetic nature and to sustain its gradual growth. Just as it is difficult for the student of voice culture to practice with his voice and yet not to let it be spoiled, so it is with a sympathetic person. While developing, he runs the risk of spoiling the faculty of sympathy; in other words, the more loving a person, the more chance he has of being disappointed. The greater the love, the greater the fragility of the heart and the more susceptible it becomes to everything, until it can break at any moment. The one who walks in the path of sympathy should take great care that his way is not blocked; everything will be trying to block his way, and it is his own perseverance that will keep it open.

By lack of development of the sympathetic nature a block is produced in the mind and in the body. In the physical body there are some nervous centers, centers that are awakened by sympathetic development. By lack of sympathetic development they remain closed. Everything that keeps man from sympathy robs him of intuition, for in these finer centers sympathy develops life, and the absence of that sympathy takes away that life.

So it is in the mind. When the heart is not sympathetic there is something missing in the mentality of man, and it is sympathy that opens it. The Sufis know the medicine for this disease, and it is the practice of the art which is called *dhikr* or *mantram*. By practicing that particular art in the right way one activates these fine centers by vibrations. By the repetition of certain mystic words the centers begin to vibrate. Very often after only a short time of doing these practices a person feels quite different, especially when a mental thought is held during that time; thus concentration is developed at the same time. It helps the love nature or sympathetic nature to be deepened or centralized, and as it begins to flow out a spiritual atmosphere is created. This all comes from the development of feeling.

During my pilgrimage to the holy men of India I saw some whose presence was more illuminating than the reading of books for a whole lifetime or arguing a thousand times about any problems. They do not need to speak; they become living lights, fountains of love. And as there is infection in disease so there is also infection in spiritual attainment. One feels uplifted and full of joy, ecstasy, happiness, enlightenment.

No doubt one person may be more impressed than another; upon one the influence is much greater than upon another. It all depends upon the individual. I remember a lady once telling me, "Since you came my husband has been very nice to me." But eight days after I had left the town where I was staying, she wrote to me that her husband was just as he had been before. It makes a great difference what person it is, for it is just like the effect of fire. On stone, on iron, on wax, on paper, on cloth, on cotton, on each object the effect of fire is different; and so on each person the effect of spiritual personality is different.

Once I met a learned man, a doctor of philosophy with a great many degrees. We spoke about the deeper side of life. He became very interested in what I said and told me that he thought very highly of me. I thought that if I were to tell him about my teacher how much more interesting it would be for him. I told him, "There is a wonderful man in this city; he has no comparison in the whole world." "Are there such people?" he asked, "I would very much like to see him. Where does he live?" And I told him, in such and such a part of the city. He said, "I live there also, where is his house? I know all the people there. What is his name?" So I told him. He said, "For twenty years I have known this man, and now you are telling me about him!" I thought to myself, "In a hundred years you would not have been able to know him." He was not ready to know him. If people are not evolved enough they cannot appreciate or understand others. They cannot even understand the greatest souls. They may sit with them, talk with them; they may be in contact with them all their life, but they do not see. While another, if he is ready to understand, needs only one moment. This philosopher had known my teacher for twenty years and yet he did not know him; I saw him once and became his pupil forever. This man was learned, he was very intellectual, but he saw him with his brain; I saw my teacher with my heart.

The one principle to be remembered in the path of sympathy is that we should all do our best with regard to the pleasure of those whom we love and whom we meet, but we should not expect the same from them. For we must realize that the world is as it is, and we cannot change it; we can only change ourselves. The one who wants others to do what he wishes will always be disappointed. That is the complaining soul, the one who all day long every day of the month is complaining. He is never without a complaint; if not about a human being, then about the climate; if not about the climate, then about the conditions; if not about someone else, then about himself.

He should remember that self-pity is the worst poverty. The person who takes life in this way, who considers his poor self to be forgotten, forsaken, ill-treated by everybody, by the planets, even by God, for that person there is no hope; he is an exile from the garden of Eden. But the one who says, "I know what human nature is; I cannot expect any better. I must only try and appreciate what little good comes from it and be thankful for it, and try and give the best I can to the others," has the only attitude that will enable him to develop his sympathetic nature. The one who keeps justice in the foreground will always be blinded by it; he will always talk about justice, but he will never really know it. For the one who keeps justice in the background, the light of justice falls on his way and he only uses justice for himself. When he has not done right towards others he takes himself to task, but if others do not do right towards him he says that this also is justice. For the just person all is just; for the unjust everything is unjust. The one who talks too much of justice is far from justice; that is why he is talking about it.

Is there then no reward at all in sympathy if it leads only to disappointment? Life's reward is life itself. A person may suffer from disease or be most unhappy and sad; but if he were asked, "Do you want to be turned into a rock?" he would say, "No, rather let me live and suffer." Therefore life's reward is life; and the reward of love is love itself. Loving is living, and the heart that closes itself to everyone closes itself to its own self.

The difference between human love and divine love is like that between drill and war. One has to drill in order to prepare for war. One has to know the phenomenon of love on this plane in order to prepare to love God, who alone deserves love. The one who says, "I hate human beings, but I love God," does not know what love means. He has not drilled; he is of no use in war. Whether a loving person loves a human being or whether he loves God, he shows no trace of hatred. The one who has hatred in him loves neither man nor God, for hatred is the sign that the doors of his heart are closed.

Is it not a great pity that we see today among the most civilized nations one nation working against the other, a lack of trust and the fear of war between them? It is dreadful to think that humanity, though it appears to be progressing, is actually going backward to a greater extent than has ever been seen in the history of the world. Are we evolving or going backward? What is missing is not intellectuality, for every day people are inventing more and more ingenious things. Then what is missing? It is the heart quality. It seems as though it is being buried more deeply every day. Therefore today the real human being is being destroyed, and the false part of his being is continuing. Better conditions can only be brought about by the individual who realizes that it is the development of the heart that can accomplish this, and nothing else.

Very often people coming to hear me say afterwards, "Yes, all you say is very interesting, very beautiful, and I too wish that the world could be changed. But how many think like you? How can you do it? How can it be done?" They come with these pessimistic remarks, and I tell them, "One person comes into a country with a little cold or influenza and it spreads. If such a bad thing can spread, could not then the elevated thought of love and kindness and good will towards all men also spread? Thus we should see to it that there are finer germs of good will going from one to the other —of love and kindness, of the feeling of brotherhood, of the desire for spiritual evolution; they will have greater results than the other ones. If we all took this optimistic view, if we all worked in our small way, we could accomplish a great deal."

There are many good, loving, and kind people whose hearts go out to every person they meet. But are they spiritual? It is important to understand that they are very close to spiritual attainment, but they are unconsciously spiritual, not consciously. Very often we meet mothers or fathers or children in whom we see a deeply loving tendency; love is pouring out from them, they have become fountains of love. Yet they do not know one word of religion or of mysticism, but this does not matter. After all, what are these names? Nothing but nets for fishes to be caught in, which may then remain in those nets for years. Sometimes these are big names with little meaning to them, but much is made of them by those who want to commercialize the finer things. Very often it is a catering to human curiosity on the part of so-called spiritual workers to create a sensation even in the spiritual world. Nevertheless truth is simple. The more simple one is and the more one seeks for simplicity, the nearer one comes to truth.

The devotional quality needs a little direction; that direction allows it to expand itself. The loving quality is just like water. The tendency of water is to expand, to spread, and so the loving quality spreads; but if a person is not well-directed or if he does not know himself, then instead of deepening it becomes limited. The love quality must be deepened first before it spreads out. If not, what generally happens to those who set out to love all human beings is that in the end they hate all, because they did not first deepen themselves enough and so lacked more and more the strength of attraction.

The Sufis have therefore considered spiritual culture to be the culture of the heart. It consists of the tuning of the heart. Tuning means the changing of pitch of the vibration. The tuning of the heart means the changing of the vibrations, in order that one may reach a certain pitch that is the natural pitch; then one feels the joy and ecstasy of life, which enables one to give pleasure to others even by one's presence because one is tuned. When an instrument is properly tuned one does not need to play music on it; just by striking it one will feel great magnetism coming from it. If a well-tuned instrument can have that magnetism, how much greater should be the magnetism of the heart that is tuned! Rumi says, "Whether you have loved a human being or whether you have loved God, if you have loved enough you will be brought in the end into the presence of the supreme Love itself."

*Chapter 26.*

# LOVE

In reality wisdom is love and love is wisdom, although in one person wisdom may be predominant and in another love. The cold-hearted man is never wise, nor is the really warm-hearted person foolish; yet both these qualities, love and wisdom, are distinct and separate, and it is possible that a person may be loving but lacking in wisdom. It may also happen that a person who is wise is lacking in love to some extent; but no one can be wise if love is absent from his heart, and no one will be truly loving if wisdom had not illuminated his heart, for love comes from wisdom and wisdom comes from love.

It is very difficult to say what love is, and how one should love. Is it embracing people and running after them and saying pleasant things to them? Not everyone finds it easy to show his love. One person perhaps has a love hidden in his heart, and another person's love comes out in his words. The love of one person changes the whole atmosphere, and that of another is like a spark hidden in a stone. To judge who has love and who has not is very difficult. There is love for instance that seems as if it comes from a firecracker, calling out. "I am love," but it burns out and is gone. There is also love like a spark in a pebble; it may never manifest, and if you hold the pebble it feels cold, but at the same time it is there, it is dependable and it lasts. Therefore one can never judge.

In the East there is a well-known story about a young man called Hakim and a princess who was renowned for her beauty. There were many who loved her and wanted to marry her, but she had made a condition: that the one who brought her a certain pearl that she longed to possess would be accepted. There was one lover of this princess who loved her perhaps more than anybody else, but he could not find a way of getting that pearl.

Now Hakim's task in life was to roam about from country to country doing what he could for those who needed his services. He met this lover, who was very unhappy, and Hakim consoled him and said, "Continue in your pursuit of love even if it be difficult, and remember that I shall go on until I have brought rest to your heart by finding for you the pearl you are looking for." Hakim went in pursuit of the pearl, and the story goes on to tell what difficulties he had in obtaining it. At last he got it and brought it to the palace, and then the princess was so impressed by Hakim that she declared that she wanted him as her husband. But Hakim told her of the promise he had made to his friend, who was her real lover. He himself was the lover of those in need.

The explanation of this story is that the princess represents God and the pearl the knowledge of God. The lover in the story is a lover of God who, however, does not want to take the trouble necessary to obtain the pearl. But there was someone else ready to delve deeper, even if it were not for himself but for others, in order to get the knowledge and give it to them. Thus there are two types of workers. The first type is the one who works for himself; but at a higher stage is the one whose task is doing work for others; he brings into the life of others that blessing which is their need.

Why is it, one may ask, that as love grows difficulties arise from all sides? This happens because before one fell in love one was unconsciously linked with the Source alone; but when once love has awakened on the physical plane, one becomes attached to someone on earth. It is like Adam and Eve being exiled from the garden of Eden. This naturally causes every influence to work against one; even the throne of God is shaken by love's outburst, for by a sincere link on earth, which is very powerful, every other influence is automatically pulled and pushed, thereby causing a commotion in the world of the heart. The soul of man is happiness; yet man is never really happy, since he is occupied with the world of woes. It is only love that can bring about that happiness which is spoken of in legends, that happiness which is beyond all the pleasures of this mortal world. Those who see or feel, consciously or unconsciously, the happiness experienced by the lover and the beloved naturally either knowingly or unknowingly react against it.

The love of God is everywhere in nature; yet we see destruction and misery and inequalities all around us. It is a difference of focus. If we focus our minds upon all that is good and beautiful we shall see God's love in spite of all the ugliness that exists in nature and especially in human nature. In doing so we will spread a cover over it; and by collecting everything beautiful in us we will be able to give to whatever lacks beauty from the supply in our own heart. But if we focus our attention upon ugliness it will grow in us, and there will come a time when we shall not be able to see any good anywhere; everywhere we look we will only see cruelty, unkindness, wickedness, and ugliness.

One may ask if in focusing one's mind on beauty alone one is not in danger of shutting one's eyes to the ugliness and suffering one might otherwise alleviate. The answer is that in order to help the poor one needs to be rich, and in order to take away evil from a person one needs to have that much more good. That goodness has to be earned as money is earned, and that earning means collecting goodness wher-

Courtesy of Raghu Rai.

Mother Teresa of Calcutta

ever we find it. What happens is that man becomes agitated by the abundance of goodness that he sees; being himself poor he cannot add to it, and then he is drawn towards evil. Although he may unconsciously develop in his own nature a craving for the goodness he sees, that does not help him in his agitation; his looking at evil only adds another wicked person to the whole.

The one whose eyes are focused on beauty in time will join the good; he is getting the same impressions, but the result is different. Besides, by criticizing, by judging, by looking at wickedness with contempt, one does not help the one who needs it. The person who is ready to overlook, forgive, and patiently tolerate all those disadvantages that he may have to meet with is the one who can help.

One should love for the sake of love, not for a return. When one serves, one should serve for the sake of serving, not for acknowledgment or appreciation in any shape or form. In the beginning such a person may perhaps seem a loser, but in the end he will be the gainer, for he has lived in the world while yet holding himself above the world; the world cannot touch him. Yet if one asks whether one can separate jealousy from love, it is like asking whether one can separate the shadow from the body. Where there is human love there is jealousy.

Furthermore, the tendency to doubt, the tendency to distress, the tendency to fear, suspicion, and confusion, where does it all come from? It all comes from the thought of getting something in return, anxiety as to whether anyone will give one back what one has given him. That is the thought behind it. And as to doubt, what is doubt? Doubt that gathers round the soul is like a cloud passing before the sun, keeping its light from shining out. But the unselfish one has good reason for his trust; he looks through the clouds and says, "What do I care if I am not rewarded. I don't mind. I know what to do: give service; that is all the satisfaction I want. I do not look for anything in return. This is where my duty ends." He is blessed because he has conquered; he has won his battle.

It is through lack of knowledge of divine justice that man doubts. He always wonders whether he will get his right portion or whether another will get it, or whether someone will get the better of him. If one would only look up and see the perfect Judge, God Himself, whose justice is so great that in the end every portion is made equal and even! Inequality is only a question of the beginning, not the end. If man saw the justice of God he would become brave, he would trust, and he would not trouble about a return; for if man will not return something, God is responsible for returning a thousandfold what one has given.

Sometimes a person cannot give the love that friends require, and he even forgets his friends when absorbed in work and his occupation. One may wonder whether this is lack of charity. But the question is, what work and occupation? There are kinds of work and occupation of a high character which ask one's whole attention, and such work requires sacrifice. And that is no lack of charity, because everyone likes to love, but if one can manage to love and be loved at the same time, it is better.

A person who is able to help others should not hide himself but do his best to come out into the world. "Raise up your light high," it is said. All that is in you should be brought out, and if conditions hinder you, break through the conditions! That is the strength of life.

If there is any power that will attract, it is the power of one's love. The only question is, is there anything one loves more than the ordinary things of life? If there is one should strive for that.

Love can take many forms, even that of indifference. I remember I went once, for a relative, to the house of a physician, an Indian physician who had a very ancient method of writing his prescriptions. Each took him nearly ten minutes. I was shown into a small room where fifteen to twenty people were already waiting, and I sat down among them. He continued to write prescriptions for all who came; and when he had finished with those who were before me, he began to write prescriptions for those who had come after me. I had thought that the physician, as a friend of the family, would have seen me first, but he went on until he had seen everyone, and I was the last.

Finally he said to me, "Now tell me what you want." I told him and he wrote out the prescription without any haste; and when I was leaving he said, "I hope you understand that I did not want to see you while all the other patients were still there. I wanted to see you at leisure." He was doing me a favor, and though he tried my patience it was still a majestic sort of favor. It gave me a good example of love in the form of indifference.

If somebody truly loves one person, he will end by loving everybody. The one who says, "I love this person, but hate that other one," does not yet know what love is. For love is not limited; it is divine and therefore unlimited. By opening the love element in oneself, one opens the divine element in oneself; and when the fountain of love begins to rise in the heart, then divine realization will rise like a fountain. The great saints, who had love for even the smallest beings, came to divine realizations without great study or meditation. Their love taught them.

Love is divine from its beginning in all aspects. Love is a conqueror who in the end will always conquer. It is not only the one we love whom love will conquer; love's conquering is the conquering of the kingdom of God. The power of love is penetrating; nothing can resist in the end. By giving love and kindness we never lose anything; love is an element that is never lessened, it is treasure that is divine.

When we stop to consider whether a person is worthy or unworthy, then we confine our love within a channel; but when we allow that feeling to flow it will develop into a continually flowing condition; then it will work out its own destiny without any intention on our part.

*Chapter 27.*

# FRIENDSHIP

Friendship is a word that we all use in our everyday language, and yet it could take one's whole life to realize its meaning. However learned a person may be, however pious, spiritual, or experienced, if he has not learned the nature and character of friendship he has not learned anything. This is the first and the last thing we have to learn. We so often use this word lightly, calling every acquaintance a friend, or professing to be somebody's friend; but the more we realize the meaning of it, the less we are able to claim friendship. For everything in life we are tested, examined, and tried, but to pass this examination of friendship is the most difficult thing in the world.

What is the reason for this? Why is it so difficult to be a friend? One would think that it was the easiest thing there is! The reason is that there is something in ourselves that is always against our being friendly. It is the self, the ego, which the Sufi calls *nafs*. As long as this ego is standing and lives, a man cannot claim to be anybody's friend. And when he is not somebody else's friend he is not even his own friend, for one learns friendship by being a friend to another.

A selfish person may seem to be a friend to himself, but that is on the surface, not in reality. He has not yet learned how to be a friend to another, so he cannot be a friend to himself. In our pursuit of truth we want to learn a great many things: the nature of life, the secret of life, the character of life; and to understand the meaning of friendship seems so easy and simple that we never trouble to think about it, nor about the responsibility of being a friend. The great error we make in our lives is that we begin to claim friendship before we have learned the meaning of friendship. In this world of illusion —where at the end of the examination we find everything to be of little importance, of little worth—if there is a sign of reality, of something that one can depend upon and in which one can recognize a sign of eternity, it is in the constancy of friendship.

Man, absorbed in the active life of this world, has a desire for friendship, though he never practices it. Yet this tendency to friendship can be found even among the animals. There is a story of a hunter who was shooting birds one day in the forest, and saw two birds sitting on a branch of a tree. He shot one bird and it dropped to the ground. As this man was at a distance it took him some time to arrive at the spot, and while he was walking towards it he saw that the other bird had come down to look at its mate. It touched it with its beak and found that it was dead, and by the time the man arrived he found both birds dead. "From that day," he said, "I gave up shooting, for I had seen a friendship among birds that one cannot find among mankind."

It is simple lesson, and a lesson that we have to learn; today when nations are against nations and races against races, when communities are against communities and one religion against another, it is now that friendship is so much needed. Besides, friendship is the first lesson of spirituality that one can learn. One may think that friendship, a personal friendship, means nothing; that one does not become spiritual through a personal friendship. But one does. A person begins his spiritual accomplishment by learning how to be a friend. For one who is really treading the path of friendship need not go anywhere to learn morals. Friendship itself teaches him sincerity, gratitude, sympathy, tenderness, appreciation; all these things that we must learn in this world, friendship teaches us. Once a person begins to learn these things through friendship with one person, he will naturally show to others the same virtues that he has acquired by going along this path; just as someone who has learned how to sing beautifully will sing every song that is given to him beautifully. The one who has cultivated his heart through friendship will naturally be inclined to be friends with others.

It is not belief in God that leads us to the goal, nor is it the analysis and the knowledge of God that bring us there. It is the friendship of God. For someone who learns the lesson of friendship in this world, this lesson develops in the end into friendship with God. But when a person exacts in return from his friend all that he does for him, then it is not friendship, it is business. It only means, "I give you a shilling and you give me twelvepence." When a person judges his friend, then the spirit of friendship is not awakened in his heart, for a friend never judges. When a person talks to another about his friend, when he blames him, when he criticizes him, he does not know what friendship is. The meaning of friendship is too sacred to realize. All other relationships and connections in this life are empty if friendship is not at the back of them to strengthen them. The relationship between mother and daughter, father and son, brother and sister, husband and wife, teacher and pupil—all these connections need a spirit behind them and this spirit is the spirit of friendship. When a daughter says, "I am friends with my mother," there is something beautiful about it. It makes the connection between a mother and daughter a different thing; it makes it living. In every relationship it is the same. When there is friendship to bind the relationship it makes it secure, it gives it life.

If one has made a friend it is not something that one has made to order, that must just fit in according to one's expectations and wishes. Every individual has his own characteristics, and as long as the spirit of forgiveness is not developed, friendship cannot last. It is a continual forgiveness that helps friendship to endure. Much can be learned by study, but not unselfishness. Unselfishness can be learned by one thing only, and that is by treading the path of friendship. It brings beauty into one's life; a friendly person, whether in business or in a profession, in whatever capacity he stands, gives one a feeling of warmth; in other words, an atmosphere of life. One is always glad to meet a friendly person in a shop, in a factory, in an office. When this spirit is awakened one can feel in his words, in his voice, in his expression, in his atmosphere that he is a friendly person, that there is something that goes out to meet others, a continual tendency to harmonize with others.

Once this spirit is developed, the ever-complaining tendency vanishes. If it is not developed then this world is full of thorns that prick. Then one will have no peace, no happiness, whatever one's position in life. If a person wants to make his life easy, if he wishes to create happiness in his life, he must try to crush that ego, that nafs, that thought of self which keeps him continually absorbed in his own thoughts and in his own affairs. By rising above it he will learn the spirit of friendship. Then for him the path that was full of thorns will become full of roses. For some souls that same world which can be hell to many others is heaven. For friendship changes man's point of view. An unfriendly man, as soon as he sees another person, sees him from his own critical point of view. He has his preconceived ideas, and therefore he is not allowed by Providence to see the good side of the other. But the one in whom the friendly spirit is awakened always overlooks little errors, faults, mistakes; his sympathy and his love naturally help him to rise above the faults of man. That is the story of Jesus Christ, the friend of humanity, before whom the greatest sinners were brought; but the attitude of the master was always forgiving. Those who brought them were unfriendly; the master was friendly.

Life is as we look at it. If we wish to find faults we can find faults in the best person in the world, and if we wish to find good points we can find good points in the worst person in the world. It is as we see life. The first lesson that one has to learn on the spiritual path is the manner of friendship. Once that is learned, then all other parts of the spiritual journey will become easy. Where do all the disturbances, such as wars, revolutions, disagreeable experiences among nations, fights among parties, come from? They all come from lack of friendship. The most extraordinary thing is that one party may perhaps have been fighting another party for years, but if we investigate their particular ideas we find that they are not even friends among themselves, for fighting against the other party produces and develops this unfriendly spirit in them. It is a kind of intoxication.

In education, in religion, or in anything else, the best thing one can do is to introduce the spirit of friendliness. And how can we introduce it? This is something that cannot arise only be reading some books about it. There exist innumerable societies and institutions of brotherhood everywhere, but they prove to be anything but brotherhood. Therefore that is not the way. The way is for an individual to be brought to understand fully that the essence of morals and of religion and of education is one, and that one essence is the manner of friendship. Sufis of all ages have named it *suluk,* which means divine manner, beneficence. That is why the best education is beneficence: how to bring pleasure and happiness to another. And one can begin to learn this by understanding fully what friendliness is and by practicing it at the same time.

Relationship is nourished by contact, kingship is maintained by reciprocity, but friendship is developed with love. There is no relationship that can be compared with friendship, for it is in learning the law of friendship that one understands ethics and morals, and also the relation between man and God.

There are three principal things to be understood in connection with friendship. The first is understanding without words. If there is no understanding between two persons, words are of no use. They may talk and talk, and discuss and discuss, and it will only go from bad to worse, for argument will never end. As it is said in the *Vadan*, "Why? is an animal with a thousand tails. At every bite you give it, it drops one of its curved tails and raises another." Can argument bring about understanding? Never. Argument only increases argument, and so one can go on till two persons turn their backs upon one another. Understanding is a gift of God, understanding is a soul's unfoldment, and understanding is the greatest fortune one can have in life. It is with understanding that the foundation of friendship is established, and it is in understanding that friendship is secure. Without understanding there is no friendship.

The next thing is a disinterested attitude. When a person thinks that by friendship he can get some benefit from the friend, or that the other may benefit by him, that is just burning the roots of friendship. In these material days so few of us understand what friendship means. Whenever there is a question of friendship the first thought is, "What shall I gain by this friendship; can his influence be of some use to me?" That is not friendship. Whenever a thought of self-interest creeps in, that means the ruin of friendship. Every little thought of profiting by it means destruction; it can never develop into a real friendship, it will only develop into a business relationship. It will last as long as the business relationship lasts, it will prosper as long as the business relationship prospers, and then it will vanish. Such a relationship can never be called friendship.

In this world every individual is helpless in some way or another, and every individual is of use in some way or another. It can happen that a person depends unconsciously upon his friend for his own interest, and even then it will turn out to be a wrong attitude. It cannot bring about fruitful results, for friendship must be built upon a solid foundation,

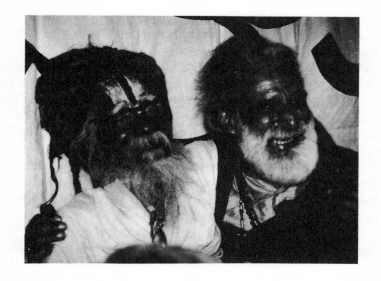

Pir Vilayat Inayat Khan and
Baba Sita Ram Das Onkarnath

a foundation where there is always a desire to give, to be helpful and serviceable to the friend: no thought of taking; always a thought of giving and keeping back nothing. A real friend holds his life cheap for his friend. The one who considers anything more important, more precious than friendship has not yet learnt the first lesson of friendship. There is no sacrifice too great, if it is made for a friend. If a sacrifice is not made for a friend, then for whom should one make it? A person would never learn how to make any sacrifice if it were not for a friend.

In our daily life we take the word friendship too lightly, and we confuse the words friend and acquaintance. An acquaintance is someone whom we have met; he has seen us, and we recognize one another. We may have been introduced at a dinner party. We use the word friend so freely in everyday language that we have forgotten the meaning of it. Generally we call anyone whom we have seen at a reception or party a friend, or anyone who belongs to our club. But to have even one friend in one's life is the greatest good fortune.

The third important thing in friendship is overlooking. No one in the world is faultless; no soul in the world is perfect. If on our part there is no desire to overlook our friends' shortcomings, there can be no more friendship. Friendship is maintained by recognizing that a human being is imperfect, that he has his faults and shortcomings. There is always something in him to overlook, and if we go on doing so, there is always the possibility that he may develop those very qualities which are lacking, for we may add to our friend qualities that are wanting in him. Sometimes people meet once and they feel they are friends. Sometimes people know each other for months and years and so they grow to be friends; their knowing one another and coming together in the end brings about the fulfillment of friendship. In such cases it develops as a result of their knowing one another.

Another odd thing sometimes happens, and that is when two persons are at daggers drawn for many months or years, and then suddenly throw their daggers away and become friends forever, but this is unusual. I myself have seen people who have been enemies working against one another for years, and from the day they became friends they have been the closest friends. Those who say, "I was his friend and he was my friend, but now we are not friends anymore," should realize that they were never friends. It was a presumption on their part, a false impression. Can friendship be such a false thing, can gold be gold at one time and not at another? Gold is gold, it never changes, it remains the same. Constancy in friendship is the soul of friendship. And that custom whereby a friend writes to another, "Yours as always," is wrong. If a plant remains as it has always been, it does not grow; and that which does not grow is not living; and that which is not living is dead.

When a person thinks, "I am too good or too kind to you; I have been too devoted to you," that person forgets that kindness, goodness, and devotion are larger than the horizon. No one can be too good, no one can be too kind, and no one can be too devoted. When there is a discussion between friends, and one says, "I have done so much for you, I have suffered so much for you, I have had so much pain on your account, I have had such a difficult life for your sake," then he is entering into business. He wants to keep a diary of what he has given in the form of love and kindness and goodness and sacrifice. A true friend makes every sacrifice he can and never thinks about it; he does not even allow his mind to ponder upon the subject. Real friendship means regard, a deep regard for the pleasure and displeasure of the friend. Is there anything in life that is more delicate than friendship—taking care that no words should hurt the friend, that no action should harm him, that not the slightest shade of coldness may fall on his heart? It is most difficult. If a person has learnt the manner of friendship he need not learn anything more; he knows everything. He has learnt the greatest religion, for it is in this same way that one will make a way to God. The one who has never learnt the manner of friendship will never know the way to God. He may be God's worshipper, but he cannot be the friend of God.

There is an attitude that one often sees in friends, and that attitude reveals a divine secret. It is the tendency to cover up from another person any fault that one's friend has committed and not only to cover it from the sight of others, but even from one's own sight. Never thinking about it, never looking at it, interpreting it differently—such a person turns the wrong of his friend into right. And every little good point of his friend, even though it may only weigh an ounce, he makes into a pound. He appreciates and admires it so much, he raises it so high, he considers it so great, that another person cannot imagine how this insignificant idea, this slight merit, can be valued so highly.

Lastly we come to that most mysterious expression, and yet an expression that is known to all on the religious path: the grace of God. What is it? It is the friendship of God. It is the friendly emotion of God. It is not the judging quality of God. When God's grace comes, it does not come by saying, "Are you worthy; are you unworthy; do you deserve it; do you not deserve it?" It comes as emotion, love, devotion, admiration come from friend to friend. There are no limits to it. It is all right for someone to say that because in the past incarnation he has done so much evil, in this life he has a bad time with much suffering; or that in the past incarnation he has done so much good, that this time he has become rich. And it is all right for others to say that when they go to hell for their sins they will be whipped and thrashed and put into the fire. But when you look at the grace of God, you forget all these things; no rules, no laws, no deserving or undeserving can be distinguished anymore. There is only one thing, and that is love, love that stands above law.

God's grace does not come specially to the pious; it does not come necessarily to people who are very good; nor does it come readily to people who are very occult or mystical. It comes as love comes from friend to friend. When love comes it comes without a conception of right and wrong. It is an emotion, it is the rising of the wave, it is a divine feeling that comes. It rises as a stream, and it falls upon the person in the form of a thousand gifts. It may be as inspiration, it may be as comfort, it may be as health, it may be as peace, it may be as rest, it may show itself in a thousand different forms.

The knowledge of what will please your friend, if it comes to you at all, will only come if you really know what friendship is. Otherwise you may presume you are a friend, and all your life you may try to please your friend, but you will never really be able to do so.

It is the same with God. You may do all possible good actions and offer a thousand prayers, and yet if you do not know what pleases God, you cannot please Him. But it does not come from knowledge; it only comes from friendship. Friendship is an automatic action, it is an innocent devotion, an unconscious outgoing, a pure feeling with depth, with life. Automatically that feeling brings about grace. Therefore no one can say why a person is another's friend. We cannot be the judge of it; we cannot understand it. And so no one can say why God is pleased with this person or that person. Sometimes we see that people who do not deserve it have great wealth; and then there are others who, if they had money, would really make the best use of it. Some do not seem to deserve the position or rank they hold; others perhaps in our eyes deserve more; and yet in the eyes of God it is different. They have it because they deserve it, though we do not see why and how. And it is the same with friendship. When someone said to Majnun, "Majnun, Leila is not beautiful; why are you so devoted to Leila?" Majnun said, "To see Leila you must borrow my eyes."

When we judge people do we see with the eyes of God, do we see what feeling God has towards them? When we cannot see in this way we have no right to question why others are in this or that position in life, why some people are rich, why they are in a big position; it is all a kind of battle with God. And those who learn this one principle—that with a friend one should do one's very best to the end, in order to prove worthy of his friendship—and those who try to do their utmost to regard the pleasure and displeasure of God without any thought of reward or of any answer from Him, it is those who really know the meaning of friendship.

Faults? Everyone has faults. Oneself, one's friend, and one's enemy are all subject to faults. The one who wishes that his own faults should not be disclosed must necessarily consider the same for the others he meets. The one who knows what the relation of friendship is between one soul and another, the tenderness of that connection, its delicacy, its beauty, and its sacredness, is the one who can enjoy life in its fullness, for he is living; and in this manner he must some day communicate with God. For it is the same bridge that connects two souls in the world which, once built, becomes the path to God. There is no greater virtue in this world than proving kind and trustworthy to one's friend, worthy of his confidence. The difference between the old soul and the young soul is to be found in this particular principle. The young soul only knows himself and what he wants, absorbed in his own pleasures and displeasures and obsessed by his ever-changing moods. The old soul regards his relation to every soul, he keenly observes his obligations towards everyone he knows in the world. He covers his wounds, if he happens to have any, from the sight of others, and endures all things in order to fulfill his duty to the best of his ability towards everyone in the world.

*Chapter 28.*

# RESIST NOT EVIL

Often one wonders at the phrase in the Bible, "Resist not evil," and it is not always given the right interpretation. To interpret it one should first explain what evil means. Is there any particular action or thing that one can point out as being evil? No doubt man is always apt to do so, but nothing can be evil according to a fixed principle. Then what is evil? It is something that is devoid of harmony, it is something that lacks beauty and love, and above all it is something that does not fit into the accommodation of life. What fits into the accommodation that life offers cannot be evil.

Evil may be likened to fire. The nature of fire is to destroy everything that lies in its path. But although the power of evil is as great as the power of fire, yet evil is also as weak as fire. For as fire does not endure, so evil does not last. As fire destroys itself, so evil is its own destruction. Why is it said, "Do not resist evil"? Because resistance gives life to evil; non-resistance lets it burn itself out. In the form of anger, passion, greed, or stubbornness one sees evil, and also in the form of deceit and treachery. But the root of evil is always one and the same: selfishness. In one person the evil is perhaps manifest on the surface; in another person it is hidden in the depths of the heart.

There is a saying in the East. "Do not invoke the name of Satan, or else he will rise from his grave." An inconsiderate or thoughtless person often falls into the error of awakening that devil even if he is asleep, for he does not know the music of life. In order to live in the world one should become a musician of life. Every person therein is a note; and when one feels that way, then one has an instrument in one's hand. The whole world is like an orchestra by which a symphony is to be played.

Even in small things one can observe the same law. Very often the greatest trouble that one has in life is not because of the difficulties others make, but because of one's own lack of comprehension of human nature. If one knew human nature one would realize that the first and the last lesson to learn is not to resist evil, for resistance becomes fuel to the fire. If we say to someone, "Do not do that; if we ask someone, "Why did you do it?"; if we reproach someone, saying, "You have done such and such a thing"—in all these ways we only make the evil stronger, we only fix the person firmer in his fault.

Everyone in this world can be a kind of teacher, but not a real teacher, for a real teacher is the one who always teaches himself. The more he teaches himself, the more he realizes that there is so much to be learnt that a whole lifetime would not be enough. And the more one learns the more one overlooks the evil in others. It does not mean that the evil is greater or less in others, it only means that one has realized that the enemy that one saw in others is really in oneself. The worst enemy one is faced with in outer life one finds to be in one's own heart. It makes one feel humiliated, but it teaches the true lesson: of finding in oneself the same element that one wished to resist in another.

Life is a place where it is necessary to move gently. Whether it be in thought, speech, or action, the rhythm must be controlled; the law of harmony must be observed in all that one does. One should know that even walking barefoot on thorns will not make one free from accusation: the thorns will accuse one of having trampled upon them. If living in this world is as delicate as that, can anyone say he has gained sufficient wisdom? Can anyone think he can afford to live in this world without giving a thought to this problem?

I was once asked how anyone at the head of a business or institution could possibly keep to the rule of not resisting evil. I said that I had seen people at the head of certain factories who had won the hearts of everyone working there, while there were other directors against whom every worker in the factory was speaking. It may be that the latter made a greater profit than the former, yet in the end they would find the gain of the former to be more enduring than their own. The ways of wisdom and tenderness cannot be made into a restricted principle for people to follow. A brush can never take the place of a knife, and therefore we all have to use every method and activity according to the circumstances. Nevertheless, the thought of not resisting evil should always be in the background.

The problem of evil is great. Many cannot bear even to hear it mentioned, although they are faced with it every moment of their lives. To leave this problem unsolved does not help. Everyone is ready to judge, to observe, or to take notice of the evil in another, not realizing that sometimes the surface of a thing is quite different from its depth. Perhaps that which seems evil has something good underneath; or what appears good may contain a spark of evil. By what standard can we determine evil and good, and who can judge the evil and good of anyone else? If one can judge at all, it is one's own evil and good. No one except God has the power to judge another. The sense of justice that is given to man is in order that he may judge his own actions; it is for this purpose that the sense of justice has been given to him.

When we look at life we shall see that it is nothing but a struggle, both individually and collectively. It seems that if there is anything worthwhile in this life it is that which is other than this struggle: the give and take of kindness and love and the doing of any action of selflessness. However well-qualified a person may be in the things of the world, his qualifications reach only to a certain point; they do not go beyond it. What is really required is qualification in the understanding of life, the understanding of the law that is working behind it. It is this qualification alone that will diminish man's continual struggle, for it will give him less to resist. It will make him more tolerant of the natural condition of human beings. As soon as one realizes that one cannot expect from anyone something of which he is not capable, one becomes tolerant.

The difficulty is that everyone demands more of another person in the way of thought and consideration, of kindness and love, than he does of himself. Man wants more justice and fairness on the part of another than he is himself prepared to give; and his standard may be so high that another person cannot keep up to it, which in turn makes him disappointed. What generally happens is that one does not just remain quiet after being disappointed but one resists, and so the struggle of life continues. One should not expect the peartree to bear roses, nor the rosebush to produce jasmine. Every person is like a certain plant, but not the same plant. We may be fond of roses, but every plant does not bear roses; if we want roses we should seek only the plant on which they grow, and we must not be disappointed if what we find is not the rose plant. In this way we can correct our own deception.

When people say that someone is bad it really means that the surface has become bad. The depth cannot be bad, however bad a person may seem. For goodness is life itself, and a person who would be all bad could not live. The very fact that he is living shows that there is a spark of goodness in him. Besides, just as there are various objects, so there are various persons; some show softness outside and hardness inside; some show hardness outside and softness inside;

some are very good in the depth and evil on the surface—
for there are as many different varieties as there are souls.

What education, what point of view, what attitude in life
is the best and will give the greatest happiness? It is the
attitude of overlooking evil instead of resisting it. There are
three ways of living one's life, which can be compared with
struggling in the sea whose waves are rising and falling all
the time. The first will struggle as long as life will permit; but
the rising and the falling of the waves in the sea continue
forever and ever, and in the end one will be drowned. And
so it is with man: struggling on, intoxicated by his struggle,
he will go on as long as his energy will permit. In this
struggle he may seem powerful, he may seem to have conquered others, he may seem to have done greater things than
others, but what does it amount to? In the end he will be
drowned. But there is another person who knows how to
move smoothly through the water, and he understands the
rhythm of moving his arms and legs; he swims with the
rising and falling of the waves. He is not struggling. This
person may hope to arrive at the port if it is near. If his ideal
is not too far distant, then he is the one to fulfill it. And the
third person is the one who walks on the water. This is the
meaning of Christ's walking upon the waters.

Life is just like waves; it is making its way continually.
The one who allows himself to be disturbed by it will be
more and more disturbed every day; the one who does not
take any notice of it will stay inwardly serene. The one who
sees all things and yet rises above them is the one who will
walk over the sea. No one can reach the highest summits of
life, of wisdom, in a moment; even a whole lifetime is too
short. Yet hope is necessary, for the one who hopes and sees
the possibilities climbs towards the summit, but the one
who has no hope has no legs on which to ascend the hill of
wisdom, the summit of which is the desired goal.

*Chapter 29.*

# RESPECT, CONSIDERATION, AND GRACIOUSNESS

There is a virtue that the Sufi calls *muruat,* a virtue that is too delicate to express in words. It means refraining from certain actions out of respect for someone else, whether in consideration for his age, position, knowledge, goodness, or piety. Those who practice this virtue do not do so only towards someone important or pious, for when this quality develops it manifests in one's dealings with everyone.

Muruat is the opposite of bluntness. It is not necessarily respect; it is something more delicate than that; it is both consideration and respect together. In its full development this virtue may even become so intense that a person out of consideration and respect tries to bear with the lack of the same virtue in another; but when one arrives at that stage the human manner ends and the saintly manner begins. Man is not born into this world only to eat, drink, and make merry; he is born in order to perfect the human character. The way he realizes this is by great thoughtfulness and consideration. Otherwise, with all power, position, wealth, learning, and all the good things of the world, he remains poor if he lacks this richness of the soul that is good manner.

All the beauty that surrounds us is outside of us; the only beauty that is dependable is to be found and developed in our own character. A person may show lack of muruat, if not in words, in his glance. One does not need to speak in order to be rude. In one's look, in one's intonation, in one's manner of standing or walking, in the way one closes the door on leaving the room, one can show one's feelings. Even if one does not speak, one can make the door speak. It is not an easy matter to control oneself when one's mind is out of hand.

Delicate ideas such as these are most difficult to learn and practice in life. And today many wonder if they are not weaknesses; but something that can only be practiced by mastering oneself can never be a weakness. There is no loss even if thought or consideration is given to someone who does not deserve it; for if such an action did not bring any profit, it was still practice; and it is practice that makes a man perfect.

There is no one in the world who does not deserve some respect. He who pays respect to another by so doing respects himself, for respect creates respect, while disrespect re-echoes in disrespect. The greatest education that can be given to a child is that of respect, not only for his friends, parents, and relations, but also for the servants in the house. Once the Prophet Muhammad, hearing his grandson call a slave by his name, told him, "Call him Uncle, for he is advanced in years." If one wishes to respect someone, one will surely find something to respect in him; and if there is nothing at all to be found, then the very fact that he is a human being quite entitles him to respect.

One form of respect is to consider another person as better than oneself; even if one does not hold that he is so; to regard another person as better than oneself, by reason of humility and also from graciousness. No person is respected who has no respect for another. Another form of respect is to recognize another person's superiority in age, experience, learning, goodness, birth, rank, position, personality, morality, or spirituality. And if one has been mistaken in recognizing another person's superiority it is no loss, for respect given to man in reality is respect given to God. He who deserves respect is entitled to it, but when someone does not deserve it and yet you respect him it shows your graciousness. To a fine person it is a matter of great regret to have lost the opportunity of paying respect when there was an occasion, while an unrefined person does not mind. There are many who, out of cleverness, wrap their disrespectful attitude in an ironical form of speech and make sarcastic but polite remarks in order to insult. In that way, they seemingly have not shown any disrespect, and yet they have satisfied their desire of being disrespectful. In some people there is a spirit of injury that feeds on hurting by a disrespectful attitude shown in thought, word, or action. If man only knew that in life what he gives he receives, only sometimes the return does not come immediately but takes time.

He is really respectful who gives respect, but he who looks for respect from another is greedy; he will always be disappointed. Even to pay respect in order to get respect in return is a kind of trade. Those who reach spiritual realization will only give respect generously, without thinking for one moment of receiving it in return. When one sincerely gives respect to anyone, not for show but from the feeling of one's heart, a happiness rises together with that, which is the product only of the respectful attitude, and nothing else can give it. There are many to whom one is indebted for their help, kindness, protection, support, for their service or assistance, and there is nothing material in the world that can express one's gratitude so fully as real respect. Remember, therefore, that for something that you cannot pay back in silver or gold you can make return only in one way, and that is by humbly offering respect.

The highest expression of love is respect. Respect is not due only to one's superior or elder, but even to a child; only one should know to what extent it should be given and in what form it should be expressed. In loving one's mate, one's friend or relation, one's parents, one's teacher, one's priest, the best expression of love that can be shown is a sincere, respectful attitude. No love offering can be more precious than a word or an act of respect.

Very often conflicts between religions have arisen because people who respected their own religion looked with contempt at the religion of another. If one did not respect one's friend's religion, one could at least respect one's friend, and out of respect for one's friend one would regard one's friend's religion respectfully. Very often, with all love and devotion and sincerity, friendship breaks only owing to disregard on the part of one or the other of the law of respect.

What is worship? Worship is not dancing before God, worship is an act of respect offered to God, to whom all respect is due. The person who worships God and disrespects man worships in vain; his piety is his mania. A true worshipper of God sees His presence in all forms, and thus in respecting others he respects God. It may even develop to such an extent that the true worshipper of God the Omnipresent walks gently on the earth, bowing in his heart even to every tree and plant, and it is then that the worshipper forms a communion with the divine Beloved at all times, when he is awake and when he is asleep.

*Khatir* means consideration for someone which is shown in the form of respect, help, or service. Very often it wants a sacrifice; it may even need self-denial. However consideration is the highest quality that can be found in human nature. Consideration of age, of experience, of knowledge, of position, consideration of some good done by a person; also consideration of somebody's feebleness, weakness—it is all included in the word *khatir*. This spirit of consideration, when developed, extends not only to the person for whom one has consideration, but as far as having consideration for that person's sake for another who is related or connected with the person in some way or other. When a king is respected and not his ambassador, that means lack of consideration to the king.

For a Sufi this quality becomes his moral. The Sufi learns consideration beginning with his murshid, but this culminates in consideration for God. When one arrives at that tenderness of feeling one considers every person in the world. To the Sufi missing an opportunity of considering another is a great disappointment, for he considers it to be a fault not only towards a human being but towards God. Verily he is pious who considers human feeling. No doubt it needs no end of endurance to consider everybody and to be considerate always; it wants no end of patience. However, by being considerate nothing is lost, if seemingly nothing is gained. The reward of this virtue is always in store. Consideration is the sign of the wise.

As soon as the soul touches the inner kingdom, which is the divine kingdom, its true nobility becomes manifest in the form of graciousness or *khulk* as the Sufis call it. Kings and those belonging to aristocratic families were trained to be gracious, yet it is a quality born in the heart of man. This means that every soul shows the aristocratic manner from the moment it touches the inner kingdom. Thus true aristocracy is the nobility of the soul: the soul begins to express in every feeling, thought, word, and action that graciousness which belongs to God Himself. Graciousness is quite different from a patronizing attitude, which is a wrong manner. A gracious person, before expressing that noble attribute, tries to hide himself even from his own eyes.

The reason why the great ones, the truly noble people, are gracious is that they are more sensitive to all the hurt and harm that comes to them from those who are unripe and try therefore out of kindness to keep themselves from doing the same to someone else, however lowly his position.

There is a great truth in what Christ has said in the Sermon on the Mount, "Blessed are the meek, for they shall inherit the earth." This will always prove true, whatever be the age and whatever the evolution of the world. Whether it be a time of aristocracy or whether it be a time of democracy, the value of that nobility of nature which is expressed in graciousness will always command its price. It is easy to use this word, but it is most difficult to practice it through life, for there is no end to the thought one has to give to every action in life in order to achieve it. It needs judgment and a sense of fairness, of weighing and measuring all one does; besides it needs a fine sense of art and beauty, for in perfecting the personality one attains to the highest degree of art. Verily, the making of the personality is the highest form of art there is. The Sufi considers the cultivation of human attributes, in which lies the fulfillment of the purpose of his life, as his religion.

A young man one day showed some impatience with his aged father, who could not hear very clearly anymore and asked him two or three times to repeat what he had said. Seeing the irritated expression on his face, the father said, "My son, do you remember that there was a day when you were a little child and you asked me what a certain bird was and I told you, a sparrow? You asked me perhaps fifty times, and I had the patience to repeat it to you again and again without being hurt or troubled about it; I was only pleased to tell you all I knew. Now when I can no longer hear so well, you can at least have patience with me and explain something twice if I did not hear you the first time." What is needed most in order to learn that noble manner of life is patience, sometimes in the form of endurance, sometimes in the form of consideration, and sometimes in the form of forgiveness.

In dealing with people who lack education, one should keep in mind that real civilization means progress. Those who are not educated should be educated to understand life better. There are only two possibilities: to go forward or to go backward. Either one will begin to think like those who are not educated, or one must help the one who is uneducated to advance one must take him gently by the hand and lead him towards more beautiful ideas.

Once in India I was staying near a Hindu temple, and

there were two porters who took care of that temple. They were Afghans, proud and rough, and rigid in their behavior; yet in their expression there was honesty and goodness. Often I passed that way, and every time they ignored my entering and leaving, lest they should have the trouble of observing the conventional politeness. One day one of them came to me with a message from his master. I got up from my seat and received him most cordially, and after that day, everytime I passed I was very well received, with smiles and cordial welcome, and they ignored me no more. This happened because education was given to him without hurting his feelings, and as that gave him pleasure he thought he would return the politeness.

To force a virtue upon anyone is pride; to let him see the beauty of good manners is an education. We should consider it our sacred task to approach the people who need improving with such gentleness in such a manner that culture and beauty are developed in them, which will then be shared by us both.

*Chapter 30.*

# JUDGING

Man is generally very ready to pass judgment without any restraint and to express his opinion instantly. He will not stop to think whether he himself has arrived at the same stage as the one whom he is judging or whether he has any right to judge him. Jesus Christ said about judging that he who was without fault should throw the first stone. This teaches a great lesson.

For the Sufi, who sees in every form the divine form, in every heart the divine shrine, to judge anyone, whatever be his position, his action, his condition, is altogether against his religion. In this way he develops the philosophy that he has first learnt intellectually.

Not blaming others is principally a question of self-restraint or self-control, of politeness, kindness, sympathy, and graciousness; of an attitude of worship towards God, the Creator of all beings, and of realizing that all are His children, good or bad. If someone's child happens to be plain in appearance, would it be polite to say before the parents, "This child is plain"?

The Father and Mother of all beings is there, comprehending and knowing what is going on in every person's heart. He sees all faults and merits before we do, and when we judge so readily it is before that Artist who has made everything, and not behind His back; it is in His presence. If we realized that, it would not be difficult to feel the personality of God everywhere.

There comes a time, after we have continually practiced the virtue of not judging, when we see the reason behind every fault we notice in anyone we meet. Then we become more tolerant, more forgiving. When a person who is ill makes a fuss by moaning and wailing, it disturbs us at first. We say how wrong it is, how annoying, what a bad nature he has. But the understanding of the reason behind it, that it is not his bad nature but the illness, will make us more tolerant. When we see no reason it makes us not only severe with that person, but blind to the light of God, blind to that forgiveness, that unique essence of God which can be found in the human heart.

The difference that exists between man's justice and God's justice can be seen in the following simile. When children are quarreling over their toys, they each have a reason. The one thinks a certain toy most attractive; why should he not possess it? The other says the toy was given to him, and why should he not keep it? Both have their reason and both are right. But the father's justice is different; the father knows the nature of each child and what he wants to bring out in the nature of that child. That is why he gave the toys to the children, to bring out something in their nature. The child does not know this, and if he were older would accuse the father of ignoring his wishes. He does not understand the justice of the father; he has to grow to another stage to do that. It is the same with the justice of God and man. Man's justice is obscured by his preconceived ideas of favor and disfavor and by his learning, which is nothing compared to the knowledge of God.

If one ever gets a glimpse of divine justice, it is only by

constantly believing in the justice of God in spite of all the proofs that seem to contradict His justice. Judging by these one might come to the conclusion that there is no justice, that everything just works mechanically. Ideas such as those of karma and reincarnation may seem satisfactory, but the fact remains that they have their root in God who is behind all. God could not be all-powerful if every individual were powerful enough to work out his own karma. Even if everything were working mechanically, there would still have to be an engineer; and is he subjected to his machine? If God is limited He can no more be God. God is perfect in His justice, in His wisdom, in His power. But if we question the cause of all those happenings which do not seem to us to be justified, we then come to another question: can a composer give a definite justification for every note that he has written in his composition? He cannot. He can only say, "It is a stream which has come from my heart. I have tried to keep to certain rules of composition, but I am not concerned with every note. I am concerned with the effort by which the whole was produced."

There is the law, but there is also love. Law is a habit, and love is being; law has been created, but love has never been created. So love is predominant. As God is beyond the law, so love is above the law. Therefore, if we would find a solution to our ever-recurring question of why it is so, it is not by the study of the law. The study of the law will only give an immense appetite; it will never bring satisfaction. If there is anything that will bring satisfaction it is diving deep into love. Then we shall realize that is not just; we shall never again say that anything is unjust. This is the point the wise reach, and they call it the culmination of wisdom.

There is a saying that God forgives more than He judges, but how do we know that God forgives? In the first place justice is born, and love has never been born; it always has been and will always be. Justice is born of a certain sense in man, the sense of fairness. As this sense matures it begins to seek for evenness, and what is not even it does not like.

In order to develop this sense we need inspiration from all that has existed before. Justice is the outcome of what we see, but this is not so with love, which is spontaneous and always present. As it is said in the Bible, God is love, and therefore, while justice is God's nature, love is God's very being. He forgives because He is forgiveness Himself; He judges because it is His nature to judge.

Justice comes from God's intelligence, and the expression of God's intelligence in this world of illusion is limited. When judging limited things our intelligence becomes limited also; we are as limited as the objects before us. The greater the object, the greater becomes our vision.

There is only one thing that is truly just, and that is to say, "*I* must not do this." When one says this to another person one may be very wrong. The mystic develops his mind in this manner, purifying it by pure thought, feeling, and action, free from all sense of separateness, only following this one line of thought. Whatever differences in principles of what is right and wrong the various religious faiths may show, no two individuals will ever differ in this one natural principle: that every soul seeks after beauty, and that every virtue, righteousness, good action, is nothing but a glimpse of beauty.

When once he has made this moral his own, the Sufi does not need to follow a particular belief or faith to restrict himself in a particular path. He can follow the Hindu way, the Muslim way, the way of any church or faith, provided he treads this royal road: that the whole universe is but an immanence of beauty. We are born with the tendency to admire it in every form, and we should not blind ourselves by being dependent on one particular line of beauty.

Forgiveness does not judge; there is only the feeling of love, and therefore, whatever be the other's fault, once a person has forgiven, the resulting happiness and joy are shared by both. Justice does not give that joy. The one who judges too much is unhappy himself, and he makes the one whom he judges unhappy too. The one who forgives is happy; he does not keep any grudge in his heart; he makes his heart pure and free from it. God's greatest attribute is forgivingness.

Man accuses God of having done many things wrong; it is often only out of respect and because of his reverent attitude that he says nothing, but if he felt free he would make a thousand accusations. There is no one who could be accused so often and for so many things as God. The reason is that it is our limited self which judges, though it is quite unable to understand.

After having acquired refinement of character and merits and virtues that are needed in life, the personality can be finished by the wakening of the sense of justice. The art of personality makes a statue, a fine specimen of art, but when the sense of justice is awakened that statue comes to life; for in the sense of justice lies the secret of the soul's unfolding. Everyone knows the name of justice; but it is rare to find someone who really is just by nature, in whose heart the sense of justice has been awakened.

What generally happens is that people claim to be just, though they may be far from being so. The development of the sense of justice lies in unselfishness; one cannot be just and selfish at the same time. The selfish person can be just, but only for himself. He has his own law most suited to himself, and he can change it. His reason will help him to do so in order to suit his own requirements in life. A spark of justice is to be found in every heart, in every person, whatever be his stage of evolution in life; but the one who loves fairness so to speak blows on that spark, thus raising it to a flame, in the light of which life becomes more clear to him.

There is so much talk about justice, so much discussion about it, and so much dispute over it. One finds two persons arguing upon a certain point and differing from one another, both thinking that they are just, yet neither of them willing to admit that the other is as just as he himself.

For those who really learn to be just, their first lesson is what Christ has taught: "Judge not, that ye be not judged." One may say, "If one does not judge, how can one learn justice?" But it is the one who judges himself who can learn justice, not the one who is occupied in judging others. In this life of limitations, if one only explores oneself, one will find within oneself so many faults and weaknesses, and when dealing with others so much unfairness on one's own part, that for the soul who really wants to learn justice, his own life will prove to be a sufficient means with which to practice justice.

Again, there comes a stage in one's life, a stage of life's culmination, a stage of the soul's fuller development, when justice and fairness rise to such a height that one arrives at the point of being devoid of blame; one has nothing to say against anyone, and if there be anything it is only against oneself. It is from this point that one begins to see the divine justice hidden behind this manifestation. It comes in one's life as a reward bestowed from above, a reward that is like a trust given by God, to see all things appearing as just and unjust in the bright, shining light of perfect justice.

*Chapter 31.*

# OVERLOOKING

There is a tendency that gradually manifests in a person who is advancing spiritually, and that tendency is overlooking, or *darguza* as the Sufis call it. At times this tendency might appear to be negligence, but negligence is not overlooking; negligence is not looking. In other words overlooking may be called rising above things. One has to rise in order to overlook; the one who stands beneath life could not overlook anything even if he wanted to. Overlooking is a manner of graciousness; it means to look and at the same time not to look, to see and not take notice of being seen, not to be hurt or harmed or disturbed by something, not even minding it. It is an attribute of nobleness of nature; it is the sign of souls who are tuned to a higher key.

One may ask, is it practical? Perhaps not always, but in the end it is practical all the same. The one who overlooks will also realize the practicality of it. Perhaps he will only realize this at last, after he has met all its numerous disadvantages; nevertheless, all is well that ends well.

Very often overlooking costs less than taking notice of something that could well be overlooked. In life there are

211

things that matter and there are things that do not matter; and as one advances through life one finds there are many things that do not matter, that one could just as well overlook. The one who takes notice of everything that comes his way will waste time on a journey that takes all his life to accomplish. While climbing the mountain of life, the purpose of which is to reach the top, if a person troubles about everything that comes along he will never be able to reach the top; he will always be troubling about everything at the foot. After having realized that life on this earth lasts only a few days, a person will not trouble anymore about little things; he will only trouble about things that really matter. By striving for little things a person loses the opportunity of accomplishing great things in life. One who troubles about small things is small; the soul who thinks of great things is great.

Overlooking is the first lesson of forgiveness. This tendency comes out of love and sympathy, for when one hates one takes notice of every little fault, but when one loves another one naturally overlooks the faults, and very often one tries to turn the faults of the beloved into merits. Life has endless things that suggest beauty, and numberless things that suggest ugliness; there is no end to merits and no end to faults, and one's outlook on life is according to one's evolution.

The higher one has risen, the wider one's horizon becomes. The tendency to sympathize, which is an analytical tendency, weighing and measuring and taking good notice of everything, brings a person the desire to overlook. "Judge not," said Christ, "lest ye be judged." The more one thinks of this lesson, the deeper it goes into one's heart. What one learns from it is to try and overlook all that does not fit in with one's own ideas as to how things ought to be in life, until one comes to a stage of realization where the whole of life seems one sublime vision of the immanence of God.

*Chapter 32.*

# CONCILIATION

Any efforts made in developing the personality or in character-building must be made not for the sake of proving oneself superior to others, but in order to become more
agreeable to those around one and to those with whom one
comes in contact. Conciliation, or *ittefaq* as it is called by the
Sufis, is not only the moral of the Sufi, but it is the sign of
the Sufi. This virtue is not learned and practiced easily, for
it needs not only good will but wisdom. The great talent of
the diplomat is to bring about the desired results by agreement. Disagreement is easy; among the lower creation one
sees it so often. What is difficult is agreement, for it requires
a wider outlook, which is the true sign of spirituality. Narrowness of outlook makes the horizon of man's vision small;
the person with a narrow outlook cannot easily agree with
another. There is always a meeting ground for two people,
however much they differ in thought, but the meeting
ground may be far off, and a man is not always willing to
take the trouble to go so far in order to come to an agreement. Very often his patience does not allow him to go far
enough to meet another. What generally happens is that

everyone wants the other to meet him where he himself is standing, and there is no desire on his part to move from there.

This does not mean that a person in order to become a real Sufi must give up his ideas so that he may meet in agreement with another. There is no benefit in always being lenient with every thought that comes from somebody else, nor is there any benefit in always erasing one's own idea from one's heart. That is not conciliation. The one who is able to listen to another is the one who will make another listen to him. It is the one who agrees easily with another who will have the power of making another agree readily with him. In doing so one really gains in spite of the apparent loss that might sometimes occur. When man is able to see both from his own point of view and from the point of view of another, he has a complete vision and a clear insight; he so to speak sees with both eyes.

No doubt friction produces light, but light is the agreement of the atoms. It is a stimulus to thought if two people have their own ideas and argue about them, and it does not matter so much. But when a person argues for the sake of argument, the argument becomes his object and he gets no satisfaction out of conciliation. Words provide the means of disagreement, reasons become the fuel for the fire; but wisdom resides where the intelligence is pliable. Then one understands all things, both the wrong of the right and the right of the wrong. The person who arrives at perfect knowledge has risen above right and wrong. He knows them and yet he does not know; he can say much, and yet what can he say? Then it becomes easy for him to conciliate each and all.

*Chapter 33.*

# GRATEFULNESS

Gratefulness in the character is like fragrance in the flower. A person, however learned and qualified in his life's work, in whom gratefulness is absent is devoid of that beauty of character which makes personality fragrant. If we answer every little deed of kindness with appreciation, we develop in our nature the spirit of gratefulness, and by learning this we rise to that state where we begin to realize God's goodness towards us. For this we can never be grateful enough to His divine compassion.

The great Sufi poet Sa'adi teaches gratefulness as being the means of attracting that favor, forgiveness, and mercy of God upon ourselves in which is the salvation of our soul. There is much in life that we can be grateful for, in spite of all the difficulties and troubles of life. Sa'adi says, "The sun and moon and the rain and clouds, all are busy to prepare your food for you, and it is unfair indeed if you do not appreciate it in thanksgiving."

God's goodness is something that one cannot learn to know at once; it takes time to understand it. But little actions of kindness that we receive from those around us we can know, and we can be thankful if we want to be. In this way man develops gratefulness in his nature, and expresses it in his thought, speech, and action as an exquisite form of beauty. As long as one weighs and measures and says, "What I have done for you," and, "What have you done for me?" "How kind I have been to you," and, "How good have you been to me?" one wastes one's time disputing over something that is inexpressible in words. Besides, one closes by this that fountain of beauty which rises from the depth of one's heart. The first lesson that we can learn in the path of thankfulness is to forget absolutely what we do for another, and to remember only what the other person has done for us. Throughout the whole journey in the spiritual path the main thing to be accomplished is the forgetting of our false ego, so that in this way we may arrive someday at the realization of that Being whom we call God.

There is a story of a slave called Ayaz, who was brought before a king with nine others. The king was to select one to be his personal attendant. The wise king gave into the hands of each of the ten a wineglass and commanded him to throw it down. Each one obeyed the command. Then the king asked each one of them, "Why did you do such a thing?" The first nine answered, "Because Your Majesty gave me the order"; the plain truth cut and dried. And then came the tenth slave, Ayaz. He said, "Pardon, Sire, I am sorry," for he realized that the king already knew it was his command; in the reply, "Because you told me to," nothing new was said to the king. This beauty of expression enchanted the king so much that he selected him to be his attendant.

It was not long before Ayaz won the trust and confidence of the king, who gave him the charge of the treasury in which precious jewels were kept. This made many jealous, this sudden rise from slave to treasurer of the king, a position that many envied. No sooner did people know that Ayaz had become a favorite of the king than they began to tell numerous stories about him in order to bring him into disfavor with the king. One of the stories was that Ayaz went every day into the room where the jewels were locked in the safe, and that he was stealing them every day, little by little. The king answered, "No, I cannot believe such a thing; you have to show me."

So they brought the king as Ayaz entered this room, and made him stand in a place where there was a hole, looking into the room, and the king saw what was going on there. Ayaz entered the room and opened the door of the safe. And what did he take out from it? His old, ragged clothes which he had worn as a slave. He kissed them and pressed them to his eyes, and put them on the table. There incense was burning, and what he was doing was something sacred to him. He then put on these clothes and looked at himself in the mirror, and said, as one might say a prayer, "Listen, O Ayaz. See what you used to be before. It is the king who has made you, who has given you the charge of this treasure. So regard this duty as your most sacred trust, and this honor as your privilege and as a token of the love and kindness of the king. Know that it is not your worthiness that has brought you to this position. Know that it is his greatness, his good-ness, his generosity that has overlooked your faults, and that has bestowed that rank and position upon you by which you are now being honored. Never forget, therefore, your first day, the day when you came to this town; for it is the remembering of that day that will keep you in your proper place."

He then took off the clothes and put them in the same place of safety, and came out. As he stepped out, what did he see? He saw that the king before whom he bowed was waiting eagerly to embrace him; and the king said to him, "What a lesson you have given me, Ayaz! It is this lesson which we all must learn, whatever be our position. Because before that King in whose presence we all are but slaves, nothing should make us forget that helplessness through which we were reared and raised and brought to life, to understand and to live a life of joy. People told me that you had stolen jewels from our treasure house, but on coming here I have found that you have stolen my heart."

*Chapter 34.*

# NOBILITY

Dignity, which in other words may be called self-respect, is not something that can be left out when considering the art of personality. When one asks what it is and how this principle can be practiced, the answer is that all manner of light-heartedness and all tendency to frivolity must be rooted out from one's nature in order to hold that dignity which is precious to one. The one who does not care for it does not need to take trouble about it; it is only for the one who sees something in self-respect. A person with self-respect will be respected by others, regardless of his power, possessions, position, or rank; in every position or situation in life that person will command respect.

There arises a question: has light-heartedness then any place in life, or is it not necessary in life at all? All is necessary, but everything has its time. Dignity does not consist in making a long face; neither is respect evoked by a stern expression. By frowning or by stiffening the body one does not show honor. Dignity does not mean being sad or depressed: it is apportioning one's activities to their proper time. There are times for laughter; there are times for seri-

Hazrat Inayat Khan

ousness. The laughter of the person who is laughing all the time loses its power; the person who is always light-hearted does not carry that weight in society which he should. Besides, light-heartedness often makes a man offend others without meaning to do so.

The one who has no respect for himself has no respect for others. He may think for the moment that he is regardless of conventionalities and free in his expression and feeling, but he does not know that it makes him as light as a scrap of paper moving hither and thither in space, blown by the wind. Life is a sea, and the further one travels on the sea the heavier a ship one needs. So for a wise man, a certain amount of weight is required in order to live, which gives balance to his personality. Wisdom gives that weight; its absence is the mark of foolishness. The pitcher full of water is heavy; it is the absence of water in the pitcher that makes it light, like a man without wisdom who is light-hearted.

The more one studies and understands the art of personality, the more one finds that it is the ennobling of the character which is going forward towards the purpose of creation. All the different virtues, refined manners, and beautiful qualities are the outcome of nobleness of character. But what is nobleness of character? It is the wide outlook.

A friendly attitude, expressed in sympathetic thought, speech, and deed, is the principal thing in the art of personality. There is limitless scope to show this attitude, and however much the personality is developed in this direction, it is never too much. Spontaneity and the tendency to give, giving that which is dear to one's heart, show the friendly attitude. Life in the world has its numberless obligations towards friend and foe, towards acquaintance and stranger. One can never do too much to be conscientious in one's obligations in life and to do everything in one's power to fulfill them. To do more than one's due is perhaps beyond the power of every person, but in doing what one ought to do one does accomplish one's life purpose.

Life is an intoxication, and the effect of this intoxication is negligence. The Hindu words *dharma* and *adharma,* religiousness and irreligiousness, signify that one's duty in life is dharma, and the neglect of the same is adharma. The one who is not conscientious in his obligations in life towards every being he comes in contact with is indeed irreligious. Many will say, "We tried to do our best, but we didn't know how," or, "We don't know what is expected of us," or, "How are we to find out what is really our due and what is not?" No one in this world can teach what is anyone's due and what is not. It is for every soul to know for himself by being conscientious in his obligations. And the more conscientious he is, the more obligations he will find to fulfill, and there will be no end to them.

Nevertheless, in this continual strife what might seem a loss to one in the beginning in the end is gain; for one will come face to face with one's Lord, who is wide-awake. The eyes of the person who, absorbed in life's intoxication, neglects his duty to his fellow men, will certainly become dazzled and his mind exhausted before the presence of God. This does not mean that any soul will be deprived of the divine vision, it only means that the soul who has not learned to open his eyes wide enough will have his eyes closed before the vision of God. All virtues come from observation of life. Nobility of soul, therefore, is signified in the broad attitude that man takes in life.

A noble-minded person shows, as something natural in his character, a respect for his word, which is called his word of honor. For that person his word is himself, and this reality can increase to such an extent that even his life could be sacrificed for his word. Someone who has reached this stage is not far from God, for many times in the scriptures it is said, "If you want to see Us, see Us in our words." If God can be seen in His words, the true soul can be seen in his word. Pleasure, displeasure, sweetness, bitterness, honesty, dishonesty, all these are to be discerned in the words man speaks. For the word is the expression of the thought, and the thought is the expression of the feeling. And what is man? Man is his thought and feeling. So what is the word? The word is man's expression, the expression of his soul.

The man on whose word you can rely is dependable. No wealth of this world can be compared with one's word of honor. A man who says what he means proves his spirituality by this virtue. To a real person, to go back on his words is worse than death, for it is going backwards instead of going forward. Every soul is going onwards towards his goal; and the person who is really going onwards shows it in his word.

At the present time it is necessary to have so many courts and so many lawyers, and hence so many prisons, which are increasing more every day. This all shows the lack of that virtue which has been valued by the noble-minded ever since the beginning of civilization; for in this quality—a quality that neither belongs to the animals nor is attributed to the angels—man shows his human virtues. What is religion? Religion in the true sense of the word is beyond explanation. It is a thin thread, too delicate and too sacred to be touched. It is the ideal, which can be polluted if it is touched; and it can be found in that sensitiveness which in other words may be called spirituality, the regard for the word.

Many in this world have undergone sacrifices; sufferings and pains have been inflicted on them, but it was only to put the virtue of their word to the test, for every virtue has to prove itself by going through a testing fire. When it has proved itself in its trial it becomes a solid virtue. This can be practiced in every little thing one does in one's daily life. If a person says one thing one moment and another thing another moment, even his own heart begins to disbelieve him.

Among the great ones who have come to the earth from time to time and have shown a great many virtues, this virtue has been the most pronounced. Muhammad, before coming before the world as a prophet, was called Amin by his comrades, which means trustworthy. The story of Haris Chandra is known to the Hindus down the ages; the example he set is engraved upon the mind of the whole race. The story of Hatim, a Sufi of ancient times, has been a great inspiration to the people of Persia. In whatever part of the world and in whatever period, by the thoughtful and by those with ideals, the word of honor will be most valued.

The spirit of generosity in nature builds a path to God, for generosity is outgoing, is spontaneity; its nature is to make its way towards a wide horizon. Generosity, therefore, may be called charity of heart. It is not necessary that the spirit of generosity be shown always by the spending of money; in every little thing one can show it. Generosity is an attitude a person shows in every little action that he does for people whom he comes in contact with in his everyday life. One can show generosity by a smile, by a kind glance, by a warm handshake, by patting a younger soul on the shoulder as a mark of encouragement, of showing appreciation, of expressing affection. One can show generosity in accommodating one's fellow man, in welcoming him, in bidding farewell to one's friend. In thought, word, and deed, in every manner and form one can show that generous spirit which is the sign of the godly.

The Bible speaks of generosity as charity, but if I were to give an interpretation of the word generosity I would call it nobility. No rank, position, or power can prove one noble; truly noble is he who is generous of heart. What is generosity? It is nobility, it is expansion of the heart. As the heart expands, so the horizon becomes wide, and one finds greater and greater scope in which to build the kingdom of God.

Depression, despair, and all manner of sorrow and sadness come from lack of generosity. Where does jealousy come from? Where do envy, aching of the heart come from? It all comes from lack of generosity. A man may not have one single coin to his name, and yet he can be generous, he can be noble, if only he has a large heart of friendly feeling. Life in the world offers every opportunity to a man, whatever be his position in life, to show if he has any spirit of generosity.

The changeableness and falsehood of human nature, besides lack of consideration and thoughtlessness for those whom he meets through life, and furthermore the selfishness and grabbing and grafting spirit that disturbs and troubles his soul—all these create a situation that is itself a test and trial through which every soul has to pass in the midst of worldly life. When through this test and trial a person holds fast to his principle of charity and marches along towards his destination, not allowing the influences that come from the four corners of the world to keep him back from his journey to the goal, in the end he becomes the king of life, even if when he reaches his destination there is not one single earthly coin left to his name.

It is not earthly wealth that makes man rich. Riches come by discovering that gold mine which is hidden in the human heart, out of which comes the spirit of generosity. Someone asked the Prophet Muhammad whose virtue was the greatest: that of the pious soul who prays continually, that of the traveler who travels to make the holy pilgrimage, that of the one who fasts for nights and days, or that of the one who learns of scriptures by heart. "None of them," said the Prophet, "is so great as the soul who shows through life charity of heart."

*Ghairat,* protection or defence of honor, is considered by the wise a great quality, a chivalry that is found as a rule in rare souls. Man regardless of this sense is no better than a domestic animal, a dog or a cat. When their master does not want them he may scold them, drive them away, and they come again, wagging their tails, for there is no sense of pride to be hurt in them. They feel the discomfort of having to move from a comfortable place and they may also feel their master's displeasure, but there is no soreness about it. In man the sense of honor is developed; with his evolution it

Pir Vilayat Inayat Khan

develops more. It is not only necessary that man should be humble, but it is also necessary that he must be proud. Pride is the sign of evolution; honor comes out of pride. If there were no pride nor honor, virtue would not exist.

Very often people confuse ghairat, this sense of honor, with conceit, sometimes with jealousy; but even the spirit of jealousy, which stands to defend one's honor, can be no other than virtue. People call it conceit, but they do not know the meaning of honor, that in the sense of honor there is a divine spark hidden; for it is the perfection of honor that is the Logos, the Ego, whom the Sufis call *Kibria.*

No doubt when this sense of honor is developed without wisdom a person might become foolishly sensitive and not only defend his honor, but die for nothing, in illusion, just as the story of Othello suggests. For a man whose sense is developed in ghairat, his honor is not only in his person, but in his friend, in his beloved, in his mother, sister, or wife, in someone whom he respects or whom he loves or with whom he connects himself. This sense of ghairat has its light and shades in dealing with friends, in give and take. Very often people prefer death to dishonor, and from a finer point of view they have reason on their side. Those who are trying to their surroundings in life, who are a burden to their relations, a trouble to their friends, an annoyance to their acquaintances, a disgust to strangers, are the one who are lacking in this sense. This shows that the sense of ghairat developed makes one's life more harmonious, for an honorable man minds his own business, keeps himself out of the way, and troubles others less, even if he has to suffer more trouble for it.

There is a story that tells that four persons were arrested for the same crime and were taken before a wise king to be judged. He saw the first person and said, "Hang him." He saw the next person and sentenced him for life. He saw the third person and said, "He must be sent out of the country." He saw the fourth person and said, "I could never have expected you to commit such a crime." The first three underwent their punishments, but this last one went home and the next morning he was found dead; that one word of the king was worse than death to him.

Ghairat is a sign of noble birth, whatever condition man may be in. He may be in rags, yet this spirit of ghairat will shine out through all conditions, proving him to be noble. Humility has its place and pride has its place in life. In the place of pride, humility cannot be fitted. Once the Nizam of Hyderabad was walking in the country, and a knight happened to see a thorn stuck in his shoe. He rushed before the attendant had seen it and took out that thorn from the king's shoe. The king looked back and said, "Were there no attendants present? It was for them, not for you. Since you have taken this work, you can no longer continue to be my knight. Please retire." It is not by the humbleness of the surroundings that the king is exalted; it is the sense of honor expressed by his surroundings that makes a king a true king.

For a Sufi, who does not give his person a greater place than dust, the central theme of whose life is simplicity, and whose moral is humility, the sense of honor is not for his personality. Yet remember that the Sufi breathes the breath of God, so he is conscious of the honor of God. His pride is greater, therefore, than the pride of any man. It is in the intoxication of this pride that he proves to be God-conscious.

*Chapter 35.*


# CONVENTIONALITY AND
# THE SENSE OF SHAME


Conventionality is no doubt manmade, as art is manmade; but as in art there is the finishing of nature, so in conventionality there is the finishing of civilization. Conventionality is no doubt acquired, not inherited, but at the same time the love of conventionality is inherited also. Children born in families in which conventionality has existed for a long time are born with a tendency towards it and it becomes natural for them to learn it; also while learning they do not feel it to be foreign to their nature.

The extreme of all good and bad things is to be avoided. Nature has helped as far as that the soul is born on earth, and then comes education, in which is the fulfillment of the purpose of life. Conventionality is not the goal, and yet since it makes civilization it is a bridge that is connected with the goal of life. Conventionality loses its virtue, as do all things when they become void of sincerity, for sincerity is the soul of every virtue.

Now coming to the question, what is conventionality? It is a law of manner that is used in life for the convenience and comfort of man. All that is manmade is as imperfect as man. Therefore if one would try to discover the mistakes of conventionality, one could find them in every civilization existing at any period of history. Nevertheless, the most civilized at any period have been the most conventional people of the time.

During the age of aristocracy conventionality increased in every part of the world and became the main part of education for that time. And when revolt arose against the spirit of aristocracy, everything good and bad that aristocracy possessed was condemned. Whatever line of reform people in the world may adopt, they cannot be free from conventionality and yet progress. These two things cannot be separated. The only thing that can be done is to break one form of conventionality and build another form. Call the first form conventionality and the next bohemian life, it all comes to the same. There is one thing that must be considered, that freedom is the soul's purpose; and if, without hindering the conventionalities, one could rise above them, so as to breathe the breath of freedom, that would be the true democracy. Democracy void of culture and refinement can very well be called anarchy.

But there are two laws that, if one considers them deeply, will become useful in living the right life. One is to strive to achieve beauty, comfort, happiness, and peace in life for oneself; the other is sharing these things with others. That is where the necessity of conventionalities comes in. The one who is a slave to conventionality is a captive; the one who is the master of conventionality is the possessor of that kingdom of which it is said in the Bible, "Blessed are the meek, for they shall inherit the earth."

The word shame is used in all different languages, and the meaning of the word understood by different people is more or less the same. But the question what, really, the word shame means could be answered by saying that shame means want. A feeling that one has in oneself of wanting something to make up one's ideal gives that feeling which one calls shame. Or when one sees in another person something wanting, it is that which brings to one's mind that sense of want, and one expresses that sense by the word shame. It is interesting to notice that in the Persian language there is a word *kam* (which can also be pronounced as shame), the meaning of which is foolish, but whose true meaning is wanting.

The question arises whether the conception of shame is inherent or acquired. That is where the point of view of the mystic differs from the conception of modern psychology. While modern psychology says that all this is acquired, the Sufi will say it is inherent. The springing up of this sense in a child is worth noticing, and is of very great interest to a seer. When one sees it from a metaphysical point of view, from a spiritual point of view, it opens up a very vast field of thought before one. One learns by thinking about this sense of wanting that the human soul by nature is perfect and the life of limitation on earth is imperfection; therefore the soul continually sees wanting in itself and want in others, and becomes unhappy over it.

The soul who sees the want in others becomes unhappy over others. Therefore there will be no end to the unhappiness of that soul, for there will be no end to the want in this life of limitation. But the soul who sees the want in himself no doubt has a chance to gain all that which is wanting; although the more a soul advances the more it will find itself wanting.

It is therefore that the nobler the soul the more sense of shame it has, for that sense is wakened in it; and the lack of nobleness of spirit is signified by the lack of that sense. There is one person who fights against that sense, which in time becomes blunted; and he might feel happier for the moment, having the sense in him so blunted. However, the limitation is there. The sense of shame is a channel that leads to that goal which is called perfection. But no doubt the more it is wakened, the more one is subject to unhappiness.

And yet true happiness is in the realization of perfection, and therefore in the end he does not lose much, in spite of the apparent gains that come to the one who is shameless. In practical life in the midst of the world the shameless apparently has more ease of action and of movement likewise. The one who has the sense of shame awakened, for him life is difficult.

But the sense of shame living in the heart of man is like a pearl in a shell. As long as it is in the shell it may not fetch its price, but it is a pearl just the same. Whatever price the pearl fetches, the marketplace is not the place of the pearl; its real place is in the crown of the king. So a person with real, living quality may not always be appreciated, may have troubles in life; and yet sometime his qualities will fetch their proper price. And if they do not fetch the proper price, still there is no loss, for beauty in all its aspects is beyond price.

Where does man learn virtue? He learns it from that sense of shame. What develops in man virtue? It is again the same sense. Often this sense works as a sharp knife upon a feeling heart; but it only makes it a cut diamond. By this we come to a realization that what is most precious in life is feeling. If the feeling sense loses its sharpness, it is as if man, who is the salt of the earth, had lost savor; and there is nothing else from which it can be gained. In all times of the world's history, whenever a civilization has touched its summits, this sense was developed in the generality. For the heights of every civilization show the fineness of human feeling, which is the highest of all aspects of culture.

The manner of the saints has been to approach God with this feeling. It was this feeling that made the Prophet Muhammad cover himself with a mantle every time the thought of God came. It is the same feeling that gives a person modesty. And all the different forms of prayer have come from this inner tendency of man in the presence of the God of perfection.

*Chapter 36.*

# TROUBLE NOT ABOUT OTHERS

There is something that belongs to human nature whose origin is in curiosity, which gives a desire for knowledge. When this tendency is abused it develops into inquisitiveness. It is wonderful that the root of every defect is a right tendency, and it is the abuse of that right tendency that turns it into a defect. If we considered how little time we have to live on this earth, we would see that every moment of our life is precious, and that it should be given to something that is really worthwhile. When time is given to inquisitiveness, wanting to know about the affairs of others, one has wasted that time which could have been used for a much better purpose. Life has so many responsibilities and so many duties, and there is so much that one has to correct in oneself, so much that one has to undo in what one has done, and so much to attend to in one's affairs to make one's life right that it seems as if a person were intoxicated who leaves all his responsibilities and duties and occupies his mind and engages his ears in inquisitiveness.

Free will is given to enable one to attend to one's own duties and affairs and to gain one's own objects, and when that free will is used in trying to find out about others—the weaknesses of others, the lacks of others, the faults of others —one certainly abuses free will. Sometimes a person is inquisitive because of his interest in the lives of others, but very often a person is inquisitive because it is his illness. He may have no interest in the matter at all; it is only because he wants to satisfy himself by hearing and knowing about others. Self-knowledge is the ideal of the philosophers, not the knowledge of the lives of others.

There are two phases in a person's development, one phase when he looks at others and another phase when he looks at himself. When the first phase has ended and the next phase begun, then one starts one's journey to the desired goal. Rumi says, "Trouble not about others, for there is much for you to think of in yourself."

Besides this, it is a sign of great respect to the aged and to those one wishes to respect to show no tendency of knowing more than one is allowed to know. Even in such a close relationship as that of parents and children, when they respect the privacy of one another they certainly show therein a great virtue.

To want to know about another is very often a lack of trust. One who trusts does not need to unveil, does not need to discover what is covered. He who wishes to unveil something wishes to discover it. If there is anything that should be discovered first, it is the self. The time that one spends in discovering others, their lives, their faults, their weaknesses, one could just as well spend in discovering one's soul. The desire to know is born in the soul, but man should discern what must be known, what is worth knowing. There are many things not worth troubling about. When one devotes one's time and thought to trying to know what one need not know, one loses that opportunity that life offers to discover the nature and secret of the soul, in which lies the fulfillment of the purpose of life.

It must be remembered that one shows lack of nobleness of character by love of gossiping. It is so natural, and yet it is a great fault in the character to cherish the tendency to talk about others. One shows a great weakness when one makes remarks about someone behind his back. In the first place, it is against what may be called frankness. Also it is judging another, which is wrong according to the teaching of Christ, who says, "Judge not, that ye be not judged." When one allows this tendency to remain in one, one develops a love of talking about others. It is a defect that commonly exists, and when two people meet who have the same tendency, they gossip together. One helps the other, one encourages the other. And when something is supported by two people of necessity it becomes a virtue, if only for the time being.

How often man forgets that although he is talking about someone in his absence, yet it is spoken in the presence of God. God hears all things and knows all things. The Creator knows about His creatures, about their virtues and faults. God is displeased by hearing about the fault of His creature, as an artist would be displeased on hearing bad remarks made by anyone on his art. Even though he acknowledged the defect of his art, he would still prefer finding it himself, and not anyone else finding it. When a person speaks against someone his words may not reach the other, but his feelings reach him, and when he sees the person, he reads all he has said in his face, if he be sensitive and of keen sight. This world is a house of mirrors; the reflection of one is mirrored upon another. In this world where so many things seem hidden, in reality nothing remains hidden; everything some time or other rises to the surface and manifests itself to view.

How few in this world know what an effect talking ill of another has on one's personality, what influence it has on one's soul! Not only is man's self within like a dome where everything he says has an echo, but that echo is creative and productive of what has been said. Every good and bad thing in one's life one develops by taking interest in it. As long as every fault one has is small, one does not notice it, and so one develops the fault till it results in a disappointment. Life is so precious, and it becomes more and more valuable as one becomes more prudent; and every moment of life can be used for a much greater purpose. Life is an opportunity, and the more one realizes this the more one will make the best of this opportunity that life offers.

The best way of working in all ways of life, at home or outside, is noiseless working, a thing that is so little thought of by many and that is so necessary in creating order, harmony, and peace in life. Very often a person does little and speaks much about it. In doing every little thing he makes a noise, and thereby very often instead of finishing something successfully he attracts difficulties.

The first thing to be remembered in character-building is to understand the secret and character of human nature. We must know that every person in the world has his own object in life, his own interest, and his point of view, and that he is concerned with himself. His peace is disturbed when you wish to interest him in your object of interest. If you wish to force upon him your point of view, however near and dear he may be to you, he is not pleased with it. Very few consider this; and they wish to pour out their own troubles and difficulties upon someone near to them, thinking, "Everyone has the same interest in my subject as I myself, and everyone has the same point of view as myself, so everyone will be glad to hear my tale."

There is a story told that a person began to speak before a new acquaintance about his ancestors. He continued so long that the patience of his hearer was thoroughly exhausted. In the end the acquaintance interrupted the story by asking, "If I do not care to know about my own ancestors, what do I care to know about yours?" There are many who are very keen to let their neighbors know about every cold and cough they may have; every little gain or loss, however small, they would be glad to announce with drums and bugles. This is a childish quality; this tendency shows a child soul. Sometimes it frightens away friends and helps foes.

People who work noisily accomplish little, for they attract by their noise ten more people who come and interfere and spoil the work that one person could easily have finished.

Noisiness comes from restlessness, and restlessness is the sign of *tamas,* the destructive rhythm. Those who have made any success in life, in whatever direction, have done so by their quiet working. In business, in industry, in art, in science, in education, in politics, in all directions of life, the wise worker is the quiet worker. He tells about things when the time comes, not before. The one who talks about things before he has accomplished them is like a cook who is announcing dishes to the whole neighborhood before they are cooked.

There is a story told in the East of an enthusiastic servant. The master had a headache, and he told the servant to go and fetch some medicine from the chemist. The servant thought it would not be sufficient only to fetch medicine, so he also made an appointment with the doctor, and on his way home he visited the undertaker. The master asked, "Why are you so late?" The servant said, "Sir, I arranged everything." Enthusiasm is a great thing in life. It is creative and it is a key to success, but too much of it sometimes spoils things. The more wise a person, the more gentle he is in everything he does. A gentleman is the quiet man.

There is a fable that a donkey went to a camel and said, "Uncle, we shall be friends, we shall go grazing together." The camel said, "Child, I enjoy my walks alone." Said the donkey, "I am most eager to accompany you, Uncle." The good-natured camel consented to it, and they both went together. Long before the camel finished grazing, the donkey had finished and was eager to express himself. He said, "Uncle, I would like to sing, if you don't mind." The camel said, "Do not do such a thing. It will be a terrible thing for both you and me. I have not yet finished my dinner." The donkey had no patience; he could not control his joy and began to sing. A husbandman, attracted by his singing, came with a long bamboo. The donkey ran away, and all the thrashing fell upon the back of the camel. When the next morning the donkey went again to invite Uncle Camel, the camel said, "I am too ill, and your way is different and my way is different. From today we shall part."

There is such a great difference between the quiet person and a noisy person. One is like a grown-up person, the other like a restless child. One constructs, the other destroys. A quiet way of working must be practiced in everything. By making too much ado about nothing one creates commotion and disturbance in the atmosphere; useless activity without any result. One also finds noise in the tendency to exaggeration, when someone wants to make a mountain out of a molehill. Modesty, humility, gentleness, meekness—all such virtues are manifest in the person who works quietly through life.

If one asked, "What is modesty?" it is difficult to explain in words. It is a feeling that rises from a living heart; the heart that is dead has not the taste of it. The modest person compared to the immodest one is like a plant standing by the side of a rock. If the heart of the immodest one is like the earth, the heart of the modest one is like the water. Modesty is life itself; a life that is conscious of its beauty, inclined to veil it in all its forms, is modesty. At the same time, modesty is the proof of sincerity and of prudence. The firecracker cries aloud, "I am the light," and is finished in a moment. The diamond, shining in its light constantly, never says a word about its light.

Modesty is not necessarily timidity or cowardice. The bravest can be modest, and it is modesty that completes bravery. Modesty is the veil over the face of the great, for the most modest is God Himself, who is not seen by anyone except those intimate with Him. Beauty in all its forms and colors, in all its phases and spheres, doubles itself, enriches itself by modesty. Modesty is not something that is learned. It is in nature, for it is natural. Modesty not only covers what is beautiful and amplifies its beauty, but it covers all that is void of beauty, in this manner fitting it into all that which is beautiful. A noble heart can even rise to such a degree of modesty that he would plead for another person's fault, trying to make out of it no fault, even knowing that it is a fault.

Yes, a modest person very often will not raise his voice, out of dignity, or say a thing, out of consideration and respect; will not argue and pull his own weight when dealing with someone who has no thought of modesty. In this case he may often lose his battle. However, one cannot hope always to ascend and descend at the same time. One should ascend sacrificing all that those who ascend will achieve. Life always demands sacrifices. In every walk of life there is a battle to be fought; and in the case of the one who loves to ascend, he may just as well ascend rather than want to descend. The Prophet Muhammad said, *Al hayya wa'l iman,* "Verily, modesty is a great piety."

*Chapter 37.*

# OPTIMISM AND PESSIMISM

Optimism represents the spontaneous flow of love; optimism also represents trust in love. This shows that it is love trusting love that is optimism. Pessimism comes from disappointment, from a bad impression that continues to be a hindrance on the path. Optimism gives a hopeful attitude to life, while with pessimism one sees darkness on one's path. No doubt sometimes pessimism shows conscientiousness and cleverness, and it may also show experience. But conscientiousness alone will never be enough to overcome the difficulties one meets in one's life; it is trust that solves life's problems. The wise have understood that cleverness does not reach far; it goes a certain distance and then no further, for cleverness is knowledge that belongs to the earth. And as to experience, what is man's experience? One is only proud of one's experience until one has seen how vast the world is. In every line of work and thought there is no moment when experience is not needed, but the further man goes in experience the more he sees how little he knows.

The psychological effect of optimism is such that it helps to bring success, for it is by the spirit of optimism that God has created the world. Optimism comes from God, and pessimism is born from the heart of man. By what little experience of life he has, man learns, "This will not succeed, that will not do, this will not come right." For the one who is optimistic it does not matter if it does not come right in the end; he will take his chance. For what is life? Life is an opportunity, and to the optimistic person this opportunity is a promise, while for the pessimistic person this opportunity is lost. It is not that the Creator makes man lose it, it is man himself who fails to seize the opportunity.

Many people prolong an illness by giving way to pessimistic thoughts. One will often find that for those who have suffered for many years from a certain illness, that illness becomes so real that its absence seems unnatural. They believe illness to be their nature, and its absence is something they do not know. In that way they keep the illness in themselves. Then there are pessimistic people who think that misery is their lot in life, that they were born to be wretched, that they cannot be anything else but unhappy, that heaven and earth are against them; but they themselves are their misery, and pessimism belongs to them. Man's life depends upon the object of his concentration, so if he concentrates upon his misery, he must be miserable. A person who has a certain habit of which he does not approve often thinks he is helpless before it as it is his nature. But nothing is man's nature except what he makes for himself. As the whole of nature is made by God, so the nature of each individual is made by himself; and as the Almightly has the power to change His nature, so the individual is capable of changing his nature. Among all the creatures of this world, man has the most right to be optimistic, for man represents God on earth, God as Judge, as Creator, and as Master of all His creation. Man is master of his life, of his own affairs—if he only knew it.

A man with optimism will help another who is drowning in the sea of fear and disappointment; while on the contrary, if someone who is ill or downhearted comes to a pessimistic person, the pessimist will pull him down and make him sink to the depths along with himself. On the side of the one is life; on the side of the other is death. The one climbs to the top of the mountain; the other descends to the depths of the earth. Is there any greater helper in sorrow or misfortune, when every situation in life seems dark, than the spirit of optimism that knows that all will be well? It is no exaggeration to say that the very spirit of God comes to man's rescue in the form of the optimistic spirit.

It does not matter how hard a situation in life may be: however great the difficulties, they can all be surmounted. But a person's own pessimistic spirit weighs him down when he is already at a low ebb. Death is preferable to being weighed down in misery by a pessimistic spirit, and the greatest reward there can be in the world is the spirit of optimism, while the greatest punishment that can be given to man for his worst sin is pessimism. Verily, the one who is hopeful in life will succeed.

There are two attitudes that divide people into two sections. The one is an ever-complaining attitude, and the other is an ever-smiling attitude. Life is the same: call it good, call it bad, call it right, call it wrong, it is what it is; it cannot be otherwise. A person complains in order to get the sympathy of others and to show them his good points; sometimes in order to show himself as more just, more intelligent, and also in the right. He complains about everything: about friends and about foes, about those he loves, and much more about those he hates. He complains from morning till evening, and there is never an end to his complaint. It can increase to such an extent that the weather is not good and the air is not good and the atmosphere is not good; he is against both earth and sky, and everything everybody does is wrong. At last it reaches the stage where that person begins to dislike his own works and it culminates when he dislikes himself. In this way he grows to be against others, against conditions, and in the end against himself.

Do not imagine that this is a character rarely to be found in the world. It is a character you frequently meet with, and certainly the one who has this attitude is his own worst enemy. The person with a right attitude of mind tries to make even wrong right, but the one with a wrong attitude of mind will turn even right into wrong. Besides, magnetism is the need of every soul; the lack of it makes life burdensome. The tendency of seeing wrong in everything robs one to a great extent of that magnetism which is needed very much in life. For the nature of life is such that naturally the multitude only accepts those who come to it with the power of magnetism, and casts out everyone else. In other words, the world is a place you cannot enter without a pass of admission, and that pass of admission is magnetism; the one who does not possess it will be refused everywhere.

Besides, you will find many who are always complaining about their health. There may be good reason, but sometimes there may be very little reason, too little indeed to speak of. When once a person has become accustomed to answer despondently when sympathetically asked, "How are you?" he certainly waters the plant of illness in himself by this complaining tendency. Our life of limitation in the world, the nature of this world's comforts and pleasures which are so changeable and unreliable, and the falseness that one finds in everything everywhere—if one complained about it, a whole lifetime would be too short to complain about it fully; every moment of our life would become filled with complaints. But the way out is to look at the cheerful side of it, the bright side. Especially for those who seek God and truth there is something else to think about. They need not think how bad a person is, when they think who is behind this person, who is in his heart, then they will look at life with hope. When we see things that are wrong, if we only give thought to this, that behind all workings there is God, who is just and perfect, then we will certainly become hopeful.

The attitude of looking at everything with a smile is the sign of the saintly soul. A smile give to a friend or even to an enemy will win him over in the end; for this is the key to the heart of man. As the sunshine from without lights the whole world, so the sunshine from within, if it were raised up, would illuminate the whole life, in spite of all the seeming wrongs and in spite of all limitations. God is happiness; the soul is happiness; the spirit is happiness. There is no place for sadness in the kingdom of God. That which deprives man of happiness deprives him of God and of truth.

One can begin to learn to smile by appreciating every little good thing that comes one's way through life, and by overlooking every bad thing that one does not like to see. Be not troubled too much about unnecessary things in life that give nothing but displeasure. But looking at life with a hopeful attitude of mind, with an optimistic view, it is this that will give one the power of turning wrong into right and bringing light into the place where all is darkness. Cheerfulness is life; sulkiness is death. Life attracts, death repulses. The sunshine that comes from the soul, rises through the heart, and manifests itself in man's smile is indeed the light from the heavens. In that light many flowers grow and many fruits become ripe.

*Chapter 38.*

# HAPPINESS

Does happiness depend upon circumstances or upon our outlook on life? This is a question that is often asked and is most difficult to answer. Many with some philosophical knowledge will say that this material world is an illusion and its conditions a dream, yet there are very few who can make themselves believe it. To know a thing in theory is different from practicing it. It is very difficult to rise above the effect that conditions produce. No doubt there is only one thing that helps us to rise above conditions, and that is a change of outlook on life; and this change is made possible by a change of attitude.

Happiness is a flourishing condition of the soul. A child who has started by being ill-mannered, hurtful, and destructive will attract the same power, and the same things will happen to it. Whatever the child gives out will rebound. How many people are acquainted with this fact? They never think that they can be hurt by their own words, their own action, thought, or feeling; they go on, and then in time it all comes back to them, sweeping them off the ground of happiness.

In Sanskrit life in the world is called *samsara.* It is pictured as living in a mist. One thinks and says and does and feels, yet all the time one does not fully know why. If a person knows one reason for it, there is another reason hidden behind it that he does not yet know. Very often conditions in life give the effect of captivity; sometimes it seems as if one has to walk between a river and a precipice. To rise above conditions one needs wings, which not everyone has. Two wings are attached to the soul: one is independence, the other indifference. It takes a great deal of sacrifice before one can feel independent in life, and indifference is against one's nature of love and sympathy. It is as if one had to cut one's heart in two before being able to practice indifference throughout life. No doubt once the soul is able to spread its wings one sees the conditions of life as being far removed; then one stands above all conditions that make man captive.

There is no difficulty that cannot be surmounted sooner or later, but even if one has achieved something one desires in life there always remains something else that seems to be incomplete; and so if a person goes from one thing to another, achieving all he desires, the objects of his desire will multiply and there will never be an end to it. The more he has to do in life the more difficulties he must meet with, and if he keeps away from the life of the world then his being here is purposeless. The more important the task, the more difficult is its accomplishment. And so the evening follows the day, and this goes on till eternity.

For a Sufi, therefore, not only is patience to bear all things necessary to relieve him momentarily from difficulty and pain, but also seeing all things from a certain point of view. Very often it is the outlook that changes a person's whole life. It can turn hell into heaven; it can turn sorrows into joy. When a person looks from a certain point of view, every little pinprick feels like the point of a sword piercing his heart; but when he looks at the same thing from a different point of view, the heart becomes sting-proof. Nothing can touch it and all the things that are thrown at him like stones drop down without having touched him.

What is the meaning of walking upon the water? Life can be symbolized as water: there is one who drowns in the water, there is another who swims in it, but there is still another who walks upon it. The one who is so sensitive that he is unhappy all day and night is of the first category. The one who takes and gives back, making a game of life, is the swimmer. He does not mind if he receives one knock, for he derives satisfaction from being able to give two knocks in return. But the one whom nothing can touch is in the world and yet above the world. He is the one who walks on the water; life is under his feet, both its joy and sorrow. Verily, independence and indifference are the two wings that enable the soul to fly.

*Chapter 39.*

# SUBTLETY

Subtlety of nature is the sign of the intelligent. If a person takes the right direction he does good with this wealth of intelligence, but a person who is going in a wrong direction may abuse this great faculty. When someone who is subtle by nature is compared with the personality that is devoid of it, it is like comparing the river and the mountain. The subtle personality is as pliable as running water; everything that comes before that personality is reflected in it as clearly as an image in the pure water. The rock-like personality, without subtlety, is like a mountain; it reflects nothing. Many admire plain speaking, but the reason is that they lack an understanding of subtlety. Can all things be put into words? Is there not anything more fine, more subtle than spoken words? The person who can read between the lines makes a book out of one letter. Subtlety of perception and subtlety of expression are the signs of the wise. Wise and foolish are distinguished by fineness on the part of the one and rigidness on the part of the other. A person devoid of subtlety wants truth to be turned into a stone, but the subtle one will turn even a stone into truth.

In order to acquire spiritual knowledge, receive inspiration, prepare one's heart for inner revelation, one must try to make one's mentality pliable like water rather than like a rock. For the further along the path of life's mystery a person will journey, the more subtle he will have to become in order to perceive and to express the mystery of life. God is a mystery; His knowledge is a mystery; life is a mystery; human nature is a mystery: in short, the depth of all knowledge is a mystery, even that of science or art.

All that is more mysterious is more deep. What all the prophets and masters have done in all ages is to express that mystery in words, in deeds, in thoughts, in feelings. But most of the mystery is expressed by them in silence, for then the mystery is in its place. To bring the mystery down to earth is like pulling a king down onto the ground from his throne; but allowing the mystery to remain in its own place, in the silent spheres, is like giving homage to the King to whom all homage is due.

Life's mysteries apart, in little things of everyday life the fewer words used, the more profitable it is. Do you think more words explain more? No, not at all. It is only nervousness on the part of those who wish to say a hundred words to explain a thing that can quite well be explained in two words; and on the part of the listener it is lack of intelligence when he wants a hundred words in order to understand something that can just as well be explained in one word. Many think that more words explain things better; but they do not know that mostly as many words as are spoken, so many veils are wrapped around the idea. In the end you go out by the same door through which you entered.

Respect, consideration, reverence, kindness, compassion, sympathy, forgiveness, and gratefulness—all these virtues can be best adorned by subtlety of expression. One need not dance in thanksgiving; one word of thanks is quite sufficient. One need not cry out loudly, "I sympathize with you, my dear friend!" One need not play drums and say, "I have forgiven somebody!" Such things are fine, subtle; they are to be felt; no noise can express them. Noise only spoils their beauty and takes away from their value. In spiritual ideas and thoughts subtlety is more needed that in anything else. If a spiritual person were to bring his realizations into the marketplace and dispute with everyone who came along about his beliefs and disbeliefs, where would he end?

What makes a spiritual person harmonize with all people in the world? The key to the art of conciliation that a spiritual person possesses is subtlety both in perception and expression. Is it lack of frankness, is it hypocrisy to be subtle? Not in the least. There are many people who are outspoken, always ready to tell the truth in a way that is like hitting another person on the head, and who proudly support their frankness by saying, "I do not mind if it makes anybody sorry or angry, I only tell the truth." If the truth is as hard as a hammer may truth never be spoken, may no one in the world follow such a truth!

Then where is that truth which is peace-giving, which is healing, which is comforting to every heart and soul, that truth which uplifts the soul, which is creative of harmony and beauty, where is that truth born? That truth is born in subtlety of intelligence in thought, speech, and action; of fineness that brings pleasure, comfort, beauty, harmony, and peace.

*Chapter 40.*

# THE SMILING FOREHEAD

By forehead I mean a person's expression, which depends solely upon his attitude to life. Life is the same for the saint and for Satan; and if their lives are different it is only because of their outlook on life. The same life is turned by the one into heaven and by the other into hell.

There are two attitudes: to one all is wrong; to the other all is right. Our life in the world from morning to evening is full of experiences, good and bad, which can be distinguished according to their degree; and the more we study the mystery of good and bad, the more we see that there really is no such thing as good and bad. It is because of our attitude and conditions that things seem good or bad to us.

It is easy for an ordinary person to say what is good or bad, just or unjust; it is very difficult for a wise person. Everyone, according to his outlook on life, turns things from bad to good and from good to bad, because everyone has his own grade of evolution and he reasons accordingly. Sometimes one thing is subtler than others, and then it is difficult to judge. There was a time when Wagner's music was not understood, and another time when he was considered the

© Sujan Singh Uban 1977. Courtesy of East-West Publications.

Baba Sita Ram Das Onkarnath

greatest of musicians. Sometimes things are good in themselves, but our own evolution makes them seem not so good to us. What one considered good a few years ago may not seem good at a later evolution. A child appreciates a doll most; later he will prefer the work of great sculptors.

This proves that at every step and degree of evolution man's idea of good and bad changes, and thus when one thinks about it one will understand that there is no such thing as right and wrong. If there is right, then all is right. No doubt there is a phase when man is a slave of what he has himself made right or wrong; but there is another phase in which he is master. This mastery comes from his realization of the fact that right and wrong are made by man's own attitude to life; and then right and wrong, good and bad will be his slaves, because he knows that it is in his power to turn the one into the other.

This opens the door to another mystery of life that shows that as there is duality in each thing, so there is duality in every action. In everything that is just, something unjust is hidden, and in everything that is bad, something good. Then one begins to see how the world reacts to all one's actions: one person sees only the good and another only the bad. In Sufi terms this particular attitude is called *hairat*, bewilderment; and while to the average man theatres, moving pictures, and bazaars are interesting, to the Sufi the whole of life is interesting, a constant vision of bewilderment. He cannot explain this to the world, because there are no words to explain it.

Can one compare any joy to that of taking things quietly, patiently, and easily? All other joys come from outer sources, but this happiness is one's own property. When a person arrives at this feeling, it expresses itself not in words but in the "smiling forehead."

There is another side to this subject, which is that man is pleased to see the one he loves and admires and respects; and if he frowns at someone, it is because it is someone he does not admire or respect. Love is the divine essence in man and is due to God alone, and love for man is a lesson, a first step forward to the love of God. In human love one begins to see the way to divine love, as the lesson of domestic life is learnt by the little girl playing with her dolls. One learns this lesson by loving one person, a friend, a beloved father, mother, brother, sister, or teacher. But love is wrongly used when it is not constantly developing and spreading. The water of a pond may turn bad, but the water of a river remains pure because it is progressing; and thus by sincerely loving one person, one should rear the plant of love and make it grow and spread at the same time.

Love has done its work when a man becomes all love— his atmosphere, his expression, every movement he makes. And how can such a man love one and refuse another? His very countenance and presence become a blessing. In the East, when people speak of saints or sages, it is not because of their miracles, it is because of their presence and their countenance, which radiate vibrations of love; and this love expresses itself in tolerance, in forgiveness, in respect, in overlooking the faults of others. Their sympathy covers the defects of others as if they were their own; they forget their own interest in the interest of others. They do not mind what circumstances they are in, be they high or humble; their foreheads are smiling. In their eyes everyone is the expression of the Beloved, whose name they repeat. They see the divine in all forms and beings.

Just as the religious person has a religious attitude in a temple, so the Sufi has that attitude before every being, for to him every being is the temple of the divine. Therefore he is always before his Lord. Whether a servant, a master, a friend, or a foe is before him, he is in the presence of God. For the one whose God is in the high heavens, there is a vast gulf between him and God; but the one who has God always before him is always in God's presence, and there is no end to his happiness.

The idea of the Sufi is that however religious a person may be, without love he is nothing. It is the same with one who has studied thousands of books: without love, he has learnt nothing. And love does not reside in a claim to love; when love is born one hears its voice louder than the voice of man. Love needs no words; they are too inadequate to express it. The small fashion in which love can express itself is what the Persians call the "smiling forehead."

# PART IV
# THE DIVINE MANNER

*Chapter 41.*

# DEITY AND DIVINITY

When distinguishing between these two concepts I should say that deity is God idealized and divinity is God personified. Deity has never been manifest on the physical plane except in the heart of man, but divinity has manifested in the physical form. Thus the secret of deity can be sought in the heart of divinity. Divinity is reduced God and enlarged man. The whole difficulty that has occurred in all periods of the world's history has been the difficulty of understanding divinity or apprehending the mystery of divinity. Man cannot think of man being God, nor can man think of God being man. Therefore the claimant of divinity has sometimes been called God, but then he was kept remote and aloof from human beings. At other times the claimant of divinity has been brought to earth and called no better than man.

In reality divinity is the expansion of the human soul; divinity is human nature in God. That is why God is one, the Only Being. But there are as many deities as there are human beings, for the deity is the enshrined God whom man has conceived by his thoughts and ideas. God is enshrined in his heart, and in that way the ideas about deity came to

differ. Some say God is the Judge and some say God is the
Father; some say God is the Creator, while to others He is
the Sustainer. Some say that God has three aspects, and that
a trinity makes God; some say gods are many. The Hindus
conceived thirty-three score *devata,* which means divinities.
The Chinese conceived numberless gods.

The believers in one God have ridiculed them, but in fact
it is one and the same conception looked at from different
points of view. Somebody can be praised by one and hated
by another, and ten people may all have a different idea of
the same person, because each understands him according to
his state of evolution. Each sees that person according to his
own point of view; each looks at him through his own eyes.
Therefore the same person is different to each being. In the
mind of one the person is a sinner; in the mind of another
he is a saint. The same person who is considered gentle and
good by one is considered the opposite by another. If this
can be so in connection with a living being, it is equally
possible that various ideas of the deity should be formed in
each heart, and that each soul should mold his own deity
according to his own evolution and his way of idealizing and
understanding. Therefore the deity of every heart is different and is as that person has imagined. But the God of every
soul is one and the same, whatever people imagine. It is the
same God that they all imagine, but their imaginations are
different. It is the lack of understanding of this that has
caused the differences in religion.

We read in the books of the past that there used to be
blood feuds, family feuds, because one family believed in
one God and another family had another, they called Him
a family God. These families used to fight with one another
because of their separate Gods, and they gave their lives for
their God. It is not very different even now when nations
fight against nations; for the time being the God of each
becomes different, or at least the people think the hostile
country is not doing the will of their own God. Man is very
much the same down the ages; he only shows his evolution
by degrees.

The deity is pictured sometimes as a spirit, sometimes as a person, sometimes as a king, sometimes as a master. The Hindus picture the deity as Creator, as Sustainer, and as Destroyer. The word divine comes from *deva,* God, and the word deva is derived from *div,* which means light. Every soul is itself a light, but a light that is surrounded by clouds, which have risen from the earthly impressions and surrounded the human heart. These clouds keep the soul covered, but the deva or div is always there.

One reads in the Bible that no one should keep his light under a bushel, and the hint to raise the light high shows us that deva or the divine spark is within man; that divinity, even when it is human, is infinite. But the expansion of this light and its disclosing are necessary. The prophets and great avatars, the messengers who have come to the world from time to time, have been examples of the expansion of this divine spark, and what they gave to the world has been the outcome of this divinity.

Divinity is like the seed that grows in the heart of the flower: it is the same seed that was the origin of that plant, and it comes again in the heart of the flower. In a similar way the same God, who was unmanifested as the seed of the plant of this creation, rises again towards fulfillment; and in that fulfillment He produces the seed in the heart of that flower which is divinity. Some religious authorities have tried to recognize the divinity of Christ while ignoring the divinity of humanity: they have tried to make Christ different from what may be called human. But by doing so they have not been able to keep the flame alight, for they have covered the main truth that religion had to give to the world, which was that divinity resides in humanity, that divinity is the outcome of humanity, and that humanity is the flower in the heart of which divinity was born as a seed. By this they have not done any good to religion; on the contrary, they have harmed religion, trying to make man something different, not knowing that all is in man—angel, djinn, and animal.

There is nothing that is not in man; for instance things

belonging to the earth such as metals—gold and silver, iron and steel—are all to be found in the body and mind of man. The one who knows alchemy can make use of it; he can make out of man a man of flesh, and he can make out of man a man of gold. And what is that stone that is called the philosopher's stone? It is the heart of the divine man: whomever it touches it turns into gold. All living beings—creatures high and low, creatures of the water, creatures of the forest, creatures that fly in the air, insects and worms; their nature, their character, their form—all can be found in man. The character of the bull, the character of the fish, the character of the insect, the character of all the animals can be seen in man. All that we can discover by going through the forest for thousands of miles we can find in one human personality. All is there. It only needs to be seen, and he can see it whose heart's eyes are open. Many in this world have their external eyes open but yet are asleep; they are moving about and think they are alive, but there is something in them that is not awakened, and so they cannot see the great treasure that is hidden.

Again, jewels, precious minerals, and pearls can all be found in man—in his character, in his external and inner being. All this is hidden—but we can discover a pearl in a person; we can see in the heart of man a diamond or an emerald. All the jewels of this world are there if only we can see it. And not only that, not only worldly treasures but all the heavenly things are there. Man represents the planets, he represents the sun and moon, he represents heaven and its angels; what does man not represent? He represents God. In that sense one may call man a miniature God, and it is the development of humanity that culminates in divinity; thus Christ is the example of the culmination of humanity. It would be hiding the greatest human virtue to hide this secret, which is the key to the mystery of the whole universe.

No doubt compared with God divinity is the imperfection of God, but it is still the perfection of man. It is just like a drop of water that is entirely and absolutely water, and yet it is a drop in comparison with the ocean. The ocean is God, but the drop is divine. If man had understood this secret of life, no wars or differences would have arisen among the followers of the various religions, who in all ages waged wars against one another's religious ideas. No prophet or master at any time would have been rejected or tortured or refused, if the world had only known this: that God always comes, that He always shows himself through the heart of the godly. The comparison of the divine with God is just like a sunglass placed before the sun. The sunglass partakes of the heat of the sun and transfers the heat to the earth, and so the divine man, the messenger in all ages, comes and partakes of God's rays and hands them down to earth in the form of the divine message.

Although a sunglass is not the sun, yet when it is exposed to the sun it partakes of the sun and begins to show the quality of the sun. And so it is with the souls who focus their hearts on God, for then God becomes reflected in their heart. The beauty and power which are to be found in God in their perfection begin to show themselves in those souls, just as the sun shows in the sunglass. They express God's qualities in their lives. The Sufis call this *akhlak-e Allah:* the divine manner. One cannot teach this manner; it comes when the heart is focused on God, and then all that is in God becomes manifest in man. When this realization comes one cannot speak anymore of the God within; then God is within and without at the same time. As soon as God is realized He does not remain within. It is before realization that God is to be found within, and this will help one to find the perfection of God, but once God is realized He is in all.

There are ages of aristocracy, and there are ages of democracy of all kinds, not only in regard to government, but also in regard to religion. And as it is natural that aristocracy should be misunderstood, so it is natural that democracy should be demoralized by the ignorant, who can only understand the outer meaning of democracy. Aristocracy of religion is belief in God, worship of God in a certain form (in the form of prayer or service, of ceremonial or ritual, whatever the form may be), and also its recognition and acceptance when it is given by an actual man; not only that, but the recognition of the illumination that completes its development in the soul of man. The Zoroastrians by their sun worship taught that the sun represents the light of the spirit, and so the son of God represents the light of God; but others misunderstood it and took it to mean something different. The son of God is he who discovers and is conscious of his inheritance from God, and not of that from man. One who is conscious of his earthly origin is an earthly man; one who is conscious of his heavenly origin is the son of God.

Man is that of which he is conscious. Man's grade of evolution depends upon the pitch he has attained; it is a certain pitch which makes him conscious of a certain phase of life. A person standing upon the earth cannot enjoy the purity of the air that exists at the top of the mountain; in order to enjoy it he must be there. That is why an insincere claim has no effect. A man who is standing upon the earth and is talking about air is talking nonsense. It will have no effect because he does not know what is in the air. He must rise to where the air is and then he must get the experience and talk from there of what he is experiencing. Then it will have an effect, because then his word is sincere. It is not by theory that a person can trace his origin; he can only do so by practice. It is not only knowing a thing but living it and being it, and this is not easy. But there is no need to separate Christ from other people for the very reason that one man is so far above the other. There is such a great gulf between the evolution of one soul and that of another that if one were to say that one man is standing on the earth and another is in the sky it would be quite right.

There is, however, no doubt that the aristocratic form of religion has also been misused. This happens when the religious authority turns religion into a means, an instrument with which to keep the people under a certain law for worldly purposes. Then naturally that aristocracy breaks down and there comes a time of democracy. And it is necessary that religious democracy should come, because it is in religious democracy that fulfillment of the religious ideal lies.

Religious democracy means that no one should ever think that he is human while someone else is divine, and that God is in heaven, unattainable, imperceptible, and far away from his soul. He must realize that divinity is in his soul, that God is within him, that he is linked with God and that God is linked with him, that his soul can expand because he is not different from God nor is God different from him. Only the danger of democracy is that when it comes too soon, before a person is ripe, then it brings disaster; for man's natural progress is to follow his highest ideal, but when he is blinded by the spirit of democracy he becomes so agitated that he wishes to break that ideal. In this way he works to his own disadvantage. He comes down instead of going up, and so it has been in all ages and with all nations and races.

The ideal must be held before us that the main purpose of life is to ennoble our soul, and that religion means to observe, to appreciate, to recognize, to respect, and to heed the ennobled soul; to learn not with the thought of following but with the ideal of becoming that which our soul recognizes as lofty and beautiful; realizing the possibility of touching that point which is attracting our soul as the light of the port attracts those who travel on the sea, giving us hope, inviting us, and telling us that the port is there.

*Chapter 42.*

# MAN'S LIFE

As man is ideal among the lower and higher creatures, among the visible as well as the invisible beings, his life, among those of all beings of the universe, is a great privilege to experience. In life man goes through two periods, that of light and that of darkness. During the period of darkness he ceases to think wherefrom he has come, where he is going, and why he is sent here to wander for a while: whether he is sent by someone or whether he came of his own will, and whether he will be here forever or whether some day his life will be extinguished; where he was before he knew himself, and where he will be hereafter. Man, by his experience of life through his senses, binds himself by a spell of greed. What he enjoys once he wants to have over and over again, and he develops this greed so much that he sacrifices others for neighbors and neighbors for surroundings and surroundings for the self. Thus he lives for self and works for self until darkness overwhelms him so much that he can satisfy neither others nor himself. The masters of humanity have prescribed only one remedy to remove this darkness, and that is charity, by the practice of which a person's sympathy

264

is broadened from his own self to the whole world. He then becomes the friend of all. In this way man journeys towards the light, and before his eyes the truth of existence is revealed. Every thing and being in life speaks with him, and he knows the language of man, beast, and bird, and even of all things in the universe. Then he realizes the illusion of his self and of the universe. His enlightened soul wants to be purified from this illusion. Therefore, by practicing wisely abstinence and control, with the help of sound, a Sufi journeys gradually towards the eternal goal.

On the journey towards the goal a *mureed* (disciple) passes through the same planes and phases that he has crossed once before and that he has had hidden in his nature all the time. A mureed commences his journey towards the goal owing to the grief and helplessness caused by contact with the world, which signifies old age. Then he becomes thoughtful in every action and move, representing middle age. In this he feels much more responsible through life, more so than a middle-aged person burdened with the responsibilities of a home. After this he enjoys a freshness, a perpetual youth increasing within him every moment of his life. Then he develops a childlike nature, regardless of the opinion of others, reveling in his playfulness. In the end he develops innocence, acquiring the qualities of an infant who is the friend of all, the enemy of no one, and who is pure from all the troubles and worries of life.

A mureed has to journey from the human plane to the animal plane, which he shows by the strength and power that he absorbs from that sphere. He feels much more vitality and experiences perfect health. He is naturally more inclined toward all material activites. A slight annoyance causes him irritation and anger. He is ready to fight for what he considers true. Then he becomes like an herbivorous animal. He serves another like a horse or a camel, not asking by what right he is controlled, and then he grows even like a sheep or a goat, living in a herd, hanging his head down by the weight of his thought, ready at any time to be sacrificed for the benefit of another. He then develops a bird-like nature and floats in the spheres of imagination, quite unconscious of the earth and its surrounding. He seeks the society of those of a like interest, just as a bird would be with a bird, and makes his home on high, in the world of thought, as the nest of a bird is in the top of a tree. He advances still further and becomes as an insect, admiring the immanence of God in nature and absorbing rapture from divine wisdom, just like a bee gathering honey from flowers. Like a moth he concentrates on and hovers round the light, until his self is sacrificed in the vision of his love. In the end he becomes like a germ, an object lying at the feet of the walker; anybody may walk upon him who so chooses. He cares for neither light nor knowledge, for he has passed far beyond all that.

A mureed then continues his return journey through the vegetable kingdom. He adopts harmlessmess, usefulness, the medicinal and healing properties, and self-sacrifice for the purpose of another—all such qualities of the vegetable. He shows in his personality the sweetness of the fruit; the perfume, color, and delicacy of a flower. Then he acquires the quality of the rock, when it has no effect upon him for what purpose he may be used, whether to crown a dome or for the base of a building. Neither climate nor day nor night can make any difference to him; neither sorrow nor joy can touch him; he becomes free from all effects. Then a mureed arrives to a condition where he sojourns in a star, planet, the moon or sun; in other words he himself becomes soul. His star quality brightens him; his planet quality produces within him a world of his own; his moon quality becomes the receiver of all divine light; and his sun quality produces in his voice, word, and glance the power of illumination.

The Sufi in his further journey also acquires the quality of *insan*, the wise one, for man cannot be insan until he realizes the nature of the world and the motive of life. Then he attains the life of the djinn, experiencing joy in knowledge, becoming free from lust. Afterwards he adopts the quality of *ghilman*, when he creates the vision of heaven within himself. Next he acquires the all-pervading quality of sound, communicating with all hearts and souls in the universe with whom he would wish. He also becomes a spirit in all its aspects. Then a Sufi acquires the quality of consciousness, being conscious and awakened in every phase of life, until he acquires the quality of unconsciousness, when he can become unaware of all signs of life. Generally many obstacles stand in the way of a Sufi during his journey. The tendency for comfort and the desire for lust; diseases; conceit; lunacy followed by an extreme interest in ecstasy; besides a curiosity for phenomena; the desire for the world's attention and adoration from the surroundings; a tendency toward a spiritual appearance; a habit of foretelling; and readiness in healing—all hinder a Sufi's progress.

Charity, independence, forgiveness, indifference, tolerance, and detachment are most useful attributes. Resignation to the will of God, together with a continuous stream of love and a constant vision of God is the quality most necessary during the journey towards the goal. An impartial justice, a sense of harmony, and a real inclination for peace are the qualities necessary for the traveler on this path.

*Chapter 43.*

# THE DIVINE ART

People belonging to different faiths very often make the mistake of considering art as something outside of religion. The fact is that the whole creation is the art of the Creator, and one sees the perfection of His art in divine man. This shows that the source of the whole creation has the spirit of art at the back of it.

In all ages man has developed his artistic faculty, and he has tried to progress in art. But in the end, where does he arrive? He remains far from touching either the beauty of nature or the art of creation. Man's art always fails to equal the art of God.

This shows that the source of every soul is the spirit of art, and art is spirit. Everything that has come out from that spirit has manifested in the form of art. Did man look more at nature—the heavens; the beauty of the stars and planets; the clouds; the sun, its rising and setting and its zenith; the waxing and waning of the moon; the different shades of color that we can see in the sky—man would always marvel at the art at work behind it all.

When one is alone with nature, near the the sea, on the river bank, among the mountains, in the forest, in the wilderness, a feeling comes over one that is never felt among a crowd, not even if one were in the crowd for years. In one moment a feeling is born, as soon as one is face to face with the true art of God. It then seems as if the soul has seen something that it has always admired and worshipped. The soul now begins to recognize One whom she has always silently worshipped, and the presence of that mighty Creator, that Artist, is realized through seeing His art. Many experience this, but few will express it. None can come back from such an experience without a deep impression, without something having been awakened to consciousness through having seen the divine art.

This shows that this creation, this manifestation that is before us, has not been made mechanically, has not been created blindly or unconsciously. As the great poet of Persia, Sa'adi, says, "The more one looks at nature, the more one begins to feel that there is a perfection of wisdom, a perfect skill behind it, which has made it. It will take numberless years for mankind to imitate that art. In fact mankind will never be able to attain it perfectly."

Whoever studies the kingdom of flowers, of vegetables, of minerals; the birds, the insects, the germs, and the worms; the animals and their forms and colors; and the beauty that each form suggests, will surely recognize as did the prophets of old, that the world is created by the Spirit, that divine Spirit who has created it with eyes wide open. It shows perfect wisdom behind it, and perfect skill in it, and a sense of beauty so perfect that man must always be incapable of achieving it.

Now the question comes, "What is man?" Man is the miniature of God, and man has inherited as his divine inheritance the tendency to art. Therefore any person with intelligence and with tender feeling—which go to make a person normal—must admit the beauty of art. One is born with that tendency. A child is born with the love of art, as is proved by the infant's being attracted to toys and beautiful colors. Lines attract him, and the first thing that he begins to like or desire is color and movement. This is the time of his life during which he is impressed by artistic things. When a person loses his sense of art, it is just as if the heart had become blind. It cannot see the art anymore because of the clouds of all manner of ugliness and undesirability and all that one does not like to look upon. All such things and impressions cover his heart and his soul, and make him, so to speak, blind to beauty, blind to art. But this is not the normal condition. The normal state of a sound mind in a sound body with tender feeling is love of beauty, is to admire art.

No doubt very often man does not live a natural life. That is, his business or profession or responsibility holds him. Some work or some thought for the needs of the body, for bread and butter or any other everyday need, holds him and absorbs the whole of his thoughts, so that he becomes useless for the discovery of the beauty and joy and happiness of life. Hence, as we see around us today, life is becoming so difficult and so full of anxiety and trouble and responsibility. From morning till evening man is just loaded with his responsibilities, toiling day and night. He has never a moment to think of the beauty of art. Since art is the first step that leads man to the cause of art, how can a person who has never admired or understood the beauty of art hope to admire or understand the Artist?

So God remains unrecognized, and not through the fault of God but through the fault of man. The Creator in the role of artist has created His beautiful art, which is not far from human eyes, but man is so engrossed in thoughts and occupations that have nothing to do with that art. All his time and thought and effort are devoted to occupations that never allow him one moment to think of art, to admire it, understand it, and appreciate it. Naturally, then, he remains as if his eyes were covered over from the vision of the Artist. The real purpose of human life is not that man be born to toil for bread and butter; the real purpose of human life is not that man should be avaricious, competing with his fellow man, hating him, viewing another with prejudice, and using the whole of his time in a spirit of rivalry and competition in which there can be no harmony or joy or peace. With the necessarily ever-increasing avariciousness there is an absence of that beauty for which the soul so constantly longs.

It would be no exaggeration to say that all the disagreeable things that go on in this world—wars, diseases, and the like —all come from the lack of an artistic attitude in life, the lack of a sense of beauty, and the lack of that vision which unites the whole humanity in one center, the center that is God. When man closes his eyes to beauty, he will never think of looking for the beautiful, although beauty is constantly beside him. Behind the beauty, as the Qur'an says, God is: "God is beautiful and He loves beauty." The natural tendency to love and admire beauty is a divine inheritance; it is the spiritual thing, that leads to spirituality. Through this tendency one accomplishes one's spiritual duty in life. When that tendency has gone and religion is left without art, then religion may perhaps be useful for an inartistic society, but it turns into a sort of formality. One does one thing, one does another. As one does weekday work, so also one does Sunday duty.

If God is not to be connected with beauty, in what form shall man idealize Him? In what form could man think of Him? In what form should he see Him? He would be kept away from Him. So when religion is covered in its form and when man keeps art aloof instead of promoting it, man's life becomes empty, for his occupation necessarily keeps art out of his life to a great extent. If then when he goes to a religious place he finds no art there either, his visit comes to be exactly like a visit to any other place to which habit may take him in daily life. There is nothing to pierce through him; there is nothing to awaken that impulse which rises from the earth to heaven; there is nothing to make him think

even for that one moment that God is beautiful and that by
beauty we reach out to God.

Man very often separates nature from art. He considers
nature different from art; he considers the one superior and
the other inferior. But in reality art is that which, by a
divinely inherited tendency, plays its role through man. God
working with His hidden hands has created nature, and He
shows His art in that nature. In that other aspect of art which
we call art, God produces beauty through the human hand
and the human mind, and so finishes that which has not yet
been finished in nature. Therefore in one respect art is a step
forward from nature, although compared with nature art is
so limited. Nature is unlimited, but at the same time art is
an improvement upon nature.

Seen metaphysically, the artistic spirit of God is satisfied
by fulfilling its artistic tendency through the art of the human being. Therefore those who consider art from a higher
point of view recognize the artistic impulse not only as a
human impulse, not only as brain work, but as a true artistic
impulse, an inspiration in itself.

In order to prepare the mind for the artistic impulse, what
is necessary? Does one need some kind of learning? Is there
some preliminary study to be made first? No. It requires a
tuning, a bringing of ourselves to an object to whose beauty
the human heart can respond, a beauty that the heart can
appreciate. When the heart can concentrate upon beauty,
then it works itself up to a certain pitch, for inspiration is
not a thing that one can pull upon to obtain as by pulling
a rope. Inspiration comes only when the heart is tuned to
that object, when it is in a position to receive it. Therefore
inspired artists have been divinely gifted, and the spirit of
art is one, though the arts are so many. When the heart is
tuned to the proper pitch, it is capable of producing or appreciating not just one kind of art and beauty, but all kinds.

Thus there can be an art in architecture. A gifted architect
can produce a great deal of beauty in his work. So too with
drawing, with embroidery, with the work of dyeing, of sew-

ing. In fact there is nothing that man does which cannot have art in it if he knows how to attune himself to that pitch which enables the art to be expressed. Poetry is an art in the same way. Unless a person is tuned to the proper pitch, he may write poetry all his life and yet it will not please either him or anyone else. So with a painter, or a musician; he will not please himself or anyone else during his whole life unless he has become tuned to that pitch.

This shows that the question as to what grade of evolution a person has attained comes in every walk of life. Whether a person be a painter, sculptor, architect, designer, singer, or dancer, whatever walk he may follow, there is no better source in nature whence to draw inspiration from above than by means of art. The more cultivated the sense of art is in man, the more able he is to respond to the beauty of art and to produce or create something beautiful in himself. The more he comes into touch with that spirit who is constantly helping every soul toward beauty, the more man can produce. Everything that helps man to approach the beauty of God is sacred. Therefore art can become religion. It would not be an exaggeration to say that there is no better religion than art itself.

When one has reached that degree of understanding, when one has reached that knowledge of art by which he can be profited, when the heart is once tuned to that pitch by which one can understand and appreciate art, and when one has changed one's outlook upon life so as to see in the beauty of art the beauty of the divine Being, then one can progress in the true art.

From this we learn that consciously or unconsciously that which our soul is really seeking is art. Yet at the same time man very frequently avoids this very thing that he is seeking. The right way and the wrong way are so near to one another. The only difference is that a person is journeying along the right way when at every step he can say, "I see the signs that support, help me to go on further, and promise that the goal is before me." When he is journeying along the wrong way every step tells him, "I am not in the right way, I must go back; I am not on the road on which I ought to be." Consciously or unconsciously every soul seeks for beauty, and if at each step of our lives we think that beauty is receiving us as we go, that beauty meets us at every step on our path, then our soul is satisfied and full of hope, knowing that the road we are on is our proper road, and that some day or other we will arrive at our goal. The person who thinks at every step of his journey, "I am not on a right road; I do not like this; I am not pleased with that," is making no progress. The beauty he is looking for, he is ever leaving behind. He is traveling in quite another way from that which he is expecting.

So we see that whether our road is right or wrong depends on our appreciation of the artistic side of life or our lack of it. But by saying this, one does not wish it to be understood that everyone must necessarily practice to become an artist or learn some branch of art. It is only to say that there is a spark of artistic faculty in every soul, there is not a single soul who does not have this spark; some have more, some have less. Yet that spark does not have to be used by everybody to that extent which cause one to be called an artist. No, but we must exhibit and utilize that faculty in our everyday life. A person with the artistic faculty is sure to show it in everything he does, even in dusting a room, keeping it tidy, or in keeping a machine in order. In all these directions a person can show art. One does not require a palace before one can begin to manifest art. If one really has the love for beauty, one can show the artistic faculty in quite small things.

Besides this there is the fact that the soul manifests outwardly that which it holds inwardly, so that it is the beauty that man has within himself which he expresses without. Man shows his artistic faculty in his manner towards his friend and towards his surroundings. A person who has no sense of art is called rude, inconsiderate, thoughtless, foolish, simple-minded, crude, coarse.

A person does not need to have much money in order to be able to express his art. He can express it in various circumstances. He may be the poorest man in the world, and yet he can express the beauty of his soul in whatever state he may be placed. Beauty will not be hidden. One shows one's art in one's words. When one is in business, in the family, or among friends, one does not know how many times during the day one hurts the feelings of others; one does not even notice them. Even though one were very learned or experienced, the lack of art would still manifest. Even a loving, kind, and good person will never be able to express the goodness that is hidden in his heart if art is lacking.

Jesus Christ taught in the Sermon on the Mount, "Blessed are they who are gentle, meek, humble, poor in spirit." What lesson does this teach us? It is this lesson of art: the lesson is, one should produce art in one's personality. Even so-called artists, musicians, poets, painters, if they have not fostered art, if art is not impressed on their souls, and if their souls have not expressed the beauty of art, they do not know art. They are profane; they claim to be something they are not.

Having thought much upon this subject, and being specially interested in art, I have come in contact with artists of different countries both in the East and West. It has always proved that those who have really attained some greatness in their art were those who showed glimpses of art in their personality. It showed in the words they spoke, in the way they received me, and in the manner in which they spoke with me: their tenderness of heart, their friendliness, their interest in my affairs. Every sign of art could be seen in such personalities. Even if not literally an artist—a painter, a singer, a poet, whatever the real occupation—it does not matter as long as one has realized beauty in that occupation, has perceived beauty around one, and has collected around one all that one finds beautiful. All this must be expressed in return, and it is that which is true art.

In the Hindu language there are two attitudes mentioned by the philosophers, namely, *hansadi* and *suhradi*. The former attitude is that of a bird of paradise, a mythical bird of the Hindus called *hausa*. If you put milk mixed with water before hausa, it will drink the milk and leave the water behind. The suhradi attitude is that of the people. It is the tendency of looking to find where there is any dirty spot and then wanting to sit in it. Such is the tendency of man; one person is always looking for what may be wrong in people, is delighted to hear something wrong about them, and is very interested in discussing their faults and hearing of their being disgraced or insulted in some way. Such persons are always wanting to see the evil around them, in whatever form it may be. This pleasure grows until the whole life becomes a burden, for the presence of evil produces its bad impression, and bad thoughts collect around him for they are reproduced just as a gramophone record produces sounds. Such a person becomes the gramophone record of the evil he collects; he utters it, he retains the bad feelings within, and he spreads them abroad wherever he goes. Nobody likes him, nor does he like anyone either; the time will come when he cannot even like himself.

Another kind of character is he who overlooks all that does not seem to be harmonious; he looks only for good in every person, and finds some good even in the worst person in the world. This person seeks for good, wishes to see it wherever he can find it, and in this way constantly gathers good impressions.

What is good? Good is beauty. What is beauty? Beauty is God. What is virtue? Virtue is beauty; what is beauty is also virtue. One does not have to learn in a book or a scripture or from some other person what is good and what is bad. We can learn from our own sense of art. The greater one's sense of art, the more it will show what is right and what is wrong, what is good and what is bad.

As soon as the senses begin to develop and understand what it is that takes away beauty and what imparts beauty, then one gathers beauty as one gathers flowers. Such persons welcome others with beauty, they express beauty, they impart it to others. Others love them. They love others. They live and move and have their being in love, just as it is said in the Bible, "They live and move and have their being in God." So a person who lives and moves and has his being in love will certainly also live and move and have his being in God.

This may be called the divine art, for which a person may study and strive. But besides this there is the art that every person must look for and develop in his own nature. The message of Sufism to the western world has this as its chief object: to awaken the spirit of the world from the thought of antagonism and mutual hatred and to bring about the feeling of human brotherhood so that all humanity may meet with one another, whatever be their nation, race, or religion, in one place, in one center, namely the thought of God. In order to rise to this ideal and tune our souls to this pitch, so necessary from beginning to end, it is necessary to seek the path of beauty and to recognize in beauty the being of God.

Hazrat Inayat Khan, founder of the Sufi Order in the West, was born in India in 1882. A master of classical Indian music by the age of twenty, he relinquished a brilliant career to devote himself to the spiritual path. In 1910, acting upon the guidance of his teacher, he became one of the first teachers of the Sufi tradition in the West. For a decade and a half he travelled throughout Europe and the United States, giving lectures and guiding an ever-growing group of seekers. In 1926, he returned to India, where he died the following year.

A catalogue of books relating to Sufism and other spiritual traditions may be obtained from the publisher by writing to:

Omega Publications, Inc.
RD 1 Box 1030E
New Lebanon, NY 12125